Potentials, Challenges and Prospects of Halal Tourism Development in Ethiopia

This book explores the potential of halal tourism development and its implementation in Ethiopia. The insights presented assist key stakeholders in making informed decisions concerning commercial strategy, profitability and feasibility of halal tourism from the secular perspective.

Being the first of its kind to assess halal tourism development in developing countries, this innovative book offers a unique contribution to halal tourism. It provides a clear understanding of halal tourism, its evolution, and the industry's current status. The book considers the prospects of halal tourism, including the conceptual and practical challenges of halal tourism development. The example of halal tourism in Ethiopia is explored to provide a lens through which deeper understandings can be drawn on where and how to develop halal tourism

This book will interest researchers, students and teachers in the disciplines of tourism, anthropology, geography, business administration and sociology. It also provides useful insights for policymakers, practitioners, planners and professionals in the hospitality and tourism industry.

Mohammed Jemal Ahmed earned his second degree from Addis Ababa University, Ethiopia, in Tourism and Development in 2012 and his Ph.D. from Izmir Katip Celebi University, Turkiye, in Tourism Management in 2021. He was a tourism and history lecturer at Jigjiga University and Wollo University, Ethiopia. From May 2021 until now, he has been an assistant professor in Tourism Management and a researcher at Wollo University, Ethiopia. His research areas include the following: Islamic tourism, halal tourism, heritage tourism, pilgrimage tourism, ecotourism, community-based tourism, Ethiopian history, and travel and migration.

Atilla Akbaba is a professor at the Faculty of Tourism at İzmir Kâtip Çelebi University (İzmir, Türkiye). He received his M.Sc. from Florida International University and his Ph. D from Dokuz Eylul University with a major in Tourism Management. He teaches hospitality and tourism-related courses. His areas of specialization include service quality, organizational culture, and management of tourism businesses. He has published widely in his areas of specialization at national and international levels.

Routledge Insights in Tourism Series
Series Editor: Anukrati Sharma, Head & Associate Professor of the Department of Commerce and Management at the University of Kota, India

This series provides a forum for cutting edge insights into the latest developments in tourism research. It offers high quality monographs and edited collections that develop tourism analysis at both theoretical and empirical levels.

Millennials, Spirituality and Tourism
Edited by Sandeep Kumar Walia and Aruditya Jasrotia

Tourism, Safety and COVID-19
Security, Digitization and Tourist Behaviour
Salvatore Monaco

COVID-19 and the Tourism Industry
Sustainability, Resilience and New Directions
Edited by Anukrati Sharma, Azizul Hassan and Priyakrushna Mohanty

Management of Tourism Ecosystem Services in a Post Pandemic Context
Global Perspectives
Edited by Vanessa G. B. Gowreesunkar, Shem Wambugu Maingi and Felix Lamech Mogambi Ming'ate

Tourism, Knowledge and Learning
Conceptual Development and Case Studies
Edited by Eva Maria Jernsand, Maria Persson and Erik Lundberg

Potentials, Challenges and Prospects of Halal Tourism Development in Ethiopia
Mohammed Jemal Ahmed and Atilla Akbaba

For more information about this series, please visit: www.routledge.com/Routledge-Insights-in-Tourism-Series/book-series/RITS

Potentials, Challenges and Prospects of Halal Tourism Development in Ethiopia

**Mohammed Jemal Ahmed
and Atilla Akbaba**

LONDON AND NEW YORK

First published 2023
by Routledge
4 Park Square, Milton Park, Abingdon, Oxon OX14 4RN

and by Routledge
605 Third Avenue, New York, NY 10158

Routledge is an imprint of the Taylor & Francis Group, an informa business

© 2023 Mohammed Jemal Ahmed and Atilla Akbaba

The right of Mohammed Jemal Ahmed and Atilla Akbaba to be identified as authors of this work has been asserted in accordance with sections 77 and 78 of the Copyright, Designs and Patents Act 1988.

All rights reserved. No part of this book may be reprinted or reproduced or utilised in any form or by any electronic, mechanical, or other means, now known or hereafter invented, including photocopying and recording, or in any information storage or retrieval system, without permission in writing from the publishers.

Trademark notice: Product or corporate names may be trademarks or registered trademarks, and are used only for identification and explanation without intent to infringe.

British Library Cataloguing-in-Publication Data
A catalogue record for this book is available from the British Library

ISBN: 978-1-032-40903-0 (hbk)
ISBN: 978-1-032-40904-7 (pbk)
ISBN: 978-1-003-35523-6 (ebk)

DOI: 10.4324/9781003355236

Typeset in Times
by SPi Technologies India Pvt Ltd (Straive)

Contents

List of Figures   ix
List of Maps   x
List of Tables   xi
List of Abbreviations   xii

Introduction   1

   References 10

1 Definitions and Dimensions of Halal Tourism   13

   Defining Tourism, Halal Tourism and Islamic Tourism 14
     Defining Tourism 14
     Defining Halal Tourism 17
     Defining Islamic Tourism 20
   Halal Tourism Vis-à-Vis Islamic Tourism 21
   Halal Tourism and the Sharia Law 27
   The Birth of Halal Tourism 28
   Trends and Prospects of Halal Tourism 29
   Halal Tourism and Non-Muslims 31
   Halal Standardization and Certification 33
   Halal Tourism and Alternative Tourism 35
   E-Marketing and Halal Tourism Websites 36
   Halal Tourism Products and Services 37
     Halal Foods and Beverages 38
     Halal Entertainment Services 42
     Halal Accommodation and Restaurants 42
     Sharia-Compliant Airport 44
     Sharia-Compliant Healthcare Centers 44
   Guidelines for Halal-Conscious Muslim Visitors 45
   References 46

2 Travel, Tourism and Worship 53

Religious Tourism and Pilgrimages 53
  Pilgrimage and Tourism 57
  Islam and Tourism 58
  Tourism from the Perspective of the Quran and Sunnah 63
Hajj and Umrah: Pilgrimage to Mecca 67
References 70

3 Major Themes and Issues in Halal Tourism Development 75

Tourism Development 75
The Theories of Tourism Development 78
  Modernization Theory 78
  Dependency (Underdevelopment) Theory 78
  Sustainable Development (Alternative Tourism) 79
Glocal Strategy and Halal Tourism Development 80
Phases of Tourism Development 82
Needs, Principles and Attributes of Halal Tourism 84
  Faith-Based Service Needs of Halal Tourism 84
  'Need to Have' Faith-Based Services of Halal Tourism 84
  'Good to have' Faith-Based Service of Halal Tourism 85
  'Nice to have' Faith-Based Service of Halal Tourism 86
Characteristics and Motivations of Halal-Conscious Visitors 91
  Characteristics of Halal-Conscious Visitors 91
  Motivations of Halal-Conscious Visitors 92
Barriers to Halal Tourism Development 94
  Lack of Awareness 94
  The Prevalence of Islamophobia and Xenophobia 94
  The Perceived Paradox of Islam and Tourism 96
  Lack of Basic Halal Tourism Infrastructure and Superstructure 97
  Unavailability of Halal Standardization and Certification 98
Identified Research Gaps and Conceptual Framework 99
  Identified Research Gaps in the Existing Literature 99
  Conceptual Framework of the Research 100
References 102

4 Ethiopia and Its Tourism Potential 106

An Overview of Ethiopian History 107
  The Legend of Queen of Sheba and King Solomon 108
  The Introduction of Religions in Ethiopia 110
  The Introduction of Christianity in Ethiopia 110
  Ethiopia and Islam 111
  Ethiopia and Its Muslim Sultanates 112
  Ethiopia and the Ottoman Turk 113
  *The First Hijra toward Ethiopia and the Image of Ethiopia
    in Islamic Eyes 113*

   The Image of Ethiopia in the Eyes of Outsiders   116
    An Overview of Tourism Development in Ethiopia   120
    Religious Tourism in Ethiopia   122
      The State of Halal Tourism Development in Ethiopia   125
      Inventory and Descriptions of Halal Visitor Attractions in Ethiopia   125
      The North Cluster   126
      The Northwest Cluster   130
      The Eastern Cluster Attractions   131
      Southeast Cluster: Halal Tourism Resources of Bale Zone   136
      Southwestern Clusters: Jimma and Its Environs   139
      Islamic Intangible Living Heritages   140
    References   141

5 Challenges and Prospects to Halal Tourism Development: Focus on Ethiopia   **145**

   Research Objectives   145
   Basic Research Questions   145
   Research Methodology   145
     Participants of the Study   147
     Sample Size and Sampling Techniques   147
     Study Area   148
     Data Collection Procedures   149
     Ethical Consideration   150
     Data Collection Techniques   150
     Interview   151
     Focus Group Discussion   152
     Observations   153
     Content Analysis   154
     The Interview Guiding Questions and Checklists   154
     Data Interpretation   155
     Methodological Integrity and Trustworthiness   155
     Problems Faced during Data Collection   156
   Data Interpretation and Findings   157
     Halal Tourism Knowledge and Awareness   157
     Tourism in Islam   159
     Experiences and Reflections of Halal-Conscious Travelers   162
     Identifying and Mapping Potential Routes of Halal Tourism in Ethiopia   166
     The North Historic Halal Tourism Route (Al-Nejashi Historic Route)   168
     The Northwest Halal Geo-Route (The Danakil Geo-Route)   170
     The East Historic Halal Tourism Route   170
     The Southeast Halal Route (Bale Eco-Route)   173
     The Southwest Halal Tourism Route (The Aba Jifar Eco-Route)   174

Ethiopia's Comparative Advantages and Opportunities to Develop Halal Tourism 175
The Availability of Unique Islamic History: Selling Stories and Legends 177
The Land of the First Hijra 178
The Homeland of Great Muslims: King Al-Nejashi, Bilal Al-Habesha and Baraka 178
The Availability of Ancient Islamic Cities and Landscapes 180
The Availability of Conducive Weather Conditions and Fertile Land 182
The Availability of Huge Domestic Demand 182
The Birthplace of Coffee Arabica 185
Barriers to Halal Tourism Development in Ethiopia 187
The Perceived Image of Ethiopia as a 'Christian Island' 187
The Availability of Islamophobia at the National and Global Level 189
The Availability of Tourismophobes 192
Lack of Muslim-Friendly Infrastructures 194
SWOT Analysis of Halal Tourism Development in Ethiopia 202
References 206

6 Conclusion, Recommendations and Implications 209

References 218

Appendix 219
Index 226

Figures

1.1	Classification of Visitors	15
1.2	The Interconnection of Mainstream Tourism, Halal Tourism and Islamic Tourism	25
1.3	Typologies of Muslim-Friendly Tourism	26
2.1	Faith-Based Service Needs 1.0 (2009)	69
2.2	Faith-Based Service Needs 2.0 (2019)	70
3.1	Maslow's Hierarchy of Needs	94
3.2	Conceptual Framework of the Research	101
4.1	The Jugol Wall of Harar & Its Main Gate	132
4.2	Hyena Feeding Man in Harar	132
4.3	Colorful Basket Collections at Harar Museums	134
4.4	The Researcher during Data Collection at Sof Omar Cave	138
5.1	Research Method Design	151
5.2	SWOT Strategies	203

Maps

5.1	Map of the Study Area	149
5.2	Halal Tourism Routes of Ethiopia	167
5.3	North Historic Halal Tourism Routes	169
5.4	North East Halal Route	171
5.5	The East Historic Halal Route	172
5.6	Southeast Halal Route	173
5.7	The Southwest Halal Route	174

Tables

1.1	Summary of Characteristics of Halal Tourism and Islamic Tourism	24
1.2	Top Ten Destinations and Origins of Halal Visitors	29
1.3	Differences between Halal Hotels and Conventional Hotels	43
2.1	Religious Food Restrictions	53
2.2	Size and Projected Growth of World Major Religious Group	56
2.3	Pilgrims into Mecca and Medina (Saudi Arabia) (2000–2019)	69
3.1	Summary of Components of Halal Tourism	87
4.1	Inbound Visitors Arrivals and Tourism Receipt (2000–2018)	122
4.2	Top Ten Arrivals by Country of Origin (2012–2015)	123
5.1	SWOT Analysis Summary	205

Abbreviations

ACES	Access, Communication, Environment and Services
ADP	Amhara Democratic Party
BMNP	Bale Mountains National Park
COMCEC	Committee for Economic and Commercial Cooperation of the Organization of the Islamic Cooperation
COVID-19	Coronavirus Disease of 2019
EARS	East African Rift System
EOC	Ethiopian Orthodox Church
EPRDF	Ethiopian Peoples' Revolutionary Democratic Front
FDRE	Federal Democratic Republic of Ethiopia
FGD	Focus Group Discussion
GCC	Gulf Cooperation Council
GDP	Gross Domestic Product
GIS	Geographic Information System
GMTI	Global Muslim Travel Index
GPS	Global Positioning System
HDC	Halal Industry Development Corporation
JAKIM	Jabatan Kemajuan Islam Malaysia
KSA	The Kingdom of Saudi Arabia
MICE	Meetings, Incentives, Conferences and Events
ODP	Oromo Democratic Party
OIC	Organization of Islamic Cooperation
PBUH	Peace Be Upon Him
PP	Prosperity Party
SEPDM	Southern Ethiopian People's Democratic Movement
SESRIC	Statistical, Economic and Social Research and Training Centre for Islamic Countries
SGIER	State of Global Islamic Economic Report
SNNPR	Southern Nations, Nationalities and Peoples Regional State
SWOT	Strengths, Weaknesses, Opportunities and Threats
SWT	Subhanahu Wa Ta'ala, Arabic for 'The most glorified, the most high'
TİKA	The Turkish Coordination and Cooperation Agency (Türk İşbirliği ve Koordinasyon İdaresi Başkanlığı)

TPLF	Tigray's People Liberation Front
UNECA	United Nations Economic Commission for Africa
UNESCO	United Nations Educational, Scientific and Cultural Organization
UNWTO	United Nations World Tourism Organization
VRF	Visiting Relatives and Friends

Introduction

Tourism has remained one of the world's largest industries. It has steadily burgeoned globally as a significant social and economic activity (Babu et al., 2008; Weaver & Lawton, 2014). Although the practice of tourism-like activities has a long history, modern tourism began only in the 1960s (Jenkins, 1994). The 21st century welcomed the tourism industry with a paradoxical status quo of shocks and uncertainties on the one hand and promising opportunities on the other (Babu et al., 2008). On the one hand, the industry's shocks have been displayed through political deterioration, such as the war in the Middle East and the 11 September 2001 terrorism attack on the World Trade Center, as well as the attacks in Bali, Spain, the UK and Egypt (Nikšić Radić et al., 2018). Natural and anthropogenic shocks such as severe acute respiratory syndrome (SARS), bird flu, mad cow disease, the tragic tsunami, hurricanes, global warming and, recently, the coronavirus (COVID-19) epidemic that broke out in China have also been experienced. These major artificial, anthropogenic and natural phenomena, coupled with the unstable global economic system and the continuous rise in oil prices, remain the major threats to the tourism industry in the 21st century. On the other hand, despite the preceding hindrances, new positive developments such as a growing middle class in emerging economies, technological advancement in communication and transportation, affordable travel costs and visa facilitation (UNWTO, 2019) help the global tourism industry grow steadily and be one of the leading global industries (Babu et al., 2008). Dann (1999) argues that lifestyle changes, a dramatic reduction in the working days and corresponding increases in leisure time, the increment of disposable income and discretionary time, as well as the emergence of new tourism niches contributed their share to the rapid proliferation and growth of the tourism industry.

Various researchers and institutions have proved that, nowadays, tourism is one of the world's largest, most complex and fastest-growing industries that surpass the conventional sectors of the economy (Camilleri, 2018; Duman, 2020; Rutty et al., 2015; Jenkins, 1994; Qaddahat et al., 2016; UNWTO, 2019). Changes have also been observed in terms of the worldwide representation of the industry. Geographically, unlike in the earlier centuries, tourism does not confine only to the traditional destination countries.

DOI: 10.4324/9781003355236-1

2 Introduction

Nowadays, new tourism destinations and generating countries are also represented on global tourism maps (World Travel Organization, 2019). Tourism has become a multi-dimensional industry that touches the lives of modern societies politically, diplomatically, economically and socially. It has widespread impacts at global, regional, national, state, local and household levels. Having both negative and positive socio-cultural, economic and environmental impacts (Kumar et al., 2015), tourism is therefore often described as a multi-faceted and multi-dimensional industry (Robinson et al., 2020) in that academicians have faced difficulties in drawing its borders (Duman, 2020). For some years now, many developing countries have recognized tourism not only as a tool of development per se but also as a driver and catalyst for other developments (Weaver & Lawton, 2014). Weaver and Lawton (2014) note that in the early periods of the development process, tourism participation, specifically pleasure tourism, was limited only to affluent elites and developed nations. Nowadays, however, millions of people travel to different countries worldwide to enjoy new experiences and impressions, engage in various businesses, and partake in governmental, religious or other missions (Kumar et al., 2015). Though the disparity has gradually been curtailed, only a few origin countries, such as Western European countries, the United States, Canada, Japan, Taiwan, South Korea, Singapore, Israel, Australia, and New Zealand, have contributed 80% of all outbound tourist traffic. In contrast, the combined population of these countries constitutes only 12% of the world's population (Weaver & Lawton, 2014).

It is reported that tourism, as a global industry, was a generator of large numbers of international arrivals, with 600 million recorded in 2000 and ascending to 1.4 billion in 2018 (UNWTO, 2019). Travel and tourism play a key role in economic development, foreign currency generation and job creation worldwide. From the suppliers' perspective, the raison d'être of tourism and the justification for its promotion in any area are its alleged economic contribution to development. The positive economic impacts of tourism convince governments, companies and investors to get involved in developing tourism destinations (Kumar et al., 2015). In 2016, travel and tourism directly contributed US$2.3 trillion and 109 million jobs worldwide; these figures increased in 2018 to US$8.8 trillion and 319 million jobs. This amount constitutes 10% of total employment and covers 10.4% of the world's GDP, and approximately one in every ten employees engages in tourism sectors (World Travel and Tourism Council [WTTC], 2019). According to the UNWTO report of 2019, worldwide international tourist arrival reached 1.4 billion, surpassing the two years of UNWTO projections. According to this report, international tourist arrivals grew 5% in 2018. In the same year, tourism contributed 1.7 trillion to the world economy. These figures have been attained two years ahead of the UNTWO forecast (UNWTO, 2019). These figures reveal the trend, and the sector's role in the world economy has been increasing. The relatively strong global economy, a growing middle class in emerging economies, technological advancement, new business models, affordable travel costs and the ease of visa facilitation have proved to be the main factors for these achievements. The gradual increment of discretionary time and income are among the most important factors that enable more people to engage in tourism (Weaver & Lawton, 2014). Tourism is the main export item and generates hard currency for many least-developed countries. In addition to the direct economic contribution, it also has secondary effects on the host communities. Secondary effects include indirect and induced economic effects. There is no doubt that in the tourism business, each dollar of direct sales generates another dollar in secondary sales in the destinations.

On top of that, since tourism is a labor-intensive industry, it creates job opportunities for locals (Brida et al., 2013). Furthermore, tourism naturally has backward and forward linkages with other sectors; therefore, it catalyzes the growth of other industries. It generates income through an economic multiplier (Gnanapala & Sandaruwani, 2016).

Tourism has a role to play from an environmental perspective as well. First, natural and manmade tourist attractions are core elements in the tourism system. Natural resources such as flora, fauna, water bodies and the aesthetical value of landscapes could satisfy visitors' emotional and spiritual thirst. Second, because of tourism, selected natural environments and historical and cultural heritages have been preserved, protected and kept from further degradation and depletion. Third, the presence of visitors in the destination may ensure the revival and survival of cultural and natural attractions that might otherwise have withered away for lack of support (Humphreys & Holloway, 2016). Fourth, visitors' interest and satisfaction in visiting the environment boost local pride and increase their awareness of natural resources. When the local people benefit from the presence of tourists who visit natural and manmade heritage, they value the environment and preserve it.

The world has gradually woken up to the fact that, like other economic activities, tourism has both negative and positive impacts (Butler, 2008); therefore, tourism is no longer a smokeless industry. He alleges that while academicians chase for the facts to disclose the negative effects of tourism, governments and their consultants are equally effective at magnifying the economic benefits, and there is relative accuracy in both camps. Not only benefits, it is unfortunate that tourism also has undesirable outcomes. Unless effective destination management that minimizes the adverse effect of tourism is implemented, tourism might cause undesirable economic, sociocultural and environmental impacts, particularly on the host community. For instance, economically, the prevalence of mass tourists in the destinations may cause inflation in the host communities, which results in a high cost of living. Seasonality is also another challenge that many destinations have faced, and many tourism employees have been tested. In some destinations, local peoples and even countries undermine other industries, such as agriculture and become over-dependent on tourism. Since tourism is the most volatile industry, it is not advisable to depend on it. A one-time blasting of a terrorist may affect a year or more inflow of tourists into that destination. Economists advise tourism not to be a primary means of income.

4 *Introduction*

Mismanaged tourism development has some undesirable impacts socially as well. Host-guest conflict is one of the major concerns, especially in saturated destination countries. Countries such as the Netherlands have planned to discourage inbound tourists' inflow for the safety and wellness of their citizens. According to Khan et al. (2020), tourism could negatively impact the environment. Visitors may pollute the air and water. Hotels could generate solid and liquid wastes. Natural resource attractions can be degraded through improper use or overuse. Invaluable movable heritages will be stolen or illegally sold. A flow of mass visitors may disrupt the wildlife cycle and ecosystem. Gnanapala and Sandaruwani (2016) highlight that the socio-cultural impacts of tourism affect the local community and therefore bring about changes in societal, collective and individual value systems, behavior, social relationships and lifestyles, modes of expression and community structure. The values and behaviors of the host community may also be influenced because of the direct contact between the residents and visitors. Tourism literature unanimously confirms that mismanaged tourism development brings about undesirable impacts such as the expansion of drugs and crime, demonstration effects and guest–host conflicts. Although the negative economic impacts are true, as described above, tourism's environmental and socio-cultural negative impacts are very noticeable and profound, while most of its positive impacts are on the economic side (Babu et al., 2008).

Traditionally, the negative impacts of tourism have been well-studied only from the perspective of the host community. The negative influences of tourism on visitors and generating countries is the most neglected area in tourism literature. However, tourism harms the visitors and generating regions as well. For instance, Humphreys and Holloway (2016) argue that visitors may bring back some undesired things, such as skin cancer due to severe sunburn, swine flu, dietary illness and infectious disease. In 2020, travelers infected by the coronavirus (COVID-19) in China brought the coronavirus back to their home countries. In so doing, they imported this highly infectious virus into their respective home countries. On top of that, their culture and behavior will also be affected.

To sum up, the tourism industry is closely interrelated with major disorders of the world today, such as poverty, migrations, conflicts, terrorism, epidemics, pollution and global warming, and reduction of biodiversity in most cases as a victim but sometimes also as a contributor (Butler, 2001, 2008; Humphreys & Holloway, 2016; UNWTO, 2019). With all its stated limitations, there exists a strong mandate for the furtherance of attempts to maximize the benefits of tourism while minimizing undesirable outcomes.

Halal Tourism Development: Focus on Ethiopia

These days, environmentally and socially responsible forms of tourism, such as ecotourism, sustainable tourism and halal tourism, are emerging. The potential of halal tourism will be discussed thoroughly in the book.

Introduction 5

Nowadays, Muslims have become the fastest-growing consumer segment in the world tourism market (Battour, 2019; Battour et al., 2010, 2017; Din, 1989). Therefore, companies not considering how to serve halal-conscious visitors have been missing significant opportunities that affect general growth. Gradually, however, many stakeholders seem to understand the potential of halal customers and that halal tourism has recently become a fast-growing tourism segment (Battour, 2019). Muslim and non-Muslim countries such as Turkiye, the UAE, Australia, Taiwan, Korea, Japan and New Zealand have given due attention to the emerging halal tourism market (Bhuiyan & Darda, 2018). As discussed in this book, the raison d'être of halal tourism is to cater to Muslims' religious considerations and address Muslims' needs. However, it also offers facilities and services to cater to the needs of non-Muslim customers who wish to consume halal tourism products and services. Recent studies have confirmed that the halal concept is an emerging cultural phenomenon and secular rather than religious (Battour et al., 2018b; Sultana, 2020). A study conducted by Qaddahat et al. (2016) in Egypt and Jordan confirms that halal is becoming a global mark for quality assurance and related to trade and other sectors; therefore, there is an increasing demand for halal products among non-Muslims as well.

The conflicts between touristic practices and Islamic values have been experienced in several destinations. According to Din (1989) and El-Gohary (2016), some unIslamic activities, such as sexual permissiveness, voyeurism, alcoholism, pork consumption and gambling, have become part of tourism. These activities are unequivocally forbidden in Islam and detract Muslims from engaging in tourism. There is also an apparent tension between religious and commercial needs (Duman, 2020). For instance, in Dubai, British tourists transgressed the value and norms of Muslims by having open sex on the beach and insulting police who sought to arrest them (Humphreys & Holloway, 2016). Battour (2019) argues that halal tourism has become popular among Muslims because Western tourism has been surrounded by alcoholism and voyeurism. Al-Munajjid (2008) also alleges that mainstream tourism nowadays causes Muslims to commit sin and immoral deeds and violate religious doctrine. It also contributes to the prevalence of nakedness and cultural decadence, permissive mixing, the prevalence of alcoholism, prostitution and Westernization.

As the best option and solution, environmentally friendly, socially responsible, and sharia-compliant tourism, known as 'halal tourism,' has emerged. In the 21st century, people want to dedicate their leisure time to travel and holidays without compromising their values, culture and faith. Therefore, halal tourism could be the best mediator in reconciling the extant conflicts between secular interests and religious values. Undoubtedly, halal tourism could make the tourism experience inclusive, responsible for the local culture, and enjoyable to halal-conscious travelers by allowing them to perform religious duties while traveling. The noble aim of halal tourism is to have customers feel comfortable, happy, and safe, thereby increasing the number of repeat visitors and attracting potential customers while promoting environmental conservation and social coexistence. Halal tourism is among the recently emerged lucrative tourism market (Battour, 2017; Battour, 2018, 2019; Battour et al., 2010, 2011, 2017), and many countries have been striving to flourish the halal tourism industry and to get benefit from it. Halal tourism is a unique market segment, with Muslim travelers seeking destinations that meet their needs in terms of food, dress and rituals (Mastercard-CrescentRating, 2019). According to Samori et al. (2016), halal tourism, one of the recent phenomena, has emerged as an option and solution over traditional mass tourism. Indeed the halal industry is not a new phenomenon. However, the concept of halal in the tourism and hospitality industry emerged dominantly in the past decade in both literature and practice. These days, Muslim and non-Muslim countries compete to capture the halal-conscious visitors market by providing tourism products and arranging facilities and infrastructures to cater to their needs (Battour, 2018; El-Gohary, 2016). Most of the customers of halal tourism are Muslims, as halal tourism has been interconnected mainly with Muslims and Islam. Contrary to the preceding claims, some Muslims question the 'halalness' of halal tourism (Eid & El-Gohary, 2015; El-Gohary, 2016).

As will be discussed thoroughly in the following chapters, academics and practitioners have tried to entertain halal tourism from Islam and Muslim perspective. However, such kind of view is riskier and not advisable for the blossoming of halal tourism. Recent studies on halal tourism prove that the interest of non-Muslim customers in consuming halal products and services increases steadily because of the quality of halal products and services. Therefore, promoting halal tourism as Islamic tourism is a mistake and myopia.

For several years, Mecca and Medina of Saudi Arabia were considered the only destinations for Muslim tourists (Fakir & Erraoui, 2019). Nowadays, this assumption does not work any longer. Halal tourism destinations and tour operators have multiplied worldwide. Halal tourism conferences have increased, and new publications on halal tourism have mushroomed. In the past decade, various factors such as national halal initiatives, conferences, expos, online networking and media have combined to bring halal tourism into the spotlight. The proliferation of halal tourism has attracted many researchers to the field (Evans & Syed, 2015). Scholars such as Battour (2019), Battour et al. (2017), Battour et al. (2010, 2012), Din (1989), Eid and El-Gohary (2015) have widely studied the relationship between the principles of tourism and that of Islam. These studies' findings reveal no contradiction between the very principles of tourism and Islam. Rather tourism and Islam 'naturally' fit each other. As to true for everybody, Muslims have their own psychological needs, such as relaxation and adventure, and physiological needs, such as food, health and climate, so Muslims may involve in tourism to satisfy their psychological needs. However, (Battour, 2019) finds that Islamic attributes and tenets are very important considerations when a Muslim decides to travel and engage in tourism. Halal tourism will fill the fractures of mainstream tourism by offering halal facilities and a halal environment to satisfy observant Muslims.

Battour (2019) identified six components of halal tourism attributes (HTA): worship facilities, halal food, Islamic entertainment, alcohol and gambling free, Islamic dress code and Islamic morality. Halal facilities include but are not limited to worship facilities, halal entertainment, and halal food and beverages. The halal environment includes alcohol-, pork- and a gambling-free environment, control of sexual permissiveness and adherence to the Islamic dress code. Tourism attributes are broadly classified into two – tangible attributes and intangible attributes. The tangible attributes include prayer facilities and halal food.

In contrast, intangible attributes include Islamic entertainment, unavailability of public consumption of alcoholic drinks, the applicability of the Islamic dress code and observation of Islamic codes of morality (Battour, 2019; p. 152). If halal facilities and services are provided, Islam advises and encourages tourism. About 13 verses of the Holy Quran explicitly encourage people to travel and visit new destinations. Indeed, as discussed thoroughly in the following chapters, some unIslamic attributes have been taken for granted in the tourism industry. Unfortunately, these attributes are seen as de facto manifestations of the sector. This situation eventually causes the existing paradoxical relationship between tourism and Islam. Hence, on the one hand, Islam inherently encourages Muslims to engage in tourism; on the other hand, haram activities and products that are not allowed to Muslims as per Islamic law and doctrine have surrounded tourism. In such a way, the tourism business has been following an approach of one-size-fits-all customers. This tradition of tourism ultimately has caused many Muslims to perceive tourism as anti-Islam.

A recent study proved that Muslims comprise 20%–25% of the world's population, and about 2 billion Muslims reside in 112 countries. Therefore, removing the above obstacles in the tourism industry is crucial to increasing Muslim visitors (Kawata et al., 2018). A growing number of Muslim countries have emphasized tourism in their development plans. For the past many years, tourism has been tailor-made for Westerners. However, recently, there has been a good initiation in the tourism industry to tailor tourism products to Muslims by developing sharia-compliant tourism. Accordingly, the interests of halal-conscious visitors began to be considered an important segment of the tourism industry; thereby, their religious needs could be catered to and satisfied not just for pilgrimage time but everywhere and at any time. Even the interest of customers with special needs, like elderly or disabled people, has been considered in the tourism industry (Farahdel, 2011).

The tourism industry in Ethiopia is promising but still in a glooming condition. Ethiopia is not enjoying its fair share of general and halal tourism in particular. In other words, not only halal tourism but also mainstream tourism in Ethiopia is in its infant stage yet. However, the country has a comparative advantage in developing halal tourism. With half of its total 115 million population, Ethiopia is Muslim and has the largest Muslim population in East Africa. In addition to the domestic market, the country is bordered by Muslim countries and is located in a strategic position to the Muslim world, which is supposed to be a major source of halal visitors. Therefore, near and distant neighbors are potential markets for halal tourism. However, the huge number of the Muslim population is not in line with the development of the halal tourism business. For countries like Ethiopia, halal tourism is a huge, viable and untapped market, and the industry stakeholders have not fully realized the huge potential of halal business in Ethiopia (Gabdrakhmanov et al., 2016). Data compiled by the researcher for the study under discussion show numerous Islamic heritages and actual and potential halal-conscious customers in the country. However, there are no halal-certified restaurants and hotels in the country.

The number of modern urban dwellers and practicing Muslims in Ethiopia is rapidly increasing. This Muslim population segment needs to be involved in halal tourism and holidays. This development per se necessitates halal tourism to emerge in the country. Moreover, Ethiopia has rich in intangible and tangible Islamic heritages. Ethiopia is the first country in Africa and the second in the world to accept Islam as a religion. It is home to the oldest mosque in Africa, dating back to the 7th century. Ethiopia's local Islamic heritage could give rise to a global opportunity and increase its visitor numbers by welcoming international Muslim travelers. As the world's fastest-growing population with a large Muslim populace, Ethiopia's place in the horn of Africa's halal economy is a subject worthy of investigation. A report by the Economist Intelligence Unit proved that Africa has a small share of the global halal travel market – 5% compared with Europe's 51%. Tanzania, Zanzibar and South Africa are relatively popular destinations in sub-Sahara Africa and are best equipped for the halal market (The Economist Intelligence Unit, 2015). The Ethiopian economy, including the Ethiopian tourism sector, has been negatively affected by poor relations between the Muslim world and Ethiopia. While countries such as Turkey, Malaysia, Indonesia, Japan and the Philippines are leading the way in halal tourism, Ethiopia has yet to exploit this infant but rapidly growing market. The halal tourism market is huge and untapped, but lack of awareness affects Ethiopia as far as halal tourism development is concerned. Some hotels already cater to halal needs but do not dare to market themselves as a halal hotel. Many halal tourism customers from India, Pakistan and the Middle East have also been there in Ethiopia. However, the locals are unaware that Islamophobic people have monopolized the travel and tourism business. If marketed well, halal travel in Ethiopia could compete with even more established destinations.

In addition to its economic contribution, halal tourism can also play a significant role in the social and political realm. It reinforces interreligious cohesion, relationship and coextensive in multi-religious, multicultural and multiethnic Ethiopia. It could strengthen Ethiopia's foreign diplomatic relationship with the Islamic world and its neighboring Muslim countries. Furthermore, it must be noted that halal tourism development is not only a profit-oriented business for Ethiopia. It is also a welfare activity for residents. The researchers also claim that in Ethiopia, the development of halal tourism should not be considered only from the economic viewpoint; rather, the human rights conditions of the residents should be taken into account. In the 21st century, tourism development is not a matter of economic contribution alone; it is increasingly perceived as a basic human right issue (Weaver & Lawton, 2014). Article 7 of the 1999 United Nations World Tourism Organization Global Code of Ethics for Tourism, for example, includes the human rights issue in tourism development. The World Tourism Organization (UNWTO) affirms the right to visit and emphasizes that obstacles should not be placed against direct and personal access to the planet's resources. Tourism resources shall be equally open to all citizens. According to Weaver Lawton (2014), the idea of perceiving tourism as a basic human right is being welcomed and encouraged by many countries.

By considering tourism as an important aspect of personal and collective wellbeing, government-sponsored programs have been arranged by some countries and organizations to help members of disadvantaged population groups to take a holiday. This phenomenon is termed social tourism. As the authors note, for example, in Belgium, over 100,000 families have been supported to engage in tourism. In 2009, the Spanish government sponsored over 1 million elder Spaniards to enjoy a seaside holiday. The European Commission's Calypso program, trial from 2009 to 2011, helped needy people such as persons with disabilities, youth aged 18–30, lower-income families and seniors to have holiday experiences. In the UK, a social charity has been arranged to help children with learning, and other disabilities engage in tourism. Generally, following the emergence of social tourism, tourism can no longer be considered a privilege. Rather it becomes a moral and human rights issue, at least in the developed world. Therefore, developing halal tourism in Ethiopia could be considered a basic right for Ethiopian Muslims.

The study under discussion is entitled 'Potentials, Challenges and Prospects of Halal Tourism Development in Ethiopia.' In this book, 'halal tourism development' refers to the establishment or flourishing of halal tourism. Studies on tourism and hospitality in a religious context are relatively limited globally (Duman, 2020) and almost none in Ethiopia. The process of tourism development, in general, and halal tourism development, in particular, has received little attention in the literature. The concept of halal tourism is vague and problematic as well. Even though halal tourism is in its theoretical infancy, there has been a relatively good amount of research on the pattern of halal tourism development in some destinations such as Malaysia, Indonesia and Turkey since the 2010s. However, these studies have been based on a shallow theoretical foundation and geographically confined only to limited destinations, mainly in Southeast Asia and Turkey. The researchers learned from various literature that there had been a lack of research that had been conducted in providing and determining the theoretical concepts of halal tourism. In this book, halal tourism is not considered from a religious perspective; this book rather aims to enable the reader to make informed decisions concerning this evolving market paradigm from the secular perspective of government policymaking or for commercial strategy, profitability and actual feasibility.

10 Introduction

This research is an exploratory study that seeks to identify the themes and patterns of halal tourism development and describe the states of halal tourism development in Ethiopia. As far as the researchers' knowledge, there has been no research on the prospects and potential of halal tourism development in Ethiopia. Nor are official data regarding characteristics of halal tourism and halal-conscious tourists available in Ethiopia. Local halal-conscious people, mainly Muslims, have traveled extensively through different parts of Ethiopia for ecclesiastical and recreational purposes but have not been considered halal visitors yet. Therefore, the purpose of this study includes exploring the halal tourism opportunities in Ethiopia and critically discussing the strategic policy for the development of halal tourism and its prospect in Ethiopia. In addition to academic literature and specific studies in this area, this book also aims to explore and illustrate the concept of halal tourism within the Islamic context by using the Holy Quran verses and Hadith as primary sources.

There are conceptual and definitional ambiguities between halal and Islamic tourism. Scholars did not clearly and properly define the boundaries of halal and Islamic tourism. Therefore, this book seeks to clarify the actual differences and similarities between the concept of halal tourism and Islamic tourism and propose a cogent definition that helps academicians and destination marketers use appropriate terminologies. Furthermore, this book empirically investigates a new perspective of halal tourism.

References

Al-Munajjid, M. S. (2008). *Travel and Tourism (Siyaahah) in Islam – Rulings and Types*. Islamhouse.Com.

Babu, S., Mishra, S., & Parida, B. B. (2008). Tourism Development Revisited: Concepts, Issues and Paradigms. In S. Babu, S. Mishra, & B. B. Parida (Eds.), *Tourism Development Revisited: Concepts, Issues and Paradigms*. SAGE Publications Ltd. https://doi.org/10.4135/9788132100058

Battour, M. (2017). Halal Tourism and its Impact on Non-Muslim Tourists' Perception, Trip quality and Trip Value. *International Journal of Culture, Tourism and Hospitality Research*. https://doi.org/10.1108/ijcthr-02-2017-0020

Battour, M. (2018). Muslim Travel Behavior in Halal Tourism. *Mobilities, Tourism and Travel Behavior - Contexts and Boundaries*. https://doi.org/10.5772/intechopen.70370

Battour, M. (2019). *Halal Tourism: achieving Muslim tourists' satisfaction and loyalty*. Author. https://books.google.com.tr/books?id=Jx-lyAEACAAJ

Battour, M., Hakimian, F., Ismail, M., & Boğan, E. (2018a). The Perception of Non-Muslim Tourists towards Halal Tourism: Evidence from Turkey and Malaysia. *Journal of Islamic Marketing*, 9(4), 823–840. https://doi.org/10.1108/JIMA-07-2017-0072

Battour, M., Hakimian, F., Ismail, M., & Boğan, E. (2018b). The Perception of Non-Muslim Tourists towards Halal Tourism. *Journal of Islamic Marketing*, 9(4), 823–840. https://doi.org/10.1108/jima-07-2017-0072

Battour, M., Ismail, M. N., & Battor, M. (2010). Toward a Halal Tourism Market. *Tourism Analysis*, 15(4), 461–470. https://doi.org/10.3727/108354210X12864727453304

Battour, M., Ismail, M. N., & Battor, M. (2011). The Impact of Destination Attributes on Muslim Tourists' Choice. *International Journal of Tourism Research*, *13*(6), 527–540. https://doi.org/10.1002/jtr.824

Battour, M., Ismail, M. N., Battor, M., & Awais, M. (2017). Islamic Tourism: An Empirical Examination of Travel Motivation and Satisfaction in Malaysia. *Current Issues in Tourism*, *20*(1), 50–67. https://doi.org/10.1080/13683500.2014.965665

Battour, M. M., Battor, M. M., & Ismail, M. (2012). The Mediating Role of Tourist Satisfaction: A Study of Muslim Tourists in Malaysia. *Journal of Travel and Tourism Marketing*, *29*(3), 279–297. https://doi.org/10.1080/10548408.2012.666174

Bhuiyan, H., & Darda, A. (2018). Prospects and Potentials of Halal Tourism Development in Bangladesh. *Journal of Tourismology*, *4*(2), 93–106. https://doi.org/10.26650/jot.2018.4.2.0007

Brida, J. G., Meleddu, M., & Pulina, M. (2013). The Economic Impacts of Cultural Tourism. In *The Routledge Handbook of Cultural Tourism*. https://doi.org/10.4324/9780203120958

Butler, R. (2001). Contemporary Issues in Tourism Development. *Tourism Management*, *22*(3), 305–306. https://doi.org/10.1016/s0261-5177(00)00056-x

Butler, R. (2008). Butler Tourism Development Revisited. In S. Babu, S. Mishra, & B. B. Parida (Eds.), *Tourism Development Revisited: Concepts, Issues and ParadigmsIssues and Paradigms* (pp. 55–64). SAGE Publications Ltd.

Camilleri, M. A. (2018). The Tourism Industry. In *Travel Marketing, Tourism Economics and the Airline Product* (Issue October, pp. 3–27). Springer Nature. https://doi.org/10.1007/978-3-319-49849-2

Dann, G. M. S. (1999). *Contemporary Issues in Tourism Development* (D. Pearce & R. Butler, eds., pp. 13–30). Routledge.

Din, K. H. (1989). Islam and Tourism. Patterns, Issues, and Options. *Annals of Tourism Research*, *16*(4), 542–563. https://doi.org/10.1016/0160-7383(89)90008-X

Duman, T. (2020). Attributes of Muslim-Friendly Hospitality Service in a Process-Based Model. In M. Hall & G. Prayag (Eds.), *The Routledge Handbook of Halal Hospitality and Islamic Tourism* (pp. 53–69). Taylor & Francis. https://doi.org/10.4324/9781315150604-3

Eid, R., & El-Gohary, H. (2015). The Role of Islamic Religiosity on the Relationship between Perceived Value and Tourist Satisfaction. *Tourism Management*, *46*, 477–488. https://doi.org/10.1016/j.tourman.2014.08.003

El-Gohary, H. (2016). Halal Tourism, is it Really Halal? *Tourism Management Perspectives*, *19*, 124–130. https://doi.org/10.1016/j.tmp.2015.12.013

Evans, A., & Syed, S. (2015). Halal Goes Global. International Trade Centre. http://search.proquest.com.ezaccess.library.uitm.edu.my/docview/224324915?accountid=42518

Fakir, F., & Erraoui, E. (2019). Moroccan Tourist's Perceptions Toward Halal Tourism. *2nd International Halal Tourism Congress/04-06 April 2019/Antalya-Turkey*, November 1–13.

Farahdel, F. (2011). Islamic Attributes and its Impact on Muslim Tourists' Satisfaction: A Study of Iran. *Business*, May, 98.

Gabdrakhmanov, N. K., Biktimirov, N. M., Rozhko, M. V., & Mardanshina, R. M. (2016). Features of Islamic Tourism. *Academy of Marketing Studies Journal*, *20*(Special Issue), 45–50.

Gnanapala, A., & Sandaruwani, J. A. R. C. (2016). Socio-economic Impacts of Tourism Development and Their Implication on Local Communities. *International Journal of Economics and Business Administration*, *2*(5), 59–67.

Humphreys, C., & Holloway, J. C. (2016). *Business of Tourism* (10th ed.). Pearson Education Limited.
Jenkins, J. (1994). Research Methods for Leisure and Tourism. *Annals of Tourism Research*, *21*(4). https://doi.org/10.1016/0160-7383(94)90104-x
Kawata, Y., Htay, S. N. N., & Salman, S. A. (2018). Non-Muslims' Acceptance of Imported Products with Halal Logo: A Case Study of Malaysia and Japan. *Journal of Islamic Marketing*, *9*(1), 191–203. https://doi.org/10.1108/JIMA-02-2016-0009
Khan, N., Hassan, A. U., Fahad, S., & Naushad, M. (2020). Factors Affecting Tourism Industry and Its Impacts on Global Economy of the World. *SSRN Electronic Journal*, January. https://doi.org/10.2139/ssrn.3559353
Kumar, J., Hussain, K., & Kannan, S. (2015). Positive Vs. Negative Economic Impacts of Tourism Development: *Developments of the New Tourism Paradigm in the Asia Pacific Region, May*, 402–413.
Mastercard-CrescentRating. (2019). *Mastercard-CrescentRating Halal Travel Frontier 2019 (HTF2019) Report*.
Nikšić Radić, M., Dragičević, D., & Barkiđija Sotošek, M. (2018). The Tourism-led Terrorism Hypothesis – Evidence from Italy, Spain, UK, Germany and Turkey. *Journal of International Studies*, *11*(2), 236–249. https://doi.org/10.14254/2071-8330.2018/11-2/16
Qaddahat, R., Attaalla, F., & Hussein, M. M. (2016). Halal Tourism: Evaluating Opportunities and Challenges in the Middle East "Jordan and Egypt". *Journal of Faculty of Tourism and Hotels, Fayoum University*, *10*(2), 343–358.
Robinson, P., Lück, M., & Smith, S. (2020). An Introduction to Tourism. In Peter Robinson, Michael Luck, Stephen Smith (Eds.) *Tourism* (pp. 3–31). CABI. https://doi.org/10.1079/9781789241488.0003
Rutty, M., Gössling, F. Scott, D. & Hall, M. (2015). The global effects and impacts of tourism. In C. Michael Hall, Stefan Gössling, Daniel Scott (Eds.), *The Routledge Handbook of Tourism and Sustainability* (pp. 36–63). Routledge. https://www.routledgehandbooks.com/doi/10.4324/9780203072332.ch3
Samori, Z., Md Salleh, N. Z., & Khalid, M. M. (2016). Current Trends on Halal Tourism: Cases on Selected Asian Countries. *Tourism Management Perspectives*, *19*, 131–136. https://doi.org/10.1016/j.tmp.2015.12.011
Sultana, S. (2020). Non- Muslims' Perception of Halal Tourism: A Conceptual Paper. *Journal of Halal Studies*, *1*(1), 1–13.
The Economist Intelligence Unit. (2015). *Mapping Africa's Islamic Economy*. The economist.
UNWTO. (2019). World Tourist Barometer: January 2019. *World Tourism Organization*, *17*(1), 1–5. http://www2.unwto.org/press-release/2019-01-21/international-tourist-arrivals-reach-14-billion-two-years-ahead-forecasts
Weaver, D., & Lawton, L. (2014). *Tourism Management* (5th ed.). Wiley & Sons.
World Travel and Tourism Council. (2019). WTTC Travel and Tourism: World Economic Impact 2019. *Current Issues in Tourism*, *75*(3), 1–20. https://doi.org/10.2167/cit/mp004.0
World Travel Organization. (2019). *International Tourism Highlights*. UNWTO, 1–24. https://www.e-unwto.org/doi/pdf/10.18111/9789284421152

1 Definitions and Dimensions of Halal Tourism

Let alone on the definitions of halal tourism and Islamic tourism, there is no consensus among academics on the definition of tourism per se. Given halal tourism is an emerging concept, theories of halal tourism are yet to build, and there are ambiguities and a lack of clarity over the concepts and definitions of halal tourism.

Scholars in their academics works, destination marketers and practitioners widely used the phrases 'halal tourism' and 'Islamic tourism' interchangeably to denote tourism products and services addressing Muslim travelers' needs (Battour et al., 2010; Fakir & Erraoui, 2019; Henderson, 2010b, 2016; Vargas-Sánchez & Moral-Moral, 2018). Battour et al. (2018); Boğan and Sarıışık (2019); and Vargas-Sánchez and Moral-Moral (2019) argue that identifying the proper terminologies and understanding the very concepts of halal tourism remain a conceptual and practical challenge for both academicians and practitioners. According to Henderson (2016); Vargas-Sánchez and Moral-Moral (2019), the concept of both halal tourism and Islamic tourism have been surrounded by definitional ambiguities. Therefore, on the one side, there are definitional ambiguities in both terminologies. On the other side, halal and Islamic tourism are the most interchangeably used phrases as far as sharia-compliant tourism is concerned, as if the two terminologies are similar but are not. Using the two terminologies interchangeably is not only a misconception but also misleading. As Boğan and Sarıışık (2019) state, since the same terminologies halal and Islamic are different, undoubtedly halal tourism differs from Islamic tourism both conceptually and practically. The book's authors also allege that the term 'Islamic' is automatically and strongly connected with religion, but the term 'halal' is not necessarily Islamic or religious. As far as religious intention is not being a prerequisite for making travel, halal tourism does not mean Islamic tourism. Duman (2020) also states that Islamic tourism is taken place purely for religious purposes.

In contrast, halal tourism may include other types of tourism activities that are acceptable by sharia law and Islamic teachings. Therefore, this study seeks to appraise the conceptual and practical usage of the phrases, namely halal tourism and Islamic tourism, in scientific research and the tourism industry and evaluate the difference between the two terminologies. This section will also try to single out the limitation of the existing definitions of

DOI: 10.4324/9781003355236-2

tourism, halal tourism and Islamic tourism. In the end, new definitions are proposed for halal and Islamic tourism.

Defining Tourism, Halal Tourism and Islamic Tourism

This section seeks to provide a thorough theoretical discussion on the definitions of tourism, halal tourism and Islamic tourism and to propose new definitions for halal tourism and Islamic tourism. It also provides a brief discussion of the major typologies of halal tourism.

Defining Tourism

Definitional paradoxes and complexities of tourism have continued until today because a universally accepted definition of tourism has not yet existed (Goeldner & Ritchie, 2012; Lohmann & Netto, 2016; Theobald, 2005; Tribe, 2009; Weaver & Lawton, 2014). However, scholars have tried to define and redefine tourism through time as per their understanding. Before directly moving on to these definitions, it is important to highlight the etymological origin of the terms 'tourism' and 'tourist.' Terminologies such as tourism and tourists are derived from the stem word 'tour,' and there are about four assumptions regarding the etymological origin of the term 'tour.' According to Theobald (2005, p. 9) and Tribe (2009, p. 31), the term 'tour' has been derived from the Latin root *tornare*, and the Greek word *tornos* both mean 'round off' or 'to turn on a lathe,' rotating or a circular movement. Accordingly, the term 'tour' implies: go and back, rounded and a circular temporal movement. Some scholars connect the term 'tour' to the French term *tourner* meaning to 'turn-about,' outdoor activity and touring trip. In English, terminologies such as *tyrnan* and *turnian* (old English) and turn (modern English) are believed to have been the genesis of the term tour. All three terms refer to going or passing around by turning or taking short walks and coming back (Tribe, 2009). All the above terminologies refer to the act of going and coming back. The key point here is that a tour in all cases implies that the starting and ending points are the same, and the travel is not a permanent one. The simplest definition given to tourism, according to the aforementioned terminologies, is, therefore, the action, the desire and the art of traveling only for recreation to return to the place of origin within a specified time (Scorțe et al., 2013; Theobald, 2005; Tribe, 2009). Medlik (2003) defines tourism as 'traveling for pleasure and spending at least one night in different places, and it tends to be synonymous with holidays.'

Hanziker and Krapf (1946) defined tourism broadly as the 'sum of the phenomenon and relationship arising from the travel and stay of non-residents in so far as they do not lead permanent residence and not connected to any earning activities.' According to Goeldner & Ritchie (2005), 'tourism can be defined as the science, art, and business of attracting visitors, transporting them, accommodating them and graciously catering to their needs and wants.' The World Tourism Organization [UNWTO] also tries to define and redefine tourism. The UNWTO is expected to generate and update a universal definition of tourism. Most organizations, including universities, use the definitions

Definitions and Dimensions of Halal Tourism

given by UNWTO though many scholars criticize the definitions thereof. The definitions given by UNWTO at different times have been presented as follows. In the Rome Tourism Conference of 1963, UNWTO defined Tourism as '...the temporary staying of visitors at least 24 hours in the country visited for leisure (recreation, holiday, health, study, religion, sport); business, family, mission, meeting ....' This UNWTO's definition of tourism has ignored visitors who are called excursionists who do not spend 24 in the area visited. In 1993, the UNWTO redefined it as the activities of people traveling to and staying in an area other than their usual place of residence for not more than one consecutive year for leisure, business, and other purposes (Goeldner & Ritchie, 2012). According to the definition of UNWTO (1993 cited in Goeldner & Ritchie, 2012), tourism excludes travels such as home-to-work commuting trips, migrations, and trips to stay more than a year. In 2007, UNWTO revised the definition of tourism as a socio-cultural and economic phenomenon involving people's movement outside their usual palaces of residence or work to other places for personal business or professional purposes. The people involved in such travel are called visitors (they may be tourists or excursionists, residents or non-residents) (United Nations, 2008).

There are also some confusing terminologies concerning tourism, such as leisure and recreation. According to Veal (1992), leisure refers to spare time or free time obtained due to the cessation of routine activities, or it is discretionary time when people are not obliged to do and when they are free to rest or do what they want. Recreation is an activity carried out during free time to refresh one's physical and spiritual needs. Therefore, leisure refers to the availability of free time, whereas recreation is activities engaged in the available free time. Recreation is dependent on the availability of free time, called leisure. Tourism is part of recreation, but not all types of reactions can be tourism. Recreations that involve travel are tourism. Therefore, travel is not always necessary for recreation, but tourism necessarily includes travel.

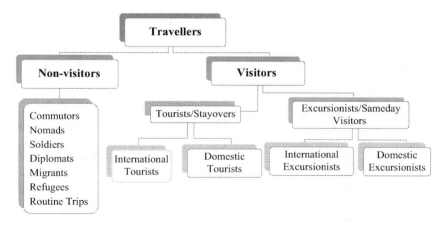

Figure 1.1 Classification of visitors.

Source: Adopted/modified from (Weaver & Lawton, 2014, p. 214).

It is also important to define typologies, such as tourists, visitors and excursionists. According to the definition of UNWTO, visitors are travelers taking a trip to a destination outside their usual environment for less than one consecutive year for business, leisure or other private tasks without earning any remuneration in the country or destination visited. Camilleri (2018) defines tourists as temporary visitors staying at least 24 hours but for less than a year in a destination. Excursionists are temporary visitors who stay in a destination for less than 24 hours.

Based on the purpose of traveling, Camilleri (2018) classified visitors into two broad groups: business and private travelers. Business travelers have little chance to choose where and when to go. The business trip is arranged for specific and brief periods, and the purpose of the trip is other than enjoying the destination's attractions and facilities. There might be some visitation after the given mission is accomplished. Business travelers are less concerned about the cost of travel because the institutions they represent could pay for them, and the demand for business visitors is predominantly inelastic (Camilleri, 2018). Private visitors are free to decide on their travel. They are price-sensitive, and such travel is highly elastic. Destination marketers, therefore, should deploy different ways of promotion and marketing. As noted by Weaver and Lawton (2014), for travelers to be tourists, they must concurrently meet certain spatial, temporal and purposive criteria. However, Theobald (2005, 2012) and Tribe (2009) raise several concerns regarding tourism, tourist and visitor definitions. For instance, how far from their homes persons should travel to be considered tourists and visitors, and what types of travels qualify as tourism are questions not well addressed yet. Especially the minimum distance thresholds are unspecified in most definitions of tourism, tourist and visitor.

Since tourism is a relatively new discipline, there have been continuing debates and contradicting concepts in its definitions. Both an unavailability of a universal definition and the availability of contradictions between existing theoretical definitions and practical activities of tourism are issues for tourism academics to be addressed. Based on the preceding definitions, one can say that the general acceptance of tourism activities is linked to going away for less than one consecutive year other than the place of usual residence and work without earning any remuneration. However, it is often difficult, if not impossible, to conclude that all people engaged in tourism do not earn any remuneration. For instance, some organizations of the visited places may pay per diem for participants in some special meetings and conferences.

Moreover, participants in some sporting events, such as the Olympics, earn some prize money. These things disqualify the phrase 'without earning any remuneration' that has been included in many definitions of tourism. Moreover, almost no definitions dare to specify a minimum distance between the origin region and destination. There is no general agreement between countries that try to specify how long a visitor must go away from his/her home and place of residence (Theobald, 2005). This issue causes the rise of questions such as 'who is a visitor?', especially for domestic visitors. Different countries have tried to put their cutting points. For instance, in the United States, visitors must travel away from their homes for a distance of at least 50 miles (one way) for business, pleasure, personal affairs, or any other purpose other than to commute to work, whether they stay overnight or return the same day while Canada reduces the distance to 25 miles. In Australia, a visitor is a person visiting a location at least 40 km away from his usual place of residence (Theobald, 2005). Even there is a disagreement within one country's organizations regarding how many kilometers/miles one should travel to be called a visitor or a tourist. For instance, the U.S. Census Bureau and the U.S. Travel Data Center propose that a tourist must travel at least 100 miles away from his/her home. In contrast, U.S. National Tourism Resources Review Commission reduces the minimum to 50 miles. Canada quantified that a tourist travels a minimum of 25 miles away from his place of residence or work (Theobald, 2005).

Defining Halal Tourism

Despite attracting a large number of global visitors, halal tourism is a relatively new concept in both tourism theory and practice (Statistical Economic and Social Research and Training Centre for Islamic [SESRIC], 2018). Therefore, it is not unprecedented that definitional, conceptual and practical challenges have been experienced in the field. Various terminologies and connotations such as Islamic tourism, sharia tourism, Muslim-friendly tourism, halal hospitality and halal-friendly travel have been used interchangeably with halal tourism throughout the literature (Battour, 2019; Boğan & Sarıışık, 2019). However, despite the availability of some commonalities, halal tourism is a different concept from all of the abovementioned terminologies.

Before venturing further into the concept of halal tourism, it is imperative to consider what the term 'halal' means and scrutinize the etymological origin of the term 'halal.' The term 'halal' is derived from the Arabic root word *halla*, which is equivalent to terms such as 'lawful,' 'legal,' 'legitimate,' 'permissible,' 'allowable,' and 'admissible' (Al Jallad, 2008). Al-Qaradawi (2013); Battour et al. (2010); Eid and El-Gohary (2015); El-Gohary (2016) state that the Arabic term 'halal' refers to anything permitted, allowed and approved according to Sharia. Borzooei and Asgari (2013) also state that the Arabic word 'halal' is equivalent to English words such as allowable and permissible. Al-Qaradawi further explains it as a permitted action concerning which no restriction exists and the doing of which is allowed by the law-giver, Allah (Al-Qaradawi, 2013, p. xxv). Evans and Syed (2015) define halal as an Arabic term meaning permissible or lawful. It is the opposite of haram, which means prohibited or unlawful.

Al Jallad (2008) further defines the term 'halal' as '[…] permissible behavior, speech, dress, conduct, manner, dietary and services and facilities.' Al Jallad claims that the halal–haram dichotomy usually applies to aspects of Muslim life. Jamal and El-Bassiouny (2018) define the word 'halal' as a comprehensive concept with a wide cultural and social connotation and encourages Muslims to use goods and services that promote goodness and welfare in all aspects of life. They further illustrate that halal encompasses goods and services such as foods, beverages, clothing, cosmetics, pharmaceuticals, entertainment, finance and financial services. Western academics have mainly considered halal from the narrow perspective of Islamic dietary laws (Al Jallad, 2008), and the large areas of halal such as halal tourism, medicines, cosmetics, halal insurance and loans, are untapped yet (Ambali & Bakar, 2014). This implies that halal must be studied from the broader context regarding its practicability and suitability for secular businesses. Halal, in the tourism context, according to Battour et al. (2017), is a practice or activity in tourism that is permissible according to Islamic teaching. Al Jallad (2008) states that the domain of halal goes beyond food and drinking and is not limited to purely a religious issue but is in the realm of business and trade. According to Suleman and Qayum (2018a), a widely held understanding exists to connect the terms 'halal' and 'haram' only to dietary requirements. Particularly non-Muslims try to confine the term only to dietary systems and law, specifically to meat and meat products. Eid and El-Gohary (2015); El-Gohary (2016) argue that even though the term 'halal' for so long connoted to food and beverages, the concept of halal is not confined only to food or food products. It includes all aspects of Muslim life. In the 21st century, it is no longer possible to confine halal solely to food and beverages because other businesses, including the halal tourism and hospitality industry, have become attractive areas of halal business. As El-Gohary (2016, p. 126) states, the concept of halal is built around the need for any Muslim to have products that are allowable, acceptable and permissible from a religious point of view that starts with food and beverages and covers many other aspects such as banking and finance, tourism, cosmetics, jobs, travel and transport services and so on. There are also similar concepts in Islam, such as *makruh* (disliked) and *haram* (forbidden). According to Duman (2020), *makruh* refers to activities that are not prescribed halal or *haram* but are disliked and discouraged.

In contrast, *haram* foods, beverages and behavioral conduct are prescribed and unacceptable in Islam. For example, Islam openly categorizes activities and actions such as adultery, gambling, consumption of pork, selling or using alcoholic products and dressing inappropriately to be *haram* (Duman, 2020). Islam has universal values that are not bounded by place, race, color or social status. It is believed that the principles of halal are among these universal values of Islam. Muslims should obey and practice sharia law irrespective of social class, nationality, race or place. The direct opposite of halal is haram, which refers to prohibited, unlawful and forbidden according to Sharia law (Jamal & El-Bassiouny, 2019). Therefore, according to Evans and Syed (2015), the defining parameter of the concept of halal is eventually evolving and expanding. Traditionally, halal refers only to meat and poultry and/or food and beverages. With the passage of time, however, halal is growing to include halal tourism, medicines, cosmetics, halal insurance and the financial system (Battour et al., 2018; Evans & Syed, 2015). In recent decades, halal has grown to include all aspects of Muslim life, including travel and tourism.

Battour et al. (2010); Battour et al. (2017, 2018); Battour and Ismail (2016); Battour et al. (2012); Vargas-Sánchez and Moral-Moral (2019) define halal tourism as any tourism phenomenon that is allowable for Muslim according to Sharia. The preceding definition is misleading because it excludes non-Muslims from halal tourism. This definition is not acceptable within the scope of the present study because the later considers halal tourism from a secular point of view. In contrast, as mentioned earlier, the definition given by the authors excludes non-Muslim visitors. Jamal and El-Bassiouny (2019) define halal tourism as tourism activities and behavior geared toward individuals and families that abide by the rules and principles of Sharia. They further explain that halal tourism is a kind of tourism that offers solutions and options for Muslim visitors by allocating prayer spaces, offering halal foods and beverages, providing separate swimming pools and avoiding alcoholic beverages. According to Battour et al. (2018), halal tourism is defined as tourism activities that are permissible under Islamic law in terms of behavior, dress, conduct and diet. Battour et al. (2011) define halal tourism as the act of designing and providing products and services at destinations to address the religious needs of Muslims. It refers to tourism products that provide hospitality services per Islamic beliefs and practices. This involves providing halal meals and beverages, assigning separate swimming pools with Islamic swimming etiquette for men and women, having alcohol-free dining areas, and arranging prayer spaces and ablution facilities (Elasrag, 2016, p. 25). World Travel Market (WTM, 2007) describes halal tourism as a type of tourism that complies with Islamic teachings in areas such as behaviorism, dress and diet. Jeffery defined halal tourism as a type of religious tourism that denotes sharia-compliant activities in terms of behavior, dress, conduct and diet (WTM, 2007). Aji (2019) defines halal tourism as 'a trip for leisure or business undertaken by Muslims towards tourist objects or at transaction either Islamic or non-Islamic countries except those countries that Sharia has banned.' The preceding definition considers Muslims as the only customers of halal tourism, and it denies the role of non-Muslim as customers; this could adversely affect the development of halal tourism. Aji argues that halal tourism is not Islamic tourism, but he fails to differentiate the peculiar behavior of Islamic tourism clients from halal tourism clients. Nor does he specify whether the products and services consumed by travelers while traveling are halal. These issues are the central point as far as halal tourism is concerned.

By thoroughly reviewing previous definitions of halal tourism by various authors from the extant literature and conducting an interview with tourism experts, the gaps in each definition have been identified and discussed earlier.

Therefore, the researchers of the study under discussion propose the following definition of halal tourism.

> Halal tourism comprises the activities of any person (Muslim or non-Muslim) who obeys Sharia law and consumes halal products and services, traveling to and staying in places other than his/her usual place of residence or work for not more than twelve months for secular and/or religious purposes.

Defining Islamic Tourism

UNWTO defined Islamic tourism as the traveling to and staying of Muslims outside their usual environment for less than 12 months for the participation of those activities that originate from Islamic motivations that are not related to the exercise of an activity remunerated in the place visited (Laderlah et al., 2011, p. 186). Duman defined Islamic tourism as 'tourism activities by Muslims that originate from Islamic motivations and are realized according to sharia principles' (Duman, 2011, p. 6). According to Jafari and Scott (2014, p. 13), Islamic tourism is the touristification of pilgrimage by merging leisure activities into a religious one. Mohamed (2018) defined it as travel that involves exploring Islamic history, arts, culture and heritage and enjoying the Islamic way of life in conformity with the Islamic faith. It could also be seen as any activity, event, experience or indulgence undertaken in a state of travel that does not transgress Islamic principles. Islamic tourism is the participation of Muslims in tourism without compromising their religious values and personal habits (Carboni et al., 2014, p. 2). According to Din (1989), Islamic tourism is a touristic activity that obeys Islamic principles undertaken by tourists with Islamic motivation.

The definition given by Din and Carboni et al. is similar to that of halal tourism. Because even though they mentioned the motivation properly, they failed to define the intention of the travelers. As to the present researchers, to be called Islamic tourism, the visitors or tourists must be Muslims, and their intention must be purely religious. The Organization of Islamic Cooperation (2011) defines it as 'Muslims tourists traveling to destinations where Islam is an official or dominant faith, often for reasons connected to religion.' This definition excludes non-Muslim countries as a destination for Islamic tourism. However, Islamic tourism could be conducted toward non-Muslim destinations. For instance, Muslims may travel to non-Muslim countries for Islamic business and preaching purposes. For Henderson (2010a), Islamic tourism generally describes tourism primarily undertaken by its followers within the Muslim world. This definition also misses that Islamic tourism could be carried out toward non-Muslim countries and destinations. Muslims may travel to non-Muslim countries to preach Islam for business or leisure. Even the very purpose of halal tourism is to meet the religious needs of Muslims in non-Muslim destinations. Because it is supposed that Muslims may face more challenges in non-Muslim countries with a lack of halal products and services as these countries have no experience with them.

In Muslim destinations, halal products and services are already available for the everyday life of the locals. Boğan and Sarıışık (2019) define Islamic tourism as 'a tourism type which has emerged as a result of individuals' preferences to travel with the purpose of gaining the consent of God.' According to Boğan and Sariisik, the traveler's intention is the main criterion for discerning Islamic tourism from halal tourism. They have overlooked other important variables, such as the behavior of the travelers and the kinds of products and services going to be consumed. Therefore, the current study argues that this definition has missed two important issues. First, they did not indicate whether travelers are Muslims or not. The term 'Islamic' per se may not indicate the faiths of the travelers. As far as Islamic tourism is concerned, the travelers must be Muslims. Second, they have failed to postulate the type of products and services visitors would rely on. Hence, to fill such gaps, the current researchers propose the following definition for Islamic tourism.

> Islamic tourism comprises the activities of practicing Muslims who strictly abide by Sharia law and principles and consume only halal products and services, traveling to and staying in places outside their usual environment for not more than one consecutive year for sacred or religious purposes.

Halal Tourism Vis-à-Vis Islamic Tourism

Various scholars have researched halal tourism and Islamic tourism (Azam et al., 2019; Battour et al., 2010; Battour, 2019; Battour et al., 2011, 2018; Battour & Ismail, 2016; Battour et al., 2010, 2012; Bhuiyan et al., 2011; Boğan & Sarıışık, 2019; Din, 1989; Duman, 2011, 2020; El-Gohary, 2016; Hassan, 2015; Jafari & Scott, 2014; Scorțe et al., 2013). However, most of these studies fail to indicate where the difference between halal and Islamic tourism lies. Among others, Boğan and Sarıışık (2019), in their article entitled 'Halal Tourism: Conceptual and Practical Challenges,' have tried to see the difference between halal tourism and Islamic tourism. However, they have also missed some important points. First, they consider all people who engage in halal tourism as 'Muslim tourists.' They suggest hotels that provide sharia-compliant services as 'halal hotels' and visitors who involves in halal tourism as "Muslim tourists.' However, some travelers who engage in halal tourism may not be Muslims. Practically some non-Muslims also participate in halal tourism.

Therefore, the tourist who engages in halal tourism could not necessarily be Muslim. They could be Muslims or non-Muslims who agree to use halal products and services. Consequently, it is recommended that tourists who engage in halal tourism be called 'halal-conscious tourists.' Boğan and Sarıışık predominantly focused on the motivation of Islamic tourism, while the concept of halal tourism received less attention. Second, the authors did propose a new definition of Islamic tourism but did not suggest halal tourism. The current study proposes 'inclusive and cogent' definitions for both. One of the most significant differences between the current paper and the previous studies is that the present study tries to see 'halal tourism' from the secular perspective as a business of Muslims and non-Muslims. The previous studies mainly consider Muslims as the only customers of halal tourism. In this book, we strongly argue that halal tourism is secular tourism that relies on halal products and services, where both Muslims and non-Muslims are equally welcomed. Moreover, the present study tries to demonstrate the classifications and interrelations of Muslim-friendly tourism. This study also tries to incorporate the opinions of tourism scholars through a new Delphi technique.

Boğan and Sarıışık (2019) point out that both academics and practitioners have not designated the cogent terminologies for sharia-compliant tourism. Therefore, halal tourism and Islamic tourism are often used interchangeably until now. Battour and Ismail (2016) conclude that sharia-compliant tourism and halal tourism have a very close meanings, if not necessarily the same. However, Battour later (2019) proclaims the difference between halal and Islamic tourism. He claims that the term 'Islamic' is used only to describe the Islamic faith and Islam's doctrine-related issues.

Nonetheless, several academics and practitioners still consider halal and Islamic tourism synonymous phrases; this is an inaccurate, misleading and faulty generalization. Halal and Islamic tourism have different meanings, each holding different roles. For a proper understanding of the science of halal tourism, it is necessary to precisely appraise the difference between halal tourism and Islamic tourism. The researchers under consideration also argue that people engage in Islamic tourism to accomplish their religious mission and please their God under any circumstance where their ultimate goal is Islamic. Therefore, it is purely religious and deserves to be called Islamic tourism. According to Duman (2020), the purposes of Islamic tourism include Hajj, Umrah, visiting relatives and friends (VRF), contemplating the greatness of God through visiting the natural beauties and other creations and cultures, learning about the religious experiences of past civilizations, to impart Islamic education, preaching and sermon. Boğan and Sarıışık (2019) emphasize the intention of the visitation to discuss whether Islamic tourism differs from halal tourism. According to them, if the intention of the visitation is other than pleasing God, it could not be said for Islamic tourism, even though they use only halal products and services throughout their trips. In Islamic tradition, it is believed that action could be Islamic only when the traveler intends to please Allah. For example, the traveling of Saudi Arabian tourists toward the halal destinations of Thailand, the Philippines, Singapore, Japan and so on cannot be Islamic tourism. However, Saudi Arabian tourists' travel toward such destinations could be halal tourism if they rely only on halal food, beverages and services while traveling. If Muslims in any destination rely on non-halal products and services, it is neither halal nor Islamic tourism.

El-Gohary (2016) considers halal tourism a subcategory of religious tourism. However, halal tourism cannot necessarily be grouped under religious tourism because the activities of those travelers, who travel for other than religious purposes, such as for pleasure and business, can be considered halal tourism as far as these visitors consume halal products and services while traveling. Therefore, halal tourism is both within and beyond the realm of religious tourism. Hence, it is important to note that halal tourism reaches beyond the boundary of Islamic or religious tourism. Mohideen and Mohideen (2008) also argue that the term 'Islamic' refers to the religious practices of Muslims per the rule of their religion. Islamic tourism considers some variables but not halal tourism. For instance, in Islamic tourism, the following points have been taken into consideration: the target customers (i.e., Muslims or non-Muslims), activities in a destination and the purpose of travel (Islamic or secular) and the product and service offered (i.e., food, facilities halal or not). However, halal tourism concerns only the last variable, the product and service offered (i.e., whether food, beverages, facilities, and services are halal or not). El-Gohary (2016) argues that practicing Muslims want to be honest about their religion wherever they are. They consume only products permitted by Sharia and fall under the jurisdiction of Islamic Sharia. The only difference between traditional (conventional tourism) and halal tourism is that the latter relies on sharia-compliant accommodations, food and beverages, activities, facilities and actions. If the visitors consume only halal products and use only halal services throughout their way and in the destinations, they can be both halal tourism and Islamic tourism. If the intention of their traveling is religious only to please Allah or to strengthen their faith either by training, learning, attending sermons or contemplating, what has been seen is Islamic tourism.

Visiting relatives and friends to please Allah is highly encouraged in Islam. There is some evidence in both the Quran and Hadith about the value of maintaining kinship ties, for it has a great role in achieving social cohesion, cooperation and love among the Muslim brethren and sistren. Therefore, visiting relatives and friends to please God will also be another main intention for the participant in Islamic tourism. Furthermore, in Islamic tourism, Muslims may travel to perform pilgrimage, teach and learn about religious causes, preach or sermonize, pray, recite Quran and strengthen the Muslim fraternity (Din, 1989). Moreover, people may also visit various wonders of natural resources, landscapes and historical sites for the religious purpose of contemplating the ultimate power of the Almighty God.

Islamic tourism can be classified into two broad dimensions. First, there is a religious tour to perform some religious duty in the place visited or transit routes such as pilgrimage toward shrines or saints. Hajj and Umra could be the best example in this regard. Second, there is also a tour for the sake of seeking and/or imparting Islamic knowledge. For instance, Muslims may travel for training, Islamic education, meetings and preaching. During this kind of visitation, knowledge is recorded and quoted for wider dissemination. As one can learn from Islamic history, books of literature, history and geography, which have never been written before by any historian or geographer, have emerged after the beginning of travel and tourism. These days, the *Tebligh* movement exemplifies this dimension. There are Muslim Jamaas known as *Tebligh* who travel to preach, teach and spread Islam accordingly. They mainly travel for less than four months (Abbasi, 2019; Haq & Wong, 2010).

Table 1.1 Summary of Characteristics of Halal Tourism and Islamic Tourism

Types of Tourism	Travel Motivations and Purposes	Type of Visitors	Type of Destinations	Activities in the Visited Areas	Consumption Preference
Halal Tourism	Secular & Religious	Muslims & non-Muslims	Muslim and non-Muslim countries, if halal products and services are available	Any halal activities	Halal products and services
Islamic Tourism	Purely religious	Only Muslims	Muslim and Non-Muslim countries, if Halal products and services are available	Religious activities such as performing pilgrimage, venerating, preaching, teaching, learning, sermonizing	Halal products and services

Sources: By the Authors, 2020.

Based on the intention of the travelers, halal tourism can be divided into two dichotomies: secular halal tourism and religious halal tourism (Islamic tourism). Both secular and Islamic tourism are similar in that both use halal products and services. At the same time, there is a distinction between secular and sacred halal tourism in that the intention of the former is not religious. In contrast, the latter can have only a religious purpose. It must be understood that Muslims also have secular life and want to enjoy it without transgressing Islamic principles. For several years, Muslim visitors were considered to visit only Islamic destinations (Fakir & Erraoui, 2019). However, this assumption no longer works in the 21st century and does not make sense. Muslims have started to engage in tourism in a halal way. Halal tourism allows Muslims to enjoy their worldly life without compromising the principles of Islam. El-Gohary (2016) argues that branding sharia-compliant tourism as 'Islamic tourism' might give rise to undesired consequences because tourism products designated only for Muslim customers could deter non-Muslim customers who might also consume halal tourism products and

Definitions and Dimensions of Halal Tourism 25

services. El-Gohary recommends 'halal tourism' as the main and the only terminology to brand and describe sharia-compliant tourism products and activities. The following diagram shows the relationship and interconnections between conventional, halal and Islamic tourism.

The desire to distance oneself from traditional religiosity and unIslamic deeds among halal-conscious visitors gives rise to the new typology known as halal tourism. The present researchers also argue that halal tourism is semantically and conceptually located both within and beyond the realm of Islamic tourism, as it has the same inward direction. Still, it welcomes secular and non-Muslim visitors as well.

Suleman and Qayum (2018b) also argue that the term 'Islamic' excludes non-Muslim customers, but halal is inclusive. They further describe that Islamic tourism strongly connects with divine guidance and worship. Another essential point that Battour (2019) raised is that of non-Muslims' traveling to destinations in Muslim countries or Islamic destinations, such as Islamic sacred place palaces, ancient mosques and shrines to visit Islamic historical religious and cultural sites. In other words, given that these travelers are non-Muslims, this kind of tourism will not be Islamic tourism. However, this kind of tourism could be halal tourism if they use halal foods and halal services while traveling and staying there. Though this issue seems debatable, it is easy to allege that it is not Islamic tourism.

As Battour suggests, the travel of non-Muslims to those areas could be termed 'Islam-related tourism.' However, the present researchers argue that it can be halal tourism if these tourists use halal products and services. Therefore, it is possible to conclude that halal tourism is a subcategory of

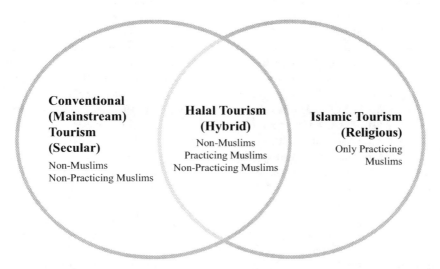

Figure 1.2 The interconnection of mainstream tourism, halal tourism and Islamic tourism.

Source: The researcher, 2020.

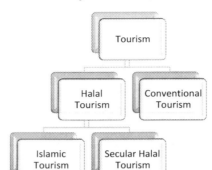

Figure 1.3 Typologies of Muslim-friendly tourism.
Source: The Authors, 2020.

tourism, and Islamic tourism is a subcategory of halal tourism. Islamic tourism is part and parcel of halal tourism, but it does not necessarily mean that all kinds of halal tourism are Islamic tourism. Therefore, mainstream tourism subsumes halal tourism, halal tourism subsumes Islamic tourism, and Islamic tourism is a branch of halal tourism.

There is also similar terminology known as Muslim-friendly tourism. The term 'Muslim-friendly' refers to the tourism experience that fits practicing Muslims. This concept is closer to halal tourism, but the two differ (Battour, 2019). The researchers under discussion argue that the term 'Muslim friendly' is not advisable from the marketing perspective to promote halal tourism because it seems exclusive to non-Muslims. It drags halal tourism toward a spiritual dimension. The term 'halal' is wider and broader than Muslim-friendly. Halal tourism is not only Muslim-friendly but also non-Muslim-friendly. For the success of halal tourism, the researchers recommend that the spiritual dimension of halal tourism should diminish, and it must excel as responsible tourism in terms of ecological, social and health dimensions. This perspective makes halal tourism sustainable and acceptable among all parties (Muslim and non-Muslims). For a destination to be recognized as a halal tourism destination, it should be fully halal and not be allowed to provide non-halal products and services. However, Muslim-friendly companies could provide halal and non-halal products and services but not in the same place or section. Muslim-friendly destinations provide halal services, products and spaces for prayer, but they are in the realm of trade.

To conclude, even though the commencement of tourism lapsed more than a half-century, the universally accepted definition of tourism has not been adopted yet. The academic and practical ambiguity is very deep in halal and Islamic tourism. Therefore, the definition and the parameters of halal and Islamic tourism have not yet been well defined and identified. In this book, the existing definitions of tourism, halal tourism and Islamic tourism were critically reviewed and evaluated. In this chapter, the authors tried to reveal the limitation of the existing definitions and propose new ones for halal and

Islamic tourism. The study approves that there is an absolute difference between halal and Islamic tourism though people still use these terminologies interchangeably. The point of difference between halal and Islamic tourism mainly lies in the intentions and actions of the travelers. If the visitors set out on a journey by shouldering a religious mission to please Allah and rely on halal products and services, there is no doubt that this kind of tourism is Islamic. Whereas if visitors consume only halal products and services, this kind of tourism can be called halal tourism irrespective of the intentions of the visitation and who the travelers are.

Halal tourism is semantically and conceptually located both within and beyond Islamic tourism. In other words, though halal tourism seems to be tourism for Muslims, it also has room for non-Muslims. Even though all kinds of Islamic tourism are part and parcel of halal tourism, it does not necessarily mean that all kinds of halal tourism are Islamic tourism. Therefore, halal tourism subsumes Islamic tourism, which is a branch of halal tourism.

The difference between halal and Islamic tourism should be well noted in academic writing and the industry. Therefore, this book suggests that academics should use appropriate terminologies in their academic writing about sharia-compliant tourism. Destination marketers are also advised to use halal tourism while promoting sharia-compliant tourism. This term is relatively secular and acceptable among both Muslims and non-Muslims who are interested in using halal products and services. Practitioners, policymakers, hoteliers and tour operators need to identify the difference between Islamic tourism and halal tourism and respond to the customers' particular interests. For instance, Islamic tourists may not be interested in worldly entertainment; rather, they may focus on religious sites and religious issues, whereas halal visitors may prefer to have more entertainment. For the success of halal tourism, it is advisable that the spiritual dimension of halal tourism should diminish, and it must excel as responsible tourism in terms of ecological, social and health dimensions. This perspective makes halal tourism sustainable and acceptable among all parties (Muslim and non-Muslims).

Halal Tourism and the Sharia Law

Sharia law, also known as Islamic law, refers to 'the clear path' or 'guide' (Bashir et al., 2008). The authors note that the sharia law includes a set of rules, regulations, teachings and values that guide one Muslim to the right path whose reward will be everlasting in worldly life and the hereafter. For Muslims to realize the divine will and to live in Islam, they must follow and abide by the sharia law. As El-Gohary (2016) states, there are two main sources of sharia law: the Holy Quran and the Sunnah of Prophet Muhammad (PBUH). The Holy Quran is the holiest book of Muslims. Muslims believe that the Quran is the actual word of Allah revealed to the Prophet Muhammad (PBUH) through Angel Gabriel, whereas Sunnah refers to what Prophet Mohammed (PBUH) said, did and approved (Bashir et al., 2008). In addition to the Holy Quran and the Sunnah, there are secondary sources of the Sharia such as *Ijmaa* (scholars' consensus), *Qiyas* (analogical deduction), *Ijtihad* (personal reasoning) and *Maslaha* (public interest) (Battour et al., 2010). Scholars of the field have unanimously agreed that for products, services and activities to be halal, they must meet the requirements of and obey the sharia principles. All halal tourism and halal travel must obey Islamic principles and Sharia. Therefore, as El-Gohary (2016); Vargas-Sánchez and Moral-Moral (2019) recommend, it is very advisable to understand Islamic Sharia and its impact on a destination to capture halal-conscious customers on tourism products and services.

The Birth of Halal Tourism

Even though halal food and service have existed for at least the past 1,400 years, the term 'halal' started to label sharia-compliant meats and poultry in the 1970s and 1980s (Evans & Syed, 2015). In due course, the terms 'Islamic tourism' and 'halal tourism' began appearing in academia in the 1990s and 2010s. Until Din published the first article on Islam and tourism in 1989, sharia-compliant tourism was treated under the terminology pilgrimage or religious tourism. In 1989, Din published an article entitled 'Islam and Tourism: Patterns, Issues, and Options.' Therefore, from 1989 to 2010, the term 'Islamic tourism' was widely utilized to refer to sharia-compliant tourism by academicians and practitioners. In 2000, the Organization of Islamic Cooperation (OIC) recognized Islamic tourism as one economic sector for the region (Kamarudin & Ismail, 2012). Since the 11 September 2001 incident, Muslims from the Middle East have preferred Muslim countries, especially Asia, to Western countries to spend their leisure time. This situation has caused a rapid proliferation of sharia-compliant tourism. In 2008, Malaysia hosted the first OIC Global Islamic Tourism Conference and Exhibition and the World Islamic Conference in Kuala Lumpur (Kamarudin & Ismail, 2012). Battour, Mohd Nazari Ismail and Moustafa Battor coined another more inclusive and compelling terminology named 'halal tourism' in 2010 to denote any kind of sharia-compliant tourism. Therefore, although halal tourism-like activities have been practiced for a relatively long period, the very terminology of halal tourism appeared in the academic literature very recently, only in 2010 (Battour et al., 2010). They employed the terminology in their journal article 'Toward a Halal Tourism Market' and introduced it to academia. Before 2010, the term 'Islamic tourism' was utilized to denote sharia-compliant tourism. From 2010 onward, both halal tourism and Islamic tourism have been used interchangeably, but the former gradually gets more recognition. It is believed that halal tourism will continue to be a convincing and dominant branded terminology to market and promote sharia-compliant tourism. Boğan and Sarıışık (2019); El-Gohary (2016); Vargas-Sánchez and Moral-Moral (2019) note that researchers and practitioners have used halal tourism and Islamic tourism interchangeably until now. However, in the past few years, many academics have been inclined to use halal tourism because the term 'halal' is secular and more acceptable by both non-Muslims and Muslims than the term 'Islamic.'

As mainstream tourism started in Europe, halal tourism was born in South East Asia. Malaysia, Indonesia, Turkiye and Singapore are the pioneers in halal tourism development. As noted by Battour (2016); El-Gohary (2016), Malaysia is the first country to identify Muslim-friendly holidays as a niche market. In 2016, she was able to attract 6 million halal-conscious tourists. Brunei, Turkiye and the UAE are also said to be among the forerunners and the leading countries in halal travel and tourism (El-Gohary, 2016). According to Mastercard-CrescentRating (2018) projection in the Global Muslim Travel Index 2019, more than 230 million Muslim tourists are expected to engage in domestic and international tourism and contribute US$300 billion to the global economy by 2026.

Trends and Prospects of Halal Tourism

According to MasterCard-CrescentRating (2019), the number of Muslim travelers has steadily increased. In 2000, there were about 25 million outbound Muslim travelers. This number climbed to 98 million travelers in 2010 and 140 million travelers in 2018 (Mastercard-CrescentRating, 2019a). Mastercard-CrescentRating (2019a) forecasts that the number of Muslim travelers will be 160 million and 230 million in 2020 and 2026, respectively. Mastercard-CrescentRating (2018) identified the following positive factors for halal tourism growth. The growing Muslim population, the increment of discretionary time and disposable income of halal-conscious tourists, the increasingly growing conscious young Muslim population, increasing access to travel information, increasing availability of Muslim-friendly travel services and facilities, and the emergence of Ramadan travel and proliferation of business travel among Muslim countries. For instance, Muslims representing growing economies such as Indonesia, Malaysia, and Turkiye and economies in the Gulf Cooperation Council (GCC) are rapidly growing to meet these new business opportunities in the MICE (Meetings, Incentives, Conferences, and Events) sector. According to Mastercard-CrescentRating Halal Travel Frontier 2019 (HTF2019) Report, it is identified that there are 17 trends that we believe will shape the next phase of development in the Halal travel space (Mastercard-CrescentRating, 2019b).

Table 1.2 Top Ten Destinations and Origins of Halal Visitors

Rank	Top 10 Destinations-GMTI2019 Rankings		Top 10 Outbound Halal Tourism Markets/2019	
	OIC Countries	Non-OIC Countries	OIC Countries	Non-OIC Countries
1	Malaysia	Singapore	Algeria	China
2	Indonesia	Thailand	Azerbaijan	France
3	Turkiye	UK	Bangladesh	Germany

(*Continued*)

Table 1.2 (Continued)

Rank	Top 10 Destinations-GMTI2019 Rankings		Top 10 Outbound Halal Tourism Markets/2019	
	OIC Countries	Non-OIC Countries	OIC Countries	Non-OIC Countries
4	Saudi Arabia	Japan	Egypt	India
5	The UAE	Taiwan	Indonesia	Italy
6	Qatar	South Africa	Iran	Russia
7	Morocco	Hong Kong	Jordan	Singapore
8	Bahrain	South Korea	Kazakhstan	The Netherlands
9	Oman	France/Spain, Philippines	Kuwait	The U.S.A.
10		Burnie	Malaysia	The U.K.

Source: Mastercard-CrescentRating, 2019b.

MasterCard-CrescentRating introduced Global Muslim Travel Index (GMTI) in 2015 to analyze the halal travel market and destinations. From 2011 to 2015, CrescentRating employed 'CrescentRating Annual Ranking' to analyze the halal travel market and benchmarked destinations (Mastercard-CrescentRating, 2019b). As it points out, the GMTI criteria are based on the following 'CrescentRating ACES model.' ACES is the acronym that stands for Access, Communication, Environment and Services. The ACES model encompasses four key factors:

- Ease of access to the destination includes visa requirements, connectivity and transport infrastructure
- Internal and external communication by the destination incorporates outreach (public education, media outreach, and Muslim visitor guidebooks), ease of communication and digital presence
- The environment at the destination comprises safety, faith restrictions, visitor arrivals and enabling climate
- Services provided by the destination refer to core needs (halal food and prayer -facilities), core services (hotels and airports) and unique experiences

Countries known to be too conservative Islamic are now engaging in halal tourism. For instance, Saudi Arabia is to offer its rich pre-Islamic and Islamic heritages for sharia-compliant tourists of any faith. According to Dinarstandard (2019), Saudi Arabia is planning to generate US$20 billion from tourism by 2035 from its proposed "Al-Ula Project," Saudi Arabia started issuing tourist visas for 90 days in 2019. According to the state of the Global Islamic Economy Report 2019–2020, the al-Ula project could help Saudi Arabia adopt a shift from a purely religious travel destination to a heritage and leisure travel destination as well (Dinarstandard, 2019). The Al-Ula project is expected to become a huge archaeological, cultural and tourism complex and an open-air living museum in a region as vast as Belgium. This major investment aims to make the Al-Ula the best visitor attraction and Saudi's cultural capital. Saudi Arabia is also developing a heritage tourism project at Souq Okaz in Taif. In such a way, Saudi Arabia is opening its door to tourism to get its fair share of the sector and retell its great history. The leading countries that have taken the initiatives of halal tourism development, such as Turkiye, Malaysia and Indonesia, have continued to capture halal-conscious customers. Besides attracting inbound ones, Muslim outbound visitors globally have increased and contributed 6.8% to the global economy in 2018. Saudi Arabia, UAE and Qatar were the top three countries in this regard (Dinarstandard, 2019). State of global Islamic economic report [SGIER] (2019–2020) confirms that Muslim spend on travel was valued at US$189 billion in 2018 and is forecast to grow to US$274 billion by 2024 (Dinarstandard, 2019). Muslims constitute a global market of approximately 2 billion potential customers (CrescentRating, 2017). The Muslim population is growing at twice the rate of the non-Muslim world, so the market for halal products and services is attracting more attention.

Indeed, according to the Pew Research Center (2015), the Muslim population is growing more than double as fast as the world population. In the decades to come, the world's population is projected to grow by 32%, but Muslim numbers will grow by 70%. Therefore, the number of Muslims has been forecasted to increase from 1.8 billion in 2015 to nearly 3 billion in 2060. In the second half of the 21st century, Muslims will likely surpass Christians as the world's largest religious group (Pew Research Center, 2015). This rapid global demographic will have an impact on the trends of halal tourism. Halal tourism has already started injecting a good proportion of dollars into the global economy. For instance, Suradin (2018) points out that in 2014 halal tourism contributed about USD 140 billion or 11% of total world expenditure on travel and tourism; this amount has not included hajj and *umrah*.

Halal Tourism and Non-Muslims

Reactions and attitudes of non-Muslims toward halal tourism receive the attention of numerous researchers (Battour, 2017; Battour et al., 2018, 2018; Hammuri & Eseynel, 2017; Kawata et al., 2018; Khan & Callanan, 2017; Sultana, 2020; Wibowo & Ahmad, 2016). Most studies on halal tourism reveal that non-Muslim countries as a destination and non-Muslim visitors as customers have been actively engaged in halal tourism development. Even though halal products and services are expected mainly to be tailored for Muslim customers, non-Muslim customers also show interest in consuming halal products and services (Gabdrakhmanov et al., 2016). Non-Muslims prefer halal products for better quality of halal products (Gabdrakhmanov et al., 2016). Similarly, non-Muslim countries and destinations supply halal products and services (Battour et al., 2018b; Kawata et al., 2018). According to Evans and Syed (2015), the practice of halal certification was started in the 1970s and 1980s to include non-Muslim entrepreneurs in the Muslim business in Malaysia. Research conducted by Evans and Syed (2015) reveals that the presence of non-Muslim Chinese in Malaysia caused the halal certification system. The presence of non-Muslim businesspersons has given rise to the beginning of halal verification and the birth of the halal certificate to guarantee the custom of Muslims. A combination of Muslim and non-Muslim countries, such as Singapore, Indonesia, Thailand and Brunei are said to have started similar systems of halal practice. Nowadays, halal foods are ubiquitous, and Muslim tourists do often order halal food and beverages in non-Muslim destinations.

Even before the proliferation of halal tourism, some Muslim and non-Muslim countries abided by halal principles. For instance, as Evans and Syed (2015) state, countries that export food products to the Muslim world, such as Australia, New Zealand, Brazil, the United States and European nations, have abided by halal principles and use halal certification. Therefore, non-Muslims are also among halal tourism's key stakeholders as suppliers and customers. According to Khoiriati et al. (2018), non-Muslim countries such as the Philippines, Singapore and Thailand have also been competing to capture the opportunity. However, halal tourism is not without its critics and challenge. The term 'halal' is highly associated with the faith of Islam; therefore, some non-Muslim tourists may decide not to travel to a halal destination. Sultana (2020) notes that the prohibition of alcohol is among the core principles of halal tourism, but this action may not favor non-Muslim customers. Therefore, marketing is one of the challenging tasks as far as halal tourism development is concerned because of the different reactions of non-Muslim and Muslim tourists to the halal tourism marketing mix (Battour, 2018). The main challenge that encounters Islamic destinations is balancing catering to non-Muslim tourists and satisfying their needs without compromising Islamic values. Non-Muslim visitors sometimes decide not to travel to a particular destination without certain attributes or because of the application of specific restrictions such as alcohol and voyeurism (Battour et al., 2013; Battour et al., 2012). In some sharia-compliant destinations, alcoholic beverages are prohibited. For instance, in Islamic resorts and beaches, alcohol and pork are not served (El-Gohary, 2016). As a result, tourists from non-Muslim countries may not travel to such destinations that practice halal tourism where such restrictions are applied though exceptions may occur if the beliefs and teachings are shared (Battour et al., 2013).

Whatever the case, halal products and services are not exclusive and are not promoted only to the Muslim market. It has rather come up with new opportunities for greater cultural and experience exchanges between Islamic and non-Islamic societies. There are also many occasions in halal hospitality where non-Muslims could be considered potential market segments (Battour, 2019). Battour et al. (2018) conducted a study in Malaysia and Turkiye to explore the perceptions of non-Muslim tourists toward halal tourism. The study tried to investigate the extent to which non-Muslim tourists are willing to purchase halal products and services. According to the study, non-Muslims have a mixed perception of halal tourism. However, gradually the majority of them start to appreciate halal tourism. According to Evans and Syed (2015), it is a fact that halal tourism is an emerging business opportunity that could satisfy Muslim and non-Muslim tourists shortly. A study conducted in Turkiye and Malaysia by Battour et al. (2018) reveals that there has been a growing interest among non-Muslims in consuming halal products. For instance, they were no complaints that alcoholic beverages had been replaced with non-alcoholic juice and tea. They also accept consuming halal food as long as its taste and quality are fine.

Moreover, the study approves that a positive perception was revealed regarding separate floors for single females and families to gender segregation at swimming pools. Furthermore, some non-Muslim tourists who cannot tolerate the noise made by children appreciate gender segregation. The study reveals that non-Muslim visitors have supported banning unIslamic activities such as prostitution, gambling and casinos. Kawata et al. (2018) studied the level of acceptance of products with halal logos by non-Muslim countries and consumers in Malaysia and Japan. The study reveals that non-Muslims have positive and neutral attitudes toward halal products like Muslims. Some non-Muslim tourists consider the halal logo to guarantee the products' quality.

Bhuiyan and Darda (2018) point out that Muslim and non-Muslim countries have been offering sharia products and entering into halal tourism. It is not uncommon for Muslim tourists to order halal food and beverages when they visit non-Muslim destinations. Non-Muslim majority countries are also increasingly marketing their countries to Muslims. Non-Muslim countries such as Thailand, Singapore and Japan seem to understand the untapped potential market. They have established halal infrastructure to cater to the fast growing-market of halal tourism. For instance, the Aerostar Hotel in Moscow, Al Meroz Hotel in Thailand and Fairmont Makati and Raffles Makati hotels in the Philippines are among the fully halal hotels in non-Muslim countries (Battour & Ismail, 2015). In addition to absorbing the normal halal-conscious tourists' influx, Japan had been promising to provide a unique Muslim-friendly environment, including movable Mosques for the 2020 Tokyo Olympics to capture event halal tourism. However, the 2020 Olympics was postponed due to the COVID-19 pandemic.

Halal Standardization and Certification

Halal standardization and certification ensure the fulfillment of the requirement demanded by the Sharia, and it ensures a quality matter for non-Muslims (Samori et al., 2016). According to Biancone and Secinaro (2019), the halal certification confirms to the consumers that products have been verified in all their ingredients and at all stages of preparation. They further explain that halal certification predominantly applies to food markets, mainly animal products, pharmaceuticals, cosmetics and personal care products. The availability of a universal halal standard with rules and regulations could help overcome many issues associated with confidence in supply chains, whereas, on the contrary, the absence of a universal halal standard and the availability of different halal standards among different countries may cause disagreements and confusion among suppliers of halal products and services (Secinaro & Biancone, 2019). According to Halim and Salleh (2012), there were about 122 halal product-certifying bodies worldwide with different halal standards and logos. SESRIC (2018) assures that the unavailability of universal halal standardization and certification system highly affects halal tourism development. A study by COMCEC (2016) reveals that the discrepancies and lack of standardization create confusion among companies seeking to address the halal market. Although the development of halal standards and certification is important, there is no global standard for halal. However, some organizations at national standards and local levels have been vested with the authority to issue halal certificates. Although there might be some minor differences from country to country based on the national jurisdiction, halal certificates can be issued by individual Muslim Islamic organizations and agencies (Secinaro & Biancone, 2019). These authors point out that, for instance, in Malaysia, issuing bodies for a halal certificate from other countries must get approval from the Department of Islamic Development of Malaysia/Jabatan Agama dan Kemajuan Islam Malaysia (JAKIM) JAKIM or MUI (Majelis Ulama Indonesia) to export products to Malaysia and Indonesia.

As noted by Biancone and Secinaro (2019), the basic requirements of the standards of food and beverages incorporate some important secular aspects such as safety, cleanliness and quality. Many marketing researchers recommend using a halal logo to easily identify and brand a product or service that has been certified halal by authorized certification bodies. A piece of information about a product on its container or package, known as 'labeling' or 'logo,' is very important to introduce halal products to the respective customers. The Arabic lettering with the word 'halal' has become the international symbol of halal products. Halal certification is increasing confidence in Muslim consumers and preserving halal integrity.

Halal Industry Development Corporation (HDC) (2015, cited in Secinaro & Biancone, 2019) proposed the following basic requirements for the Malaysian Standard (MS) of halal foods.

1 Does not contain any parts or products of animals that are haram to Muslims or products of animals that are not slaughtered according to Sharia law
2 Does not contain any ingredients that are 'najis' (filth or unclear) according to sharia law
3 Is safe and not harmful
4 Is not prepared, processed or manufactured using equipment that is contaminated with things that are najis (filth or unclean) according to Sharia law
5 Preparation, packaging, storage or transportation must comply with Sharia (Adapted from HDC, 2015).

Che Musa et al. (2013) propose the following Halal Quality Standard (HQS) for halal hotels

1. The standard bedroom has a Qibla indicator, prayer mat, prayer place, prayer time table and halal meal
2. Restaurants serving halal food
3. Serving halal food at all times
4. Having separate swimming pools for males and females or scheduling swimming pools or spas according to gender
5. Spacious bedroom for prayer, prayer rooms available by gender, and with a Qibla indicator
6. Spa and gymnasium by gender; additional facilities, for example, separate saloons for males and females, boutique arcades, suhoor (pre-dawn meal) and Iftar (fast-breaking) during Ramadan.
7. Swimming pool by gender, spa by gender, prayer rooms made available for hotel guests, restaurants of halal international cuisine, entertainment for family and gender, and bathrooms equipped with bidets.

It must also be noted that halal standardization and certifications are not limited only to foods and beverages. As noted by Oyelakin and Yusuf (2018), health items, cosmetics products, services such as logistics, finance and others are also included in the scope of the halal industry. Moreover, services including marketing, packaging, branding and rebranding, financing, travel and hospitality fashion products are also areas of the halal industry that must be addressed by halal standardization and certification system.

Halal Tourism and Alternative Tourism

For the past several years, tourism has mainly depended on the sea, sand and sun (3S). This kind of tourism is traditionally known as mass tourism, conventional or mainstream tourism (Weaver & Lawton, 2014). However, alternative tourism, sometimes called 'new tourism,' has emerged to supersede mass tourism (Leslie, 2012). Alternative tourism refers to tourism that ensures the equitability of tourism development to benefit the concerned stakeholders, such as local populations, governments, tourists and investors (Leslie, 2012). Alternative tourism subsumes responsible tourism, ecotourism and sustainable tourism. Leslie further explains the three principles of alternative tourism: understand the locals' culture, respect the guest and maintain the environment. According to the principle of alternative tourism, the local people shall not be treated as servants or exotic photo opportunities in tourism development. Mastercard-CrescentRating (2019a) states that social justice is one principle of halal tourism. Social justice refers to the ability to improve the lives of the host communities and appreciate various green initiatives to protect the environment and eco-friendly tourism practices. Driven by the teachings of Islam and global tourism trends toward sustainable tourism development, Muslims have become more conscious of being socially responsible during their travels (Mastercard-CrescentRating, 2019a). Vargas-Sánchez and Moral-Moral (2019) suggest halal tourism to incline toward a healthy and eco-friendly perspective. Halal tourism, therefore, can be grouped among alternative or responsible tourism typologies. Like the concept of ecotourism, halal tourism emphasizes environment conservation, environmental education, local community welfare and respect for locals (Wildan & Sukardi, 2017).

To materialize the principles of responsible tourism, including respecting the cultures of both sides and maintaining the environment, stakeholders in the tourism industry should be responsible for their actions. Ecotourism is one type of responsible tourism that has overlapping objectives with halal tourism. Ecotourism can be defined as a responsible journey to natural and cultural areas that never compromise the environment conservation and the well-being of local people (Leslie, 2012). Ecotourism comprises principles including stakeholders must be prior informed, there must be equal, effective and active participation of all stakeholders, indigenous peoples communities' rights to say 'no' or 'yes' to tourism development should be acknowledged, and there must be special affirmative action to increase the wide participation of indigenous peoples and local communities in many aspects. Likewise, halal tourism is environmentally friendly and socially responsible (Leslie, 2012). Driven by the very nature of the Islamic faith and the current global attention given to sustainability, Muslim travelers are becoming more conscious, disciplined, environmentally friendly, and socially responsible (Mastercard-CrescentRating, 2019b). Muslim-friendly travel and sustainable travel practices have overlapping objectives, including promoting jobs and economic growth, educating their customers on responsible tourism and investing in ecotourism projects (Dinarstandard, 2019). Halal tourism educates customers on sustainable tourism and encourages them to implement responsible tourism practices, which include social, environmental, conservation and economic impacts (Battour, 2019). Halal tourism is guided by the win-win principle, also known as 'balanced consumption,' wherein social responsibility is preferred to conspicuous consumption and profit-seeking in that the local environment is guaranteed (Secinaro & Biancone, 2019).

Halal tourism also has some points of connection with thanatourism or dark tourism. Dark tourism could be defined as a type of tourism where notorious sites become the primary attractions. These sites could be infamous sites associated with torture, accident, war, massacre or any kind of tragedy. It is motivated by a fascination with death or tourist sites, including visiting civil visual depictions of death, massacres, burial locations and places where religious figures died (Akbulut & Ekin, 2018). As mentioned in various surah of the Holy Quran, such as Surah Al-An'am: 11, Surah Yusuf: 109, and Surah An-Naml: 69, Muslims are encouraged to visit past civilizations and historical sites to learn from them (Adie, 2020).

E-Marketing and Halal Tourism Websites

Given halal tourism has emerged in the era of digital and internet-based technologies, it is not surprising that it widely utilizes internet-based technologies. Mastercard-CrescentRating (2019a) noted that the halal tourism market has witnessed significant changes in recent years. The rapid pace of technological innovation realizes the rapid proliferation of halal tourism. Online halal booking through websites is also among the emerging concepts of halal tourism (Battour, 2018). Many websites provide information on halal tourism. MasterCard, CrescentRating, and HalalTrip are the leading in online halal tourism marketing and promotion. CrescentRating website (www.crescentrating.com) was established in 2006 to inform business tourists of halal-friendly destinations (Battour, 2018). Halal websites such as www.muslim-friendly.jp.net and www.Halalbooking. com have been offering online halal tourism. Mastercard is a worldwide financial-technological company that facilitates worldwide electronic payments for individuals and governmental and non-governmental organizations (Mastercard-CrescentRating, 2019a).

Furthermore, Mastercard facilitates the authorization, clearing and settlement of payment transactions and delivers related products and services. HalalTrip aims to be a reliable global online platform for halal travelers. Halalrip has been working to be the most inclusive, reliable and innovative online platform with a next-generation mobile app. It aims to make destination discovery and trip planning fun and more intuitive for those looking for a Halal-friendly travel experience (www.mastercard.com. www.crescentrating. com. www.halaltrip.com).

Moreover, Have-Halal-Will Travel, an online travel guide, has launched on its platform named Sophia (Dinarstandard, 2019). The British travel agent serendipity tailor-made also launched a new online Muslim-friendly travel agency, Rihaala.com (https://www.rihaala.com), that offers halal services, including Umrah bookings. The platform has focused on targeting Muslim millennials' needs to curate their trips online. Halal Holiday was launched only in 2019 in Malaysia to render halal-friendly services for travelers. It focuses on online selling by replacing packages offered by traditional travel agencies, including hajj and umrah agencies. The Gulf countries-based online travel agency, known as UmrahMe, was launched in January 2019, which provides customizable umrah packages that include flights, hotels and online visas. It is one of the first travel agencies licensed by the Saudi Ministry of Hajj and Umrah. Several new digital solutions have also emerged to address the needs of Muslim travelers and visitors. Generally, halal digital travel solutions technology transforms halal travel (Dinarstandard, 2019).

Halal Tourism Products and Services

Sharia-friendly hospitality is a burgeoning research area within the halal and Islamic tourism domain (Duman, 2020). In halal hospitality, halalness of food and beverages, cleanliness of prayer areas, halalness of earnings (free from usury), modesty in dress code and behavior and shunning of voyeurism matters a lot. Halal tourism is all about halal products and services. The preceding discussions focused more on describing the concept of halal tourism, whereas, in this section, components of halal tourism will be discussed rigorously. Halal products and services refer to sharia-compliant products and services (Battour, 2016, 2019a; Duman, 2020; Khan & Callanan, 2017). Halal destinations are expected to offer various halal products and services to visitors. Battour further states that investigating and understanding some of the popular forms of halal tourism products and services help destinations satisfy the needs of halal-conscious customers, and researchers assess the profit potential of halal tourism investment. As described by Duman (2020), deeds, utilization and consumption are classified into five groups in Islam. These are compulsory/obligatory (*fard/wajib*), recommended (*mustahabb/mandub*), neutral or indifferent (*mushbuh*), disliked (*makruh*) and forbidden (*haram*). According to Din (1989), *mushbuh* refers to actions not officially designated haram or halal but *makruh* actions that are discouraged, disliked and recommended to abstain from. Haram activities, services and products are openly ruled out, condemned and unacceptable in Islam. For example, activities such as gambling, adultery, stealing or other crimes, and foods such as pork and alcoholic beverages are haram in Islam. Bergeaud-Blackler (2016) states that halal benefits humankind, whereas haram refers to what is detrimental, and Muslims are expressly forbidden from consuming.

Halal Foods and Beverages

Religion and culture significantly shape consumer behavior, including food types and cooking. Sharia highly influences the consumption behavior of Muslims. Islam orders Muslims to follow a halal dietary system (Riaz & Chaudry, 2004). Accordingly, in most cases, Muslim travelers want to use halal foods and beverages. Therefore, the relationship between visitors' beliefs and their food preference has important implications for halal tourism developers that the issue of food should be managed wisely, and the religious aspect of food must be addressed seriously (Bon & Hussain, 2010).

According to Evans and Syed (2015), halal food and beverages have existed for more than 1,400 years but only in the past few decades that the concept of halal foods and beverages begun to be studied. Nowadays, halal food and beverages are ubiquitous in non-Muslim countries and have received the attention of several researchers (Bon & Hussain, 2010; Evans & Syed, 2015; Krishnan et al., 2017; Riaz & Chaudry, 2004; Wibowo & Ahmad, 2016). As noted in the earlier discussion, 'halal' is an Arabic term meaning permissible or lawful. Hence, halal food and beverages refer to foods and beverages that are compliant with sharia principles and permissible for use and consumption by Muslims. In other words, foods and beverages that meet the Islamic dietary code and are consumed by Muslims are called halal food and beverages (Bergeaud-Blackler, 2016; Bon & Hussain, 2010).

Foods and beverages are among the top criteria of all general visitors and Muslim visitors (Bon & Hussain, 2010; El-Gohary, 2016; Henderson, 2010a). In some cases, food and beverages themselves are also the core attractions.

For example, some types of tourism, such as gastronomy and culinary tourism, food tourism and wine tourism, depend on food and beverages. Therefore, food and beverages are core attractions per se for many destinations in their tourism marketing. Hence, food and beverages are a central part of tourism development in one way or another. In addition to this, given that eating and drinking are physiological needs, visitors consider food and beverages in every walk of their life.

Furthermore, dining out has become a touristic activity. However, many religions, including Islam, Christianity and Judaism, prescribe the prohibited and permitted foods and beverages to their respective adherents (Bon & Hussain, 2010). For instance, foods and beverages permitted to Muslims are called 'halal,' whereas Jewish call their permitted foods and beverages '*kosher.*' The scope of the research under consideration, however, is only about halal food and beverages. In Islam, sharia law unequivocally prescribes the halalness or harmness of food and beverage. In Muslim-minority countries, halal food has also become a defining element of Muslim identity (Evans & Syed, 2015). These days, some countries started certifying halal foods. Malaysia already started halal certification of food products in the 1970s and 1980s. The Department of Islamic Development Malaysia (Jabatan Kemajuan Islam Malaysia [JAKIM]) has been vested with the authority to certify halal products. Singapore, Indonesia, Thailand and Brunei have followed in the footstep of Malaysia and all developed similar systems. Evans and Syed (2015) point out that in addition to meat and poultry, a variety of processed food and personal-care products such as baked goods, dairy products, soft drinks, bottled water, tea bags, pharmaceuticals and cosmetics are subjected to certification.

Islam is not only a religion of rituals but also a way of life that guides every aspect of Muslims' personal and social behavior (Duman, 2020). Accordingly, any activity, including eating, can be considered a matter of worship of God, like ritual duties. Islam has its own peculiar Islamic dietary code; foods that meet these codes are called halal (lawful or permitted). Halal foods and beverages refer to foods and beverages allowed for Muslims to consume by Sharia (Bon & Hussain, 2010; Riaz & Chaudry, 2004). All foods of plants and their byproducts, except those that the Quran and the Sunnah have specifically prohibited, are considered halal. Therefore, for Muslims, it is obligatory to consume only halal foods. It should also be clear that non-Muslim consumers often prefer halal food for its high quality and organic standards (Riaz & Chaudry, 2004). The study of Riaz and Chaudry (2004) reveals that many visitors are interested in healthy foods, low in calories, cholesterol, and fat and organically produced. Generally, the following five terminologies are adopted to denote the permissibility of foods and beverages (Riaz & Chaudry, 2004).

- Halal: refers to food and beverages that are permissible and lawful according to Sharia. It also entails items beyond meat and poultry, such as cosmetics, drugs and personal care products.

- Haram: entails prohibited foods and beverages. It is the direct opposite of halal and includes anything prohibited by Sharia. Sharia prohibits Muslims from consuming haram foods such as pork, alcohol and any food that harm the health of human beings, such as toxic foods and beverages.
- *Mashbuh* is a gray area between halal and haram. It is questionable or doubtful and open for interpretation either due to the differences in scholars' opinions or the presence of unidentified ingredients in a food product.
- *Makruh* refers to a dislike for a food product that deserves to be discouraged but is not designated haram. For instance, tobacco-related products can be mentioned in this category. Generally, Muslims are recommended to stay far away from *makruh*.
- *Zabiha* is related to a system of slaughtering. It is used to differentiate the slaughters such as Muslims, *Ahlul Kitab* (Jews or Christians) or without religious connotation. Some Muslims consider meat slaughtered by Jews and Christians also halal. There is a Quranic verse that reinforces this one. The food of the people of the scripture is allowable for Muslims (The Holy Quran, 5:5).

The prohibited foods are specified in the Holy Quran Chapter II, Verse 173 as follows:

> ... foods such as carrion, blood, and any product of swine and flesh that is not slaughtered in the name of Allah are not halal ...
> (the Holy Quran, 2:173)

Allah also openly prohibited the consumption of alcohol and other intoxicants in the Holy Quran, chapter 5, verse 90, as follows: '... you who believe! Alcoholism and gambling ... are actions of evil so avoid them ...' (the Holy Quran, 5:90).

As stated by Riaz and Chaudry (2004), all pure and clean foods are permitted for consumption by Muslims except the following categories.

- Carrion or dead animals
- Flowing or congealed blood
- Swine, including all byproducts of swine
- All types of intoxicants such as alcohol and drugs
- Carnivorous animals with fangs such as lions, dogs, wolves and tigers
- Birds with sharp claws (birds of prey) such as falcons, eagles, owls, or vultures
- Land animals such as frogs or snakes (Riaz & Chaudry, 2004, p. 22).

In general, Muslims consider the following circumstance to be *makruh* at best.

- Animals slaughtered while pronouncing a name other than God
- Animals slaughtered without pronouncing the name of God on them
- Animals that are killed in a manner that prevents their blood from being fully drained from their bodies

Sea creatures, all marine animals and locusts are considered halal by some denominations of Muslims, such as Sunni groups, even if they die spontaneously (Bergeaud-Blackler, 2016). The jurists of sharia law have recommended avoiding consuming others, such as pigs, crocodiles, weasels, pelicans, otters, foxes, elephants, ravens and insects. By definition, plants, vegetables and their derivatives are generally halal except for alcoholic drinks or other intoxicants (Riaz & Chaudry, 2004). Marzuki et al. (2020) note that plants and their derivatives, as well as all kinds of water and beverages, are halal except those that are poisonous, intoxicating, or hazardous to health. However, nowadays, some processed and packed plant products might use prohibited chemicals or ingredients or be contaminated with such stuff. Contamination can also involve the utensils used during production (Razalli, 2020). Therefore, serious precautions must be taken while processing halal foods and beverages.

Riaz and Chaudry (2004) discuss that a particular foodstuff or beverage can be halal or haram in a different situation. The nature of the foodstuff and the way it is processed and obtained all matter a lot. For instance, food such as pork is haram because the materials per se prescribed in the Quran are haram. However, beef and poultry are not harams by their very nature. However, how they are obtained, how they are slaughtered, and how they are processed and cooked may make them haram. For instance, if it is not slaughtered according to Sharia and/or obtained through stolen or other illegal ways incompatible with Islamic teaching, the beef or the chicken would be considered unacceptable. For animal products to be halal, an animal must be halal species, slaughtered properly, obtained and processed through halal means. To maintain customer loyalty, precautions must be taken from the beginning of production to the end food product 'farm-to-fork.'

Moreover, harmful food and beverage that are poisonous or intoxicating are harams. According to Marzuki et al. (2020), halal food, certification and labeling have become important attributes in convincing consumers that the food they purchase is good quality and safe to consume. However, some issues may not be solved even by certification. Even though some Muslims tolerate it, the slaughtering system remains a point of disagreement. Hand slaughter, stunning and mechanical blades are still debatable among industry certifiers and the public (Evans & Syed, 2015). Some customers want to know whether stunning or mechanical slaughter was used. Policymakers and meat suppliers seem uncertain about how to respond. This is an important issue to be addressed by stakeholders.

Hygienic, safety and cleanliness are also among the key issues of halal food and beverages (Ambali & Bakar, 2014). Nutritionists prove that most food classified as haram in Islam is harmful to humankind in modern science too (Riaz & Chaudry, 2004). For instance, Carrion and dead animals, blood, pork and intoxicants proved dangerous for health. Therefore, in addition to religious values, halal foods have become preferable for health and quality matters. Thereby the number of non-Muslims for halal food is steadily increasing. For instance, in Ethiopian Universities, meat was prepared for Muslims (by default halal) and Christians separately for religious purposes. However, some non-Muslims prefer Muslims' food to Christians' for its perceived quality. A study conducted by Ambali and Bakar (2014); Oyelakin and Yusuf (2018) also proved that the interest of non-Muslims in consuming halal products is increasing. The reason for choosing halal food for those who do not abide by Sharia is the relevant connection of halal products to hygiene, safety and the quality of halal goods and services.

Halal Entertainment Services

Duman (2020) suggests that halal entertainment is one component of halal tourism development. Visitors enjoy pleasure and develop a sense of belonging through entertainment. Service providers could create a pleasing experience and retain visitors by offering various halal entertainments. Islam does not forbid sharia-compliant leisure and entertainment. However, recreation and entertainment services must be designed based on halal standards without transgressing Islamic principles. The first step in flourishing halal entertainment must be avoiding haram activities such as sexual permissiveness, voyeurism, nightclub, consumption of pork, alcoholic beverages and gambling. Unfortunately, these activities have become entertainment's default features, so doing is wrong. In addition to the haram, as mentioned earlier, activities of entertainment, pious Muslims forbid listening to music, song and dance because of the concerns that these things can cause Muslims to disregard their religious duty (Duman, 2020). However, as noted by the authors, instead of secular songs, dancing and music, it is possible to use religious songs such as *Menzuma* and *Neshida (Neshid)*, which are mainly integral to the Sufi traditions of Islam. Hospitality providers can provide a range of entertainment facilities to customers, such as television with halal channels, dining areas, and swimming pools per sharia law.

Halal Accommodation and Restaurants

Nowadays, the accommodation and hospitality industry that fits with the emerging market and Muslim tourist demands is a strategic approach to outplaying local and global halal tourism (Duman, 2020; Razak et al., 2020; Šuligoj & Maruško, 2017). Muslim tourists pay due attention to products and services that do not transgress Islamic principles (Akbaba & Çavuşoğlu, 2017). One of the most important factors influencing the success of the halal tourism industry is the availability of sharia-compliant accommodation (Razalli, 2020; Razzaq et al., 2016). Accommodations should employ the halal concept to achieve a competitive advantage by adding value to their products and service portfolios. According to Razalli (2020), a sharia-compliant hotel consists of five main practices, namely (1) administrative, (2) common areas, (3) bedrooms, (4) service and (5) food and beverage. Accordingly, the administrative section is responsible for making financial and policy issues with Sharia complaints. The common area focuses on entertainment activities. For instance, an unnecessary intermingling of men and women in common areas such as a spa, gymnasium, recreational/sport, swimming pool, lounge and prayer room for guests must be avoided by offering separate facilities or arranging schedules for males and females. Halal products and services should not be served in common areas. Only sharia-friendly architecture and design should be displayed in common areas (Razalli, 2020). The bedroom is expected to include *the Qibla* direction indicator, a copy of the Quran, a prayer mat and schedule, a bidet, halal toiletries, halal in-room food, and Islamic in-room entertainment (El-Gohary, 2016). The fourth category of service practices is related to those practices in the context of Islamic marketing and arranging some special halal events such as wedding packages, tours and seminars/conferences. The last category of halal accommodation is responsible for providing certified halal foods and beverages.

Table 1.3 Differences between Halal Hotels and Conventional Hotels

S. No.	Halal Accommodations	Conventional Accommodation
1	Target to cater to a specific niche market of halal-conscious visitors	Open to all categories of customers
2	Decoration must be in keeping with Islamic architecture and design principles	Hotel design is not specified or not limited
3	Rooms are larger than industry standards to accommodate the need for Muslims to pray inside the room	A standard room ranges from 30 to 40 m2, a junior suite from 55 to 65 m2, and a presidential suite from 200 to 220 m2
4	Must serve halal food only	No limitation on food served within the hotel
5	No alcoholic beverage at all	Alcohol is served throughout the hotel. Alcohol sales bring 80–90% to gross profit in food and beverage sales figures
6	Gender-specific staff to serve customers and the majority should be Muslims	No limitation in staffing requirement
7	Revenue from room 80–85%	Revenue from room 40–60%
8	Revenue from food and beverage 10–20%	Revenue from food and beverage 30–40%
9	Revenue from other departments 5–10%	Revenue from other departments 5–10%

(*Continued*)

Table 1.3 (Continued)

S. No.	Halal Accommodations	Conventional Accommodation
10	In-room facilities must facilitate Muslims in performing their religious duties, such as water-bidet and prayer mat	Some hotels provide these facilities upon request

Source: Modified from (Wibowo & Ahmad, 2016).

Even though there is a widely held perception that sharia-compliant hotels suit only Muslims, a study conducted in Malaysia proves that the number of non-Muslim consumers who choose sharia-compliant hotels is also increasing (Razalli, 2020). As Battour (2018) alleges, several sharia-compliant hotels are recently burgeoning both in Muslim and non-Muslim destinations. For example, Al Meroz Hotel in Thailand, Aerostar Hotel in Moscow, Fairmont Makati, and Raffles Makati hotels in the Philippines are fully halal hotels in non-Muslim countries (Battour, 2016). These hotels provide facilities and services such as *Qibla* direction, halal food, alcohol-free beverages and a prayer room with a call for prayers.

According to Battour (2018), sharia-compliant hotels should fulfill the following items: a copy of the Quran, *Qibla* direction indicator, a prayer mat, a prayer timetable, Islamic or Muslim-friendly viewing TV and alcohol-free beverages in the fridge and water usage-friendly washroom. In addition to these items, he suggests the following serves to offer: certified halal food, well-trained staff to cater to Muslims' needs, female staff for women, segregated floor and swimming pool/gym for females, prayer room (small mosque if possible) and Ramadan services and facilities.

Sharia-Compliant Airport

The present study approves that some Muslim countries such as Turkiye, Saudi Arabia and Egypt have sharia-compliant airports. However, it is reported that observant Muslims have faced difficulties in many airports in practicing their religion due to a lack of Muslim-friendly facilities (Battour, 2018). A study conducted by Battour in 2019 proved that there are no sharia-friendly facilities inside airport toilets in many destinations. Therefore, practicing Muslim visitors requested Muslim-compliant toilets and washrooms to be provided at airports. Battour (2018); El-Gohary (2016) claim that sharia-compliant toilets are very important in airports because regular toilets provide only tissue paper. It is Muslims' etiquette to use water after the toilet, and there must be a suitable water supply inside the toilet. Besides, prayer places must also be assigned to both females and males inside the airports.

Sharia-Compliant Healthcare Centers

Prophet Muhammad (PBUH) says, 'disease is part of fate, and so is its cure.' He also stated, '… for every ailment there is a cure,' so searching for treatment is recommendable. Sharia urges Muslims to have their ailment treated. At the same time, Muslims are commanded to observe the teaching of Islam everywhere throughout their lives. Therefore, staff, patients and individuals' families of nursing patients must be helped to fulfill their religious duty on time. Sharia-compliant healthcare services must be designed to provide halal-conscious patients with medical treatment that respect Islamic principles. According to Rahadian et al. (2019), a halal healthcare center must fulfill at least the following basic elements. First, there must be a place where staff, patients and their nursing (families) perform their religious duties, mainly prayer. Second, to avoid undesired cross-gender interactions, women patients should be treated by women doctors and males by males as much as possible. Although Sharia does not strictly forbid treatment by the opposite sex, treating the patients with a nurse or physician of the same gender whenever possible is highly recommended (Zawawi & Othman, 2017). Third, pharmaceuticals and drugs are expected to be halal if possible. Fourthly, all the processes of the treatment are advised to be sharia-compliant. It is recommended that halal principles be parts and parcels of medical ethics in halal healthcare centers. As true for other halal products and services, quality, trustworthiness and hygienic issues are among the main concern of halal healthcare centers. Zawawi & Othman (2017) recommends that the buildings of halal health centers follow architecture that displays religious beliefs, social and economic structure, aesthetic motivation and artistic sensibility.

In contrast, offensive things and activities have to be avoided. According to Zawawi and Othman (2017), in addition to pharmaceutical products supplied to the patients, materials for personal sanitary care of patients, as well as the food and beverages offered to the patient, staff and visitors at the hospital, must also be halal. A study by Battour (2018) reveals that halal healthcare facilities and services have become the pull factors in attracting destinations. He proposes the following attributes of halal healthcare facilities and services: the same gender of nurses and doctors with patients, halal drugs and pharmaceutics, prayer rooms, halal food and Muslim-friendly toilets (Zawawi & Othman, 2017). However, Sharia is not rigid but rather conditional as per the situation. In cases of necessity or if the patient will be harmed if she does not take the haram treatment, Islam makes forbidden things permissible. For instance, in Islam, eating haram food, such as dead meat, for one who cannot find anything else and fears that he will die of hunger is permitted. Likewise, non-halal pharmaceuticals can be taken to save one's life if refraining from taking these medicines would result in the patient's death (Rahadian et al., 2019; Zawawi & Othman, 2017). Generally, sharia-compliant healthcare services have not been fully implemented in many destinations yet, and this may negatively affect halal tourism development.

Guidelines for Halal-Conscious Muslim Visitors

Based on Al-Munajjid's (2008) proposal, the present researchers propose the following guidelines for halal tourism. (1) Muslims should not travel to seek the blessing of Allah except in the three specified Holy Mosques. Islam forbids Muslims from traveling to venerate shrines except for the three mosques: Masjedel Haram (Bayt Allah) of Mecca, Masjid Nebawi of Medina and Masjedel Aqsua of Jerusalem. The hadith narrated by Abu Hurairah said, '*No journey should be undertaken to visit any mosque but three: al-Masjid al-Haram, the Mosque of the Messenger (peace and blessings of Allah be upon him) and the Mosque of al-Aqsa.*' In Islam, it is forbidden to venerate any place, such as graves, shrines, tombs or mausoleums, other than these three mosques. Nothing in Sharia suggests places deserve to be revered apart from the three mosques. However, this does not mean that visiting mosques and Islamic heritage sites is forbidden in Islam. Rather what is forbidden is setting out on a journey with that aim and venerating them. (2) Muslims are forbidden to travel just for leisure and fun to a country where haram activities are practiced, and halal products and services are unavailable. However, Muslims could travel to those places for medical treatment, education, business, and so on. (3) Muslims are advised to refrain from visiting places where corruption, alcoholism and voyeurism are common practices. Islam forbids its adherent to visit places of corruption, where alcohol is drunk and immoral actions are taken place, and sins are committed: they can be beaches and parties or other immoral places. Muslims are advised to avoid sin and block all means that lead to sin. (4) A Muslim woman is forbidden to travel alone without her *Muhrim* (*Muhrim* refers to her close men relatives such as her husband, father, brothers, son and husband). Even it is not allowed for a Muslim woman to travel for hajj or umrah without a *Muhrim*. (5) Non-Muslims can visit Muslim countries, and then they are granted safety until they leave. However, during their stay in Muslim countries, they should respect Islam, Islamic morals and the culture of the Muslims. A semi-naked and decadent dress code also is not advisable. Moreover, it must be noted that non-Muslims are not allowed to visit the two holy sanctuaries in Mecca and Medina (adapted and modified from Al-Munajjid, 2009).

References

Abbasi, A. S. (2019). Tablighi Jamaat: A Multidimensional Movement of Religious Travellers. In A. Jamal, R. Raji, & K. Griffin (Eds.), *Islamic Tourism: Management of Travel Destinations* (pp. 228–243). CABI.

Adie, B. A. (2020). Marketing Europe to Islamic Heritage Tourists. In C. M. Hall & Girish Prayag (Eds.), *The Routledge Handbook of Halal Hospitality and Islamic Tourism* (pp. 157–169). Routledge. https://doi.org/10.4324/9781315150604-26

Aji, M. H. (2019). Aji Halal Tourism is Not Islamic. *TheJakartaPost*, 7.

Akbaba, A., & Çavuşoğlu, F. (2017). Halal Hotel Concept and Halal Hotel Certification in Turkey. *International Journal of Contemporary Tourism Research*, *1*(1), 48–58. https://doi.org/10.30625/ijctr.309145

Akbulut, O., & Ekin, Y. (2018). Battlefield Tourism: The Potential of Badr, Uhud and the Trench (Khandaq) Battles for Islamic Tourism. In Razaq Raj and Kevin Griffin (Eds.), *Islamic Tourism: Management of Travel Destinations* (pp. 168–180). CABI.

Al Jallad, N. (2008). The concepts of al-halal and al-haram in the Arab-Muslim culture: a translational and lexicographical study. *Language Design*, *10*, 77–86.

Al-Munajjid, M. S. (2009). *Travel and Tourism (Siyaahah) in Islam – Rulings and Types*. Islamhouse.Com.

Al-Qaradawi, Y. (2013). *The Lawful and the Prohibited in Islam*. Shoruuk International. https://books.google.com.my/books?id=iXCNAQAAQBAJ

Ambali, A. R., & Bakar, A. N. (2014). People's Awareness on Halal Foods and Products: Potential Issues for Policymakers. *Procedia – Social and Behavioral Sciences*, *121*(October), 3–25. https://doi.org/10.1016/j.sbspro.2014.01.1104

Azam, M. S. E., Abdullah, M. A., & Razak, D. A. (2019). Halal Tourism: Definition, Justification, and Scopes Towards Sustainable Development. *International Journal of Business, Economics and Law*, *18*(3), 23–31.

Bashir, M., Afzal, M. T., & Azeem, M. (2008). Reliability and Validity of Qualitative and Operational Research Paradigm. *Pakistan Journal of Statistics and Operation Research*, *4*(1), 35. https://doi.org/10.18187/pjsor.v4i1.59

Battour, M. (2016). *Muslim Friendly Tourism*. Islamic Tourism Centre. doi.10.13140/RG.2.1.4915.6084

Battour, M. (2017). Halal Tourism and its Impact on Non-Muslim Tourists' Perception, Trip quality and Trip Value. *International Journal of Culture, Tourism and Hospitality Research*. https://doi.org/10.1108/ijcthr-02-2017-0020

Battour, M. (2018). Muslim Travel Behavior in Halal Tourism. In L. Butowski (Ed.), *Mobilities, Tourism and Travel Behavior – Contexts and Boundaries* (Issue October 2017, pp. 1–16). I InTech. https://doi.org/10.5772/intechopen.70370

Battour, M. (2019). *Halal Tourism: Achieving Muslim Tourists' Satisfaction and Loyalty*. Author. https://books.google.com.tr/books?id=Jx-lyAEACAAJ

Battour, M., Battor, M., & Bhatti, M. A. (2013). Islamic Attributes of Destination: Construct Development and Measurement Validation, and their Impact on Tourist Satisfaction. *International Journal of Tourism Research*, *16*(6), 556–564. https://doi.org/10.1002/jtr.1947

Battour, M., Hakimian, F., Ismail, M., & Boğan, E. (2018). The Perception of Non-Muslim Tourists towards Halal Tourism: Evidence from Turkey and Malaysia. *Journal of Islamic Marketing*, *9*(4), 823–840. https://doi.org/10.1108/JIMA-07-2017-0072

Battour, M., & Ismail, M. N. (2015). Halal Tourism: Concepts, Practises, Challenges and Future. *Tourism Management Perspectives*, *9*(May), 150–154. https://doi.org/10.1016/j.tmp.2015.12.008

Battour, M., & Ismail, M. N. (2016). Halal Tourism: Concepts, Practises, Challenges and Future. *Tourism Management Perspectives*, *19*, 150–154. https://doi.org/10.1016/j.tmp.2015.12.008

Battour, M., Ismail, M. N., & Battor, M. (2010). Toward a Halal Tourism Market. *Tourism Analysis*, *15*(4), 461–470. https://doi.org/10.3727/108354210X12864727453304

Battour, M., Ismail, M. N., & Battor, M. (2011). The Impact of Destination Attributes on Muslim Tourist's Choice. *International Journal of Tourism Research*, *13*(6), 527–540. https://doi.org/10.1002/jtr.824

Battour, M., Ismail, M. N., Battor, M., & Awais, M. (2017). Islamic Tourism: An Empirical Examination of Travel Motivation and Satisfaction in Malaysia. *Current Issues in Tourism*, *20*(1), 50–67. https://doi.org/10.1080/13683500.2014.965665

Battour, M. M., Battor, M. M., & Ismail, M. (2012). The Mediating Role of Tourist Satisfaction: A Study of Muslim Tourists in Malaysia. *Journal of Travel and Tourism Marketing*, *29*(3), 279–297. https://doi.org/10.1080/10548408.2012.666174

Bergeaud-Blackler, F. (2016). Florence Bergeaud-Blackle. In F. Bergeaud-Blackler, J. Fischer, & J. Lever (Eds.), *Halal Matters: Islam, Politics and Markets in Global Perspective* (pp. 91–105). Routledge.

Bhuiyan, H., & Darda, A. (2018). Prospects and Potentials of Halal Tourism Development in Bangladesh. *Journal of Tourismology*, *4*(2), 93–106. https://doi.org/10.26650/jot.2018.4.2.0007

Bhuiyan, M. A. H., Siwar, C., Ismail, S. M., & Islam, R. (2011). Potentials of Islamic Tourism: A Case Study of Malaysia on East Coast Economic Region. *Australian Journal of Basic and Applied Sciences*, *5*(6), 1333–1340.

Biancone, S. & Secinaro, S. (2019). The Halal Tourism: A Business Model Opportunity. In K. A. Jamal, Raj, R., Griffin (Ed.), *Islamic Tourism: Management of Travel Destinations* (pp. 192–201). CAB. https://doi.org/10.1079/9781786394132.0010

Boğan, E., & Sarıışık, M. (2019). Halal Tourism: Conceptual and Practical Challenges. *Journal of Islamic Marketing*, *10*(1), 87–96. https://doi.org/10.1108/JIMA-06-2017-0066

Bon, M., & Hussain, M. (2010). Halal Food and Tourism: Prospects and Challenges. *Bridging Tourism Theory and Practice*, *2*, 47–59. https://doi.org/10.1108/S2042-1443(2010)0000002007

Borzooei, M., & Asgari, M. (2013). The Halal Brand Personality and its Effect on Purchase Intention. *Interdisciplinary Journal of Contemporary Research in Business*, *5*(3), 481. http://journal-archieves34.webs.com/481-491.pdf

Camilleri, M. A. (2018). The Planning and Development of the Tourism Product. In M. A. Chamilleri (Ed.), *Tourism Planning and Destination Marketing* (1st ed., Issue November, pp. 1–23). Emerald Publishing Limited. https://doi.org/10.1108/978-1-78756-291-220181001

Carboni, M., Perelli, C., & Sistu, G. (2014). Is Islamic Tourism a Viable Option for Tunisian Tourism? Insights from Djerba. *Tourism Management Perspectives*, *11*, 1–9. https://doi.org/10.1016/j.tmp.2014.02.002

COMCEC. (2016). Muslim Friendly Tourism: Developing and Marketing MFT Products and Services In the OIC Member Countries. In *Standing Committee for Economic and Commercial Cooperation of the Organization of Islamic Cooperation (COMCEC)* (Issue August). www.comcec.org

Crescentrating. (2017). Global Muslim Travel Index (GMTI) 2017. *Crescentrating. Com*, *May*, 1–5. https://doi.org/10.1016/j.jweia.2015.05.010

Din, K. H. (1989). Islam and Tourism. Patterns, Issues, and Options. *Annals of Tourism Research*, *16*(4), 542–563. https://doi.org/10.1016/0160-7383(89)90008-X

Dinarstandard. (2019). State of the Global Islamic Economy Report 2019/20. In *Dubai International Financial Centre*. https://haladinar.io/hdn/doc/report2018.pdf

Duman, T. (2011). The Value of Islamic Tourism: *Islam and Civilisational Renewal*, *July*, 12–13.

Duman, T. (2020). Attributes of Muslim-Friendly Hospitality Service in a Process-Based Model. In M. Hall & G. Prayag (Eds.), *The Routledge Handbook of Halal Hospitality and Islamic Tourism* (pp. 53–69). Taylor & Francis. https://doi.org/10.4324/9781315150604-3

Eid, R., & El-Gohary, H. (2015). The Role of Islamic Religiosity on the Relationship between Perceived Value and Tourist Satisfaction. *Tourism Management*, *46*, 477–488. https://doi.org/10.1016/j.tourman.2014.08.003

Elasrag, H. (2016). MPRA. *Economic Policy*, *2116*, 33. https://doi.org/10.1227/01.NEU.0000349921.14519.2A

El-Gohary, H. (2016). Halal Tourism, is it Really Halal? *Tourism Management Perspectives*, *19*, 124–130. https://doi.org/10.1016/j.tmp.2015.12.013

Evans, A., & Syed, S. (2015). Halal Goes Global. International Trade Centre. http://search.proquest.com.ezaccess.library.uitm.edu.my/docview/224324915?

Fakir, F., & Erraoui, E. (2019). Moroccan Tourist's Perceptions Toward Halal Tourism. *2nd International Halal Tourism Congress/04-06 April 2019/Anatalya-Turkiye*, November, 1–13.

Gabdrakhmanov, N. K., Biktimirov, N. M., Rozhko, M. V., & Khafizova, L. V. (2016). Problems of Development of Halal Tourism in Russia. *Journal of Organizational Culture, Communications and Conflict*, *20*(2), 88–93.

Gabdrakhmanov, N. K., Biktimirov, N. M., Rozhko, M. V., & Mardanshina, R. M. (2016). Features of Islamic Tourism. *Academy of Marketing Studies Journal*, *20*(Special Issue), 45–50.

Goeldner, C. R., & Ritchie, J. R. B. (2012). Tourism: Principles, Practices and Philosophies. In *John Wiley & Sons, Inc., Hoboken, New Jersey*. John Wiley & Sons, Inc. https://doi.org/10.1159/000470892

Halim, M. A. A., & Salleh, M. M. (2012). The Possibility of Uniformity on Halal Standards in the Organization of Islamic Countries (OIC) Country. *World Applied Sciences Journal*, *17*, 6–10.

Hammuri, G., & Eseynel, I. (2017). The Analysis of Hoteliers Attitude towards the Establishment of Islamic Hospitality Policies: North Cyprus. *Journal of Humanities and Social Sciences*, *2*(2), 124–131. https://doi.org/10.21276/sjhss.2017.2.2.3

Hanziker, W., & Krapf, K. (1946). Guest Editorial. *Tourism Review*, *75*(1), 1–3. https://doi.org/10.1108/TR-02-2020-405

Haq, F., & Wong, H. Y. (2010). Is Spiritual Tourism a New Strategy for Marketing Islam? *Journal of Islamic Marketing*, *1*(2), 136–148. https://doi.org/10.1108/17590831011055879

Hassan, Z. (2015). Factors affecting Muslim Tourists Choice of Halal Concept Hotels and Satisfaction in Malaysia: Moderating effect of Religious Devotedness. *International Journal of Accounting and Business Management*, *3*(2), 133–144. https://doi.org/10.24924/ijabm/2015.11/v3.iss2/133.144

Henderson, J. C. (2010a). Islam and Tourism: Brunei, Indonesia, Malaysia, and Singapore. *Bridging Tourism Theory and Practice*, *2*, 75–89. https://doi.org/10.1108/S2042-1443(2010)0000002009

Henderson, J. C. (2010b). Islam and Tourism. In *Tourism in the Muslim World: Bridging Tourism Theory and Practice* (pp. 75–89). Scott, N. and Jafari, J. (Ed.). https://doi.org/10.1108/s2042-1443(2010)0000002009

Henderson, J. C. (2016). Halal Food, Certification and Halal Tourism: Insights from Malaysia and Singapore. *Tourism Management Perspectives*, *19*, 160–164. https://doi.org/10.1016/j.tmp.2015.12.006

Jafari, J., & Scott, N. (2014). Muslim World and its Tourism. *Annals of Tourism Research*, *44*(1), 1–19. https://doi.org/10.1016/j.annals.2013.08.011

Kamarudin, L. M., & Ismail, H. N. (2012). Muslim Tourists' Typology in Malaysia: Perspectives and Challenges. *Tourism and Hospitality International Conference, Thic*, 1–8.

Kawata, Y., Htay, S. N. N., & Salman, S. A. (2018). Non-Muslims' Acceptance of Imported Products with Halal Logo: A Case Study of Malaysia and Japan. *Journal of Islamic Marketing*, *9*(1), 191–203. https://doi.org/10.1108/JIMA-02-2016-0009

Khan, F., & Callanan, M. (2017). The 'Halalification' of Tourism. *The Journal of Islamic Marketing*, *8*(4), 558–577.

Khoiriati, S. D. S., Krisnajaya, I. M., & Dinarto, D. (2018). Debating Halal Tourism Between Values and Branding: A Case Study of Lombok, Indonesia. *KnE Social Sciences*, *3*(5), 494–515. https://doi.org/10.18502/kss.v3i5.2352

Krishnan, S., Omar, C. M. C., Zahran, I., Syazwan, N., & Alyaa, S. (2017). The Awareness of Gen Z's toward Halal Food Industry. *Management*, *7*(1), 44–47. https://doi.org/10.5923/j.mm.20170701.06

Laderlah, S. A., Rahman, S. A., Awang, K., & Man, Y. C. (2011). A Study on Islamic Tourism: A Malaysian Experience. *IACSIT Press*, *17*, 184–189.

Leslie, D. (2012). The Responsible Tourism Debate. In D. Leslie (Ed.), *Responsible Tourism Concepts, Theory and Practice* (pp. 17–43). CABI. http://library1.nida.ac.th/termpaper6/sd/2554/19755.pdf

Lohmann, G., & Netto, P. (2016). *Tourism Theory Concepts, Models and Systems*. CABI.

Marzuki, S. et al. (2020). Islamic Tourism: The Practices Ofa Shariah-Compliant Hotel in De Palma Hotel, Malaysia. In C. Michael Hall and Girish Prayag (Eds.), *The Routledge Handbook of Halal Hospitality and Islamic Tourism* (pp. 109–1015). Routledge. http://library1.nida.ac.th/termpaper6/sd/2554/19755.pdf

Mastercard-CrescentRating. (2018). Global Muslim Travel Index 2018. In *Mastercard-Crescentrating* (Issue April). https://www.crescentrating.com/download/thankyou.html?file=X7UrOM8Y_GMITI-Report-2018-web-version%281%29.pdf

Mastercard-CrescentRating. (2019a). *Global Muslim Travel Index 2019* (Issue April).

Mastercard-CrescentRating. (2019b). *Halal Travel Frontier2019 Report*.

Medlik, S. (2003). Dictionary of Travel, Tourism and Hospitality. In S. Medlik (Third Edit). Butterworth-Heinemann.

Mohamed, N. (2018). *The Influence of Religiosity upon Muslim Tourists' Travel Decision-Making Processes for an Islamic Leisure Destination* (Issue September). Heriot-Watt University.

Mohideen, H., & Mohideen, S. (2008). The Language of Islamophobia in Internet Articles. *Intellectual Discourse*, *16*(1), 73-87.

Omar, C. M. C., Islam, M. S., & Adaha, N. M. A. (2013). Perspectives on Islamic Tourism and Shariah Compliance. *Paper Proceeding Islamic Economics and Business*, *1*(1), 1–8.

Organization of Islamic Cooperation. (2011). *International Tourism in OIC Member Countries: Prospects and Challenges*. SESRIC

Oyelakin, I. O., & Yusuf, A. H. (2018). Prospects of Halal Products in Developing Countries: Comparison between Nigeria and Malaysia. *International Journal of Business Society*, *2*(8). https://doi.org/10.30566/ijo-bs/2018.285

Pew Research Center. (2015). *The Future of World Religions: Population Growth Projections, 2010–2050*. http://www.pewforum.org/2015/04/02/religious-projections-2010-2050/

Rahadian, B., Hakim, N., Kurniawan, A., Putri, A. R., & Adienda, C. (2019). Implementation of Halal Product Guarantee in Dental Health Services in Islamic Hospital. *International Journal of Human and Health Science*, *3*(2), 3–6. http://ijhhsfimaweb.info/index.php/IJHHS/article/view/77/76

Razalli, M. R. (2020). Shariah-Compliant Hotel Operations Practices (SCHOP). In C. M. Hall & G. Prayag (Eds.), *The Routledge Handbook of Halal Hospitality and Islamic Tourism* (pp. 93–109). Taylor & Francis. https://doi.org/10.4324/9781315150604

Razzaq, S., Hall, C. M., & Prayag, G. (2016). The Capacity of New Zealand to Accommodate the Halal Tourism Market – OR Not. *Tourism Management Perspectives*, *18*, 92–97. https://doi.org/10.1016/j.tmp.2016.01.008

Riaz, M. N., & Chaudry, M. M. (2004). Food Production. In *Canadian hospital* (Vol. 35, Issue 11). CRC Press. https://doi.org/10.4324/9781315626796-26

Samori, Z., Md Salleh, N. Z., & Khalid, M. M. (2016). Current Trends on Halal Tourism: Cases on Selected Asian Countries. *Tourism Management Perspectives*, *19*, 131–136. https://doi.org/10.1016/j.tmp.2015.12.011

Scorțe, C., Dragolea, L., & Paschia, L. (Dincă) (2013). Tourism – The Main Component of Hospitality Industry. *Annales Universitatis Apulensis Series Oeconomica*, *15*(2), 703–715.

Secinaro, P. Pietro, & Biancone, S. (2019). The Halal Tourism: A Business Model Opportunity. In K. A. Jamal, A. Raj, & R. Griffin (Ed.), *Islamic Tourism: Management of Travel Destinations*. (pp. 192–201). CAB. https://doi.org/10.1079/9781786394132.0010

Statistical Economic and Social Research and Training Centre for Islamic, & (SESRIC). (2018). *OIC ECONOMIC OUTLOOK 2018: Challenges and Opportunities towards Achieving the OIC-2025*. Organisation of Islamic Cooperation. www.idi.org.il

Suleman, R., & Qayum, B. (2018a). Religion and Islamic Tourism Destinations. In *Islamic Tourism: Management of Travel Destinations*. https://doi.org/10.1079/9781786394132.0026

Suleman, R., & Qayum, B. (2018b). Religion and Islamic Tourism Destinations. In A. Jamal, R. Raj & K. Griffin (Eds.), *Islamic Tourism: Management of Travel Destinations* (pp. 26–37). CABI. https://doi.org/10.1079/9781786394132.0026

Šuligoj, M., & Maruško, H. (2017). Hotels and Halal-oriented Products: What Do Hotel Managers in Slovenia Think? *Organizacija*, *50*(4), 314–323. https://doi.org/10.1515/orga-2017-0023

Sultana, S. (2020). Non- Muslims' Perception of Halal Tourism: A Conceptual Paper. *Journal of Halal Studies*, *1*(1), 1–13.

Suradin, M. (2018). Halal Tourism Promotion in Indonesia: An Analysis on Official Destination Websites. *Journal of Indonesian Tourism and Development Studies*, *6*(3), 143–158. https://doi.org/10.21776/ub.jitode.2018.006.03.01

Theobald, W. F. (2005). Global Tourism. In W. F. Theobald (Ed.), *Global Tourism* (3rd ed.). https://doi.org/10.1016/b978-0-7506-7789-9.50011-x

Theobald, W. F. (2012). Global Tourism. *Global Tourism*. https://doi.org/10.4324/9780080478043

Tribe, J. (2009). *Philosophical Issues in Tourism* (J. Tribe, ed., Vol. 53, Issue 9, pp. 3–25). Channel View Publications.

United Nations. (2008). *International Recommendations for Tourism Statistics 2008*. United Nations.

Utomo, S. B., Scott, N., & Jin, X. (2019). The Impacts of Hajji Satisfaction on Islamic Religious Commitment: A Theoretical Framework. In A. Jamal, R. Raj, & G. Kevin (Eds.), *Islamic TourIsm: Management of Travel DesTInaTIons*. CABI.

Vargas-Sánchez, A., & Moral-Moral, M. (2018). Halal Tourism: Insights from Experts in the Field. In *Islamic Tourism: Management of Travel Destinations*. https://doi.org/10.1079/9781786394132.0154

Vargas-Sánchez, A., & Moral-Moral, M. (2019). Halal Tourism: Literature Review and Experts' View. *Journal of Islamic Marketing*, *11*(3), 549–569. https://doi.org/10.1108/JIMA-04-2017-0039

Veal, A. J. (1992). Definitions of Leisure and Recreation. *Australian Journal of Leisure and Recreation*, *2*(52), 44–48. http://funlibre.org/biblioteca2/docs_digitales/investigacion/definiciones_ocio_y_recreacion

Weaver, D., & Lawton, L. (2014). *Tourism Management* (5th ed.). Wiley & Sons.
Wibowo, M. W., & Ahmad, F. S. (2016). Non-Muslim Consumers' Halal Food Product Acceptance Model. *Procedia Economics and Finance*, *37*(16), 276–283. https://doi.org/10.1016/s2212-5671(16)30125-3
Wildan, W., & Sukardi, S. (2017). *Ecotourism Model Based on Social Capital (Halal Tourism) as the Strengthening Factor for the Economy of Lombok Community*. January. https://doi.org/10.5220/0007303703290333
World Travel Market. (2007). *WTM Global Trends Report 2007*.
Zawawi, M., & Othman, K. (2017). An Overview of Shari'ah Compliant Healthcare Services in Malaysia Majdah. *Malaysian Journal of Consumer and Family Economics An*, *2*, 91–100.

2 Travel, Tourism and Worship

In the doctrine of most religions, traveling is considered worship because, in most cases, adherents travel to access sacred places, to be educated or to spread their faiths. For instance, in Islam, the greatest journeys were undertaken during the first decades of Islam to seek and spread knowledge (Fahim & Dooty, 2014). Allah encourages people to travel through His Quran that travels on earth and see the end of those who rejected the truth (the Holy Quran, 6:11). Adherents of almost every religion have traveled from one place to other perceived sacred places for worship.

Religious Tourism and Pilgrimages

Religious tourism, sometimes called faith tourism or spiritual tourism, has emerged as an attractive thematic area in tourism literature (Battour, 2019; Din, 1989). The relationship between tourism and religion has been addressed in the large body of tourism literature (El-Gohary, 2016; Öter & Çetinkaya, 2016). The findings of these studies reveal that religion is among the key motivating factors for tourists to travel and affects the behavior of tourists during visitation. Duman (2020) also contends that religion affects the host–guest relationship in tourism and hospitality. They further illustrate that religions have some shared norms and rules. For instance, in every religion, some foods are permitted for adherents, and some specified foods are not allowed for religious customers.

Table 2.1 Religious Food Restrictions

Major Religion	Prohibited Foods and Beverages	Remarks
Islam	<ul><li>All kinds of swine products</li><li>Blood</li><li>Carrion and carnivorous animals</li><li>Any alcoholic beverages and other addictive drugs</li><li>Any contamination of halal (permitted) and haram (prohibited) utensils for kitchen use is not allowed</li></ul>	During Ramadan, which lasts about a month, Muslims must abstain from any kind of intake, such as eating, drinking and smoking, from dawn until sunset

(*Continued*)

DOI: 10.4324/9781003355236-3

Table 2.1 (Continued)

Major Religion	Prohibited Foods and Beverages	Remarks
Christianity	• All kinds of swine products • Blood • Drinking alcohol is strongly discouraged by many denominators of Christianity • Eastern Orthodox Church members prohibit meat intake on Wednesdays or Fridays during the liturgical year, and the very observant also refrain from eating fish, poultry, and dairy products these days • Roman Catholics prohibit red meat or poultry products or their derivatives on Fridays during Lent; fish, eggs, and dairy products are allowed. On the two mandatory fast days, Ash Wednesday and Good Friday	• Various denominators of Christianity have different restrictions
Hinduism	• All kinds of swine products • Foods including beef, eggs, root vegetables such as onions, garlic and mushrooms • Alcoholic beverages are strongly discouraged	• Fasting is held only during events, such as marriages
Judaism	• Any non-kosher food • Food is cooked without following the food preparation rules of Judaism • Meat products other than cloven hooves and chew their cud. For instance, a properly butchered beef is kosher whereas pork is not kosher inherently • Pork and its byproducts, including lard and bacon, and flesh • Blood • Not all products from non-kosher animals are allowed. Only one-fourth of flesh from kosher animals is permitted • Only domesticated birds are permitted and must come from a certified kosher farm • Meat and dairy products cannot be consumed or served together • Fishes and their byproducts are non-kosher except for fish with fins and scale	• A butcher (approved by the Jewish community) must slaughter animals humanely and according to a set process with specific equipment. The blood is worn out, and the flesh is slated to remove all traces of blood • The following 6 days are fasting days of Judaism: Fast of Esther, Yom Kippur, Tisha, Tzom Gedaliah, the Seventeenth of Tammuz & the Tenth of Teves

Source: Adapted from Hall and Prayag (2020).

For instance, Jews are allowed to eat only *kosher* food, while Muslims are expected to consume only halal food and beverages, and Hindus look for vegetarian offerings (Hall & Prayag, 2020). Consuming pork is strictly forbidden in all Abrahamic religions of Judaism, Christianity and Islam, and, similarly, Hindu teaching strictly forbids its followers to consume beef (Battour, 2019). The tourism industry must understand and consider all these restrictions while providing food, and attention must be paid to dishes ingredients and food preparation procedures as well.

These days, religious tourism has received much attention in the field of tourism. According to Rinschede (1992); Öter and Çetinkaya (2016), religious tourism is as old as religion itself, and religious tourism is among the pioneer forms of tourism, dating back thousands of years. Monotheist religions such as Judaism, Christianity and Islam, as well as traditional and polytheist religions have practiced religious tourism and pilgrimages for centuries now. Buddhism, Hinduism and Shintoism are also not exceptional. It has been reported that over 10 million Muslims perform Hajj and Umrah per year (Dinarstandard, 2019), about 5 million Catholic Christians visit Lourdes in France, and 28 million Hindu pilgrims travel to River Ganges in India annually (Ojo & Busayo, 2017). The World Tourism Organization (UNWTO) reported that about 330 million pilgrims visit major global religious sites each year and inject about US$18 billion into the world economy (University of Venda [UNIVEN], 2015). Religion has long been an integral motive for undertaking journeys, and the religion-driven journey is usually considered the oldest form of tourism (Timothy & Olsen, 2006). According to Durán-Sánchez et al. (2018), traveling for fervor and religious devotion has existed in humanity since immemorial times. Rinschede (1992) states religious tourism is a type of tourism wherein religion is the main motive of its participants. Rinschede suggests two taxonomies of religious tourism based on time involved and distance traveled, namely short-term and long-term religious tourism.

Lefebvre, in Blackwell (2007), defines religious tourism as tourism consisting of a range of spiritual sites and associated services, which are visited for both secular and religious reasons. Based on this definition, Blackwell (2007) identifies two kinds of sites: shrines and pilgrimage sites. Shrines refer to sites where a relic or image is 'venerated,' whereas pilgrimage sites are recognized places where a miracle has occurred, still occurs and may do so again. However, Battour (2019) disagrees with the above definition. According to Battour, the visiting of secular tourists toward shrines or sacred sites other than the purpose of pleasing God cannot be considered religious tourism. He referred to this kind of tourism as 'religious-based tourism.' Shackley (2008) classified religion-based attractions into the following categories: (1) natural phenomena of sacred lakes, mountains, islands and groves; (2) buildings and sites originally constructed for religious purposes; (3) buildings with a religious theme; (4) special events with religious significance held at non-religious sites and (5) sacralized secular sites associated with tragedy or politically significant events. Santos (2003) identified the following characteristics of religious tourism: the travel is voluntary, temporary and unpaid; the motivation of traveling is religion; it might be supplemented by other motivations; and the destination is a religious site and sacred sites (Cited in Blackwell, 2007).

Despite the worldwide trend toward secularization, there has been a rejuvenation of places and routes of religious sites in recent years (Álvarez-García et al., 2018). Blackwell (2007) argues that recently religious travel has revived, and more people are traveling to visit sacred sites in search of sacredness, spiritual guidance and reaching holy places. A study conducted by UNIVEN (2015) confirmed that about 330 million people travel for religious reasons annually and inject many dollars into the global economy. Religious tourism is promising for the development of many destinations. Blackwell (2007) concludes that, unlike hedonistic tourism, religious tourism is less affected by various shocks. Recent studies in India confirm that even in areas with recognized higher risks of dangers, pilgrims did not deter from visiting sacred sites (Bhattarai et al., 2005, cited in Blackwell, 2007). Another study conducted on the Hajj pilgrimage also proves that religious sites generally are less responsive to the threats to personal safety posed by global and internal security matters than secular, hedonistic attractions. For example, during the hajj pilgrimage of 1990, it was reported that more than 1,400 Muslim pilgrims suffocated and/or were trampled to death (Gambrell, 2015). Again, in 2015 about 700 pilgrims died due to suffocation and trampling at the hajj pilgrimage to Mecca. However, these fatal incidents did not have a significant impact on the subsequent year's inflows of the pilgrim because people perform pilgrimages to please their God and reciprocally receive His blessings and rewards in the hereafter rather than for worldly enjoyment. When the pilgrims set out on the pilgrimage journey, they expect that sometimes the journey will be difficult and those fatal incidents will emerge, but they mostly do not cancel traveling by fearing it.

Table 2.2 Size and Projected Growth of World Major Religious Group

Major Religions	2010 Population	% of World Population in 2010	Projected 2050 Population	% of World Population in 2050	Population Growth 2010–2050
Christianity	2,168,330,000	31.4	2,918,070,000	31.4	749,740,000
Islam	1,599,700,000	23.2	2,761,480,000	29.7	1,161,780,000
Unaffiliated	1,131,150,000	16.4	1,230,340,000	13.2	99,190,000
Hindus	1,032,210,000	15.0	1,384,360,000	14.9	352,140,000
Buddhists	487,760,000	7.1	486,270,000	5.2	−1,490,000
Folk Religions	404,690,000	5.9	4449,140,000	4.8	44,450,000
Other Religions	58,150,000	0.8	61,450,000	0.7	3,300,000
Jews	13,860,000	0.2	16,090,000	0.2	2,230,000
World Total	6,895,850,000	100.0	9,307,190,000	100.0	2,411,340,000

Pilgrimage and Tourism

Pilgrimage is the most studied subcategory of religious tourism. Utomo et al. (2019) define pilgrimage as a religious journey to holy sites for spiritual purposes to seek the blessing of God. Various people travel toward various holy sites to practice pilgrimage. For instance, Muslims to Mecca in Saudi Arabia, Christians to Santiago de Compostela in Spain, Jews to Israel, Catholics to Lourdes in France and Hindus to the Ganges in India (Utomo et al., 2019). Given the interconnectedness of religion and tourism has eventually increased, no longer possible to treat the nature of their association only under pilgrimage. In recent studies of tourism, religious tourism was recognized as one type of tourism and received good attention (Battour et al., 2010; Din, 1989; Rinschede, 1992). The UNWTO definitions given to tourism and tourist seem wide enough to include both pilgrimage and religious tourism. Both pilgrims and religious or sacred tourists fit into the UNWTO definition of tourism. Both involve the decision to travel from home toward a destination to return. Therefore, according to the UNWTO definition, both pilgrimage and religious tourism are parts of tourism. However, there is a substantially undergoing debate about whether pilgrimage differs from tourism (Battour, 2019, Battour, et al. 2010; Blackwell, 2007; Din, 1989). Some academicians try to differentiate tourism and pilgrimage and/or tourists and pilgrims based on the motivations and expectations of tourists and pilgrims (Blackwell, 2007). These authors have tried to place tourism and pilgrimage at the opposite ends of a continuum of travel – between the sacred and the secular. It is believed that pilgrims perform some formal elements such as chanting the Lord's name, bowing down and prostrate to God, kiss the so-called sacred walls of buildings and materials, but the tourists might not accomplish such ritual activities at the destination, rather trample, debase and discredit these sacred places. When the sacred sites become too touristic, then the religious virtues that motivated the original devotees to communicate the message of the holy places are undermined and debased (Blackwell, 2007). Pilgrims believe that pilgrimages have the power to reconcile body and spirit. There are also debates about what is meant by religious tourism and whether it differs from a pilgrimage. Kadhim et al. (2008) allege that pilgrimages have been part of religious history throughout the ages. A pilgrimage is a ritual journey toward sacred sites and shrines with a sacred purpose. For pilgrims, every movement along the way has a meaning. The pilgrims set out on the journey of pilgrimage not to have fun but to face challenges that they know the journey will be difficult and that life-giving challenges will emerge. Pilgrims believe that pilgrimage is not a vacation; it is a journey to receive blessings and rewards for the hereafter. Some conservative religious leaders have rejected the association of religion with tourism. This means that they do not accept pilgrims as tourists for both possess contrary motivations and ends (Tală & Pădurean, 2008). During an international Christian Conference of Asia, a religious father stated that '… tourism is not pilgrimaging because pilgrims step the sacred soil smoothly with humility and patience, while tourists trample these places, photographing them, traveling with arrogance and in a hurry' (Ambrósio, 2007, p. 84). According to his explanation, tourists are materialists and hedonists whereas pilgrims are spiritualists.

Moreover, Tală and Pădurean (2008) argue that mass tourism might cause those holy places to lose their sacredness. For Gendron (1972, p. 81, cited in Ambrósio, 2007), tourist travels to escape from mundane life and to enjoy more pleasure and fun; however, the pilgrims depart their home not for worldly fun but for their soul to be close to God. Some authors also argue that the presence of many tourists at sacred sites could lead to the commercialization and commodification of sacred sites, religious festivals and events. The suppliers of tourism could modify and commercialize religious festivals and events to suit the needs of secular tourists (Egresi et al., 2012).

The economic contribution of religious tourism has been underestimated for the past several years. Today the spending habits of pilgrims have been changing. For instance, Saudi Arabia earns 75% of its visitor export from pilgrims (Egresi et al., 2012).

Islam and Tourism

In the Islamic faith, the boundaries of spiritual and secular activities are transcended. They are closely intertwined because the Quran and Sunnah are sources of all aspects of human activities (Jafari & Scott, 2014). A brief description of the Islamic belief system is necessary to understand the characteristics of Muslim travelers and the very concept of Islam. In other words, to introduce the concept and clarify the perceived misconceptions, it is important to describe what Islam and Muslims mean, especially for non-Muslim readers. It should be clear that Islam includes both a belief system and a complete way of life from womb to tomb. Battour et al. (2012); El-Gohary (2016) state that Islam is the name of the religion whose first and last prophets were Adam (may Allah be pleased with him) and Prophet Muhammad (PBUH), respectively. The term 'Islam' originated from the Arabic stem word 'Salama,' which means peace, purity, submission, and obedience. In the religious sense, Islam means submission to the will of God and obedience to His law, whereas 'Muslim' refers to a person who submits to God or is an adherent of Islam. As discussed by El-Gohary (2016), Islam comprises five pillars. The first pillar of Islam is the profession of faith (*Shahada*). This refers to giving witness that there is no god but Allah and Muhammad is His last messenger (*la ilaha illa-llahu muḥammadun rasulu-llah*). The *Shahada* is the central statement of Islam and the principal mark of Islamic orthodoxy or oneness of God and the door to enter into Islam. The second pillar is prayer (*Salah*). According to Islamic principles, Muslims must pray five times a day, facing the direction of *Qibla* (Mecca) alone or congregational with others. Alms-giving (*Zakah*) is the third pillar. The term *zakah* is derived from the Arabic word, which means 'purification,' therefore, in Islam, giving charity is considered as purifying one's wealth. Giving charity to those who deserve it is part of the Muslim character and one of the five pillars of Islamic practice.

Zaka is a compulsory charity in Islam. It is an obligation for those who have the specified quantity of wealth to give to those members of the community who deserve it. Scholars of Hadith and the Holy Quran suggest that *zakat* is about 2.5% of one's annual capital assets. Only the poor, those who collect the alms and needy people deserve alms. It could also be used to free captives and debtors for the sake of Allah (the Holy Quran, 9:60). In another Quranic verse, Allah says, '…and in whose wealth there is a right acknowledged for the beggar and the destitute…' (Quran 70:24–25). The fourth one is fasting (*Sawm*). Fasting one month a year, during Ramadan, the ninth lunar month or the ninth month of the Islamic calendar, is mandatory except for those who have been exempted because of their age, health conditions and so on. The ill, travelers and others who are unable to fast also are exempted from fasting. Quran is believed to have been sent down by God to Muhammad through the angel Gabriel during the month of Ramadan. Fasting in Islam involves abstaining from all kinds of food, beverages, smoking and sexual activity between dawn and sunset. The fifth pillar of Islam is the pilgrimage to Mecca (Hajj). Since Hajj is one aspect of the study under consideration, it will be discussed thoroughly later in this chapter. These five pillars of Islam are accepted and adhered to by Muslims everywhere, by all sects of Islam and are obligatory for capable Muslims. All five pillars appear in different chapters of the Qur'an and their details in Hadith (www.islamreligion.com website).

Other concepts to be clarified concerning Islam are the Quran, Sunnah and Hadith. As Battour and Ismail (2016), Din (1989), and El-Gohary (2016) explain, the Holy Quran is the holiest scripture to Muslims on earth. All Muslims unanimously believe Quran is the 'word' of God that has come down through angel Gabriel to Prophet Mohammed as a revelation, whereas 'Sunna' refers to what the Prophet Muhammad (PBUH) said, did approve, and disapproved of, explicitly or implicitly. Hadith, on the other hand, denotes the reports and the compilation of such narrations. Generally, the Sunnah of Prophet Muhammed (PBUH) has been collected and compiled in the form of a book or literature called Hadith.

For Muslims, Islam is a comprehensive way of life from birth to death. In addition to religious issues, it affects recreation, travel, the motivation of visitors and tourism development at large directly and indirectly (Jafari & Scott, 2014; Zamani-Farahani & Musa, 2012). Islam has rules and regulations that its adherents must follow and practice (Hall, 2011). For instance, Islam forbids Muslims from visiting some specified places, such as places where corruption is practiced, alcohol is consumed and, immoral acts are taken place, varied sins are committed; and therefore, the teachings of Islam have direct and indirect impacts on tourism and travel industry (Battour, 2016). Rashid (2007) proposes three types of Islamic tourism: The first one is an obligatory visit to Mecca. In Islam, those physically and finically capable Muslims must visit Mecca (perform Hajj) at least once in a lifetime. The second is highly recommended, such as Umrah, and the last is a journey performed in search of knowledge, research, commerce, health, leisure and recreation. Therefore, in Islam, tourism could be seen as 'a must-do' mandatory activity such as Hajj and 'a nice to do' activity such as a journey in search of Islamic knowledge and a journey to learn about what Allah creates in the universe and to contemplate. In such a manner, Islam encourages tourism in different ways. Above all, tourism is one of the central tenets of Islam. As Hajj is one of the five pillars of Islam, Muslims from all corners of the world and all generations need to perform the pilgrimage to Mecca to fulfill their religious duty and consolidate their commitment to their religion.

As highlighted by Henderson (2016); Zamani-Farahani and Musa (2012), the very principles of Islam and tourism do not contradict, but they are compatible. Al-Munajjid (2009) alleges that the Arabic term *siyaha* has been used in Islamic literature to denote tourism. The term is taken from the Arabic verb *Saha*, which means 'move or flow.' Thus, in Muslim countries, the traveling of a person from one place to another for tourism is addressed by the word *siyaha*. The word *rihlah* is also used to denote tourism-like activities, especially business tourism. For example, Ibn Battuta's journey and the Prophet Muhammad's (PBUH) travel between Mecca and Syria are recorded as *rihlah*. Hence, the teaching of Islam encourages travel and visitation in many ways, except those travels that contradict the tenet of Sharia.

In several of its verses, the Holy Quran deals with the issue of tourism (Fahim & Dooty, 2014). There are at least 13 verses scattered in various chapters of the Qur'an (Quran, 3:137; 6:11; 12:109; 16:36; 22:46; 27:69; 29:20; 30:9; 30:42; 35:44; 40:21; 40:82; 47:10) that encourage Muslims to travel and visit various destinations and attractions such as historical sites, various natural features and landscapes. These Quranic verses call humankind to travel to different countries of this globe, not for the sake of encouraging hedonism but to learn from the previous generation's mistakes and to contemplate the unlimited power of the Almighty God (El-Gohary, 2016). For instance, the following Quranic verse encourages people to visit historical sites. 'There have been examples that have passed away before you: Travel through the earth, and see what the end of those who rejected truth was [...]' (the holy Quran, 3:137). Allah through his holy Quran encourages Muslims to visit historical places to know about the deeds of the previous generation. He encourages them to visit various natural creatures, landscapes and topographies and to praise Him with the following verse of the Quran. 'Travel through the earth and see how Allah did originate creation [...]' (the holy Quran 29:20). Scholars of the holy Quran and Hadith state that this verse aims to let people understand God's unlimited and ultimate power so that adherents can contemplate accordingly. In the early days of Islam, traveling and visitations were among the strategies for spreading Islam to the rest of the world. The companions of Prophet Muhammad (PBUH) have traveled worldwide, teaching the people and calling them to Islam (Al-Munajjid, 2009). Duman (2020) states that humans as caliphs in this world have been encouraged to know and explore the creations of God by traveling on earth.

Regarding this, Allah (SW) says in his holy Quran '[...] travel through the earth and see how God did originate creation [...]' (The Holy Quran, 29:20). Moreover, halal recreation and entertainment are also not prohibited in Islam. Islam offers special tips for tourists or guests in that they are allowed to postpone Ramadan fasting and shorten regular prayers or combine some prayers (Battour et al., 2010; Din, 1989). However, at the same time, Islam orders the adherents to continue practicing worship and respecting Islamic values such as Islamic code dress, food and prayer even during traveling (Zamani-Farahani & Henderson, 2010). Therefore, Muslims who want to travel must accomplish his/her religious duties per the sharia principles in the transit route and destinations as well. This has finally given rise to the birth of Muslim-friendly niche tourism, such as Islamic tourism, Halal tourism, and Sharia-friendly tourism.

According to the Pew Research Center, Islam was the second religion in the number of adherents, with 1.6 billion adherents of the global population, comprising one-fourth of the world's population. If the current demographic trends continue, Islam will surpass Christianity by the middle of the 21st century (Pew Research Center, 2011). According to the projection of the Pew Research Center (2015), the number Muslim population will be 2.8 billion by 2050, which covers then 30% of the world population (Lipka, 2015). Given both numbers of the Muslim population and their disposable income steadily increasing, destinations cannot overlook Muslims as potential customers any longer. According to the Pew Research Center Projection (2015), Muslims will grow more than twice faster as the overall world population in the coming five decades; therefore, in the second half of this century, Muslims are expected to surpass Christians as the world's largest religious group (Lipka, 2015). In 2015, Muslims share 24.1% of the global population. In 2013, 10% of outbound tourists were reported to have been Muslim tourists and generated 140 billion USD in revenues (Çetin & Dinçer, 2016). Mujahidin (2020) claims that new tourism trends that align with religious observances and Islamic lifestyles have emerged recently. Hakim (2019) also points out that niche tourism such as halal tourism and Islamic tourism have emerged to meet the needs and desires of Muslim travelers. According to Elseidi (2018), the steadily increasing halal visitors made many destinations reconsider their marketing strategies, restructure their products and services, cater to Muslim visitors' needs and meet the growing market segment. Statistical Economic and Social Research and Training Centre for Islamic (SESRIC, 2018) found that the major source market for the global halal tourism industry is the 57 Member Countries of the Organization of Islamic Cooperation (OIC), in general, members of the Gulf Cooperation Council (GCC), in particular.

According to the State of the Global Islamic Economy Report (2014/2015), Global Muslim spending on tourism, excluding Hajj and Umrah was US$140 billion in 2013, which comprises 11.5% of global expenditure (Reuter, 2015). The top generating countries of Muslim tourists based on 2013 expenditure include Saudi Arabia, Iran, the United Arab Emirates, Qatar, Kuwait, Turkey and Indonesia. Mastercard-CrescentRating (2018) points out that for destinations to plant unforgettable memories for Muslim travelers, it is important to cater to the faith-based needs of Muslim travelers in touch-points, including restaurants, hotels and airports. Mastercard-CrescentRating advises that adding value to destinations by offering world heritage sites and places with a showcase of Islamic history or culture as unique experiences can achieve high satisfaction of the Muslim visitors.

To sum up, in the last couple of years, a large body of literature has been produced on the topic of Islam and tourism. The most referenced journal articles in the area include Battour et al., 2010; Battour, 2019; Battour et al., 2018; Din, 1989; El-Gohary, 2016; Henderson (2010). An article entitled 'Islam and Tourism: Patterns, Issues and Option' is one of the pioneer studies in tourism and Islam. Din wrote this article in 1989. It is the most referenced and cited article in the succeeding related or similar works. For the first time, the paper tries to reveal the relationship between Islam and tourism and paved the way for subsequent researchers in the area; in such a way, Din broke the silence in the area. Other contemporaneous studies of Din's work did not touch on such themes. In this and other publications, Din introduced the concept of Islamic tourism to academia.

The author utilized some verses of the Quran to confirm the positivity of Islam to travel and tourism. At the same time, the author did not hide the default characteristics of tourism, such as sexual permissiveness, voyeurism, consumption of pork and alcohol and gambling. These activities are naturally against Islamic values and naturally unIslamic. According to Battour et al. (2010); Din (1989); El-Gohary (2016); Henderson (2010), though by definition Islam encourages traveling, it does not, however, mean that Islam allows travel and visitation toward the areas where unIslamic activities are seen as norms and everyday actions. According to the preceding authors, tourism in Islam is meant to be spiritually purposeful, to make Muslims aware of the greatness of God through observing the signs of history and natural and manmade wonders, all of which are gifts of God. Muslims are also encouraged to visit and to be visited by their Muslim brethren and mainly Muslim countries. As Din (1989) describes in his article, the governments of some Muslim countries, such as Libya and Saudi Arabia, sponsored travel toward Muslim countries and domestic tourist as well. The preceding authors concentrated mainly on tourism development in Muslim countries and destinations. According to their studies, some Muslim countries disregarded and/or discouraged tourism development. However, this negative perception of indifference seems to change over time. Nowadays, many countries in the world understand the benefits of tourism and envision the development of the tourism industry. Authors such as Battour et al. (2010), El-Gohary (2016), Henderson (2010) and others have followed the footstep of Din in this regard. They have studied the relationship between Islam and tourism. Their works have been reviewed throughout this paper, especially Battour has contributed a dozen journal articles and books to the field.

The works of these preceding authors and other literature reveal that in Islam, the purposes of traveling include but are not limited to the following. (1) To contemplate and praise Allah: Sharia encourages Muslims to observe the amazing creations of God by traveling through the earth. Creation, in this case, includes various landscapes, flora and fauna. (2) To learn a lesson from the deeds of the past generation and repent: visiting historical sites helps humankind to learn from the mistakes of their predecessors and to repent and contemplate. (3) Seeking and/or imparting knowledge: Islam associates traveling with knowledge, teaching and learning. Islam orders humankind to travel through the earth and seek knowledge, disseminate and impart knowledge and or spread religion. For instance, during the reign of Prophet Mohammed (PBUH), his companions vastly traveled to seek and spread knowledge. Allah also apparently orders people to travel through his Quran repeatedly by saying, 'travel through the earth.' (4) Business and trading: partaking in different businesses it might be economic activities such as trade, or conferences and meeting or visiting relatives and friends to strengthen fraternity and sorority. This kind of travel is known as *Rihla* in Islamic tourism; and meetings, incentives, conferences and exhibitions (MICE) in conventional tourism. (5) Pilgrimage: performing pilgrimage toward the three mosques: Kaaba (Mesjidel Haram) of Mecca, Masjid Nebawi of Medina and Masjidel Aqsua of Jerusalem are mentioned in Hadiths. Hajj is one of the five pillars of Islam. There is also a tradition of Sufi and Shia Muslims known as *Ziyara*. *Ziyara* is a Muslim's travel to visit holy places such as shrines, mosques, mausoleums, and famous spiritual people and saints to seek spiritual growth and devotion (Haq & Wong, 2010). However, such kind of practices is highly discouraged by some sects of Sunni Muslims known as *Selefi*. Indeed such actions are unmentioned both in the Quran and in Sunnah. Nor has it been endorsed by the Islamic school of thought (Haq & Wong, 2010). Of course, Muslims can visit such sacred and historic sites simply for their historical significance (Al-Munajjid, 2008). However, visiting such places and personalities by seeking physical and spiritual healing, recovery from illness, family affairs and family development is not acceptable in Islam. (6) Tourism in Islam also includes traveling to contemplate the wonders of Allah's creation and enjoy the beauty of this great universe, to fulfill the obligations of life known as relaxation. Relaxation is essential to refresh oneself and enable one to strive hard after that (Al-Munajjid, 2008).

Tourism from the Perspective of the Quran and Sunnah

The relationship between Islam and the tourism industry is increasingly getting attention in scholarly work published under the title of Islamic tourism and halal tourism (Jamal & El-Bassiouny, 2019). These studies have tried to scrutinize tourism from the perspectives of the primary sharia sources of the Quran and Sunnah. Most researchers have discovered the positive relationship between tourism and Islam in their very nature though some contradictions are inevitable during implementation. All Muslims unanimously agreed that for Muslims, the Quran and Sunnah provide guidance in all aspects of humankind's activities and, therefore, observant Muslims make any decision, including travel as per the rule of the Quran and Sunnah. As Battour et al. (2010); El-Gohary (2016) explain, the Quran is the holiest scripture of Muslims on earth. All Muslims unanimously believe the Quran is the 'word' of Allah that has come down through angel Gabriel to Prophet Mohammed as a revelation, whereas 'Sunnah' refers to what the Prophet said, did, approved and disapproved of explicitly or indirectly. Hadith, on the other hand, denotes the reports and the compilation of such narrations. Generally, the Sunnah of Prophet Muhammed (PBUH) has been collected and compiled in the form of a book or literature called Hadith. Scholars such as Al-Munajjid (2009); Battour et al. (2010); El-Gohary (2016); Griffin and Raj (2017) and others have studied tourism from the perspective of the Quran and Sunnah in the last couple of years.

Tourism from the Perspective of the Holy Quran

As has been noted, more than 13 verses scattered in various chapters of the Quran inspire and encourage Muslims to travel and visit various destinations and attractions such as historical sites, various natural features and landscapes. These Quranic verses call humankind to travel to different places of this globe not for the sake of engaging in hedonism but for contemplation (*tefekur*) and to appreciate the unlimited power of the Almighty God. For instance, the verse of the Holy Quran, 3:137 encourages people to visit historical sites: '[…] earth has faced believers and disbelievers before you so that travel through the earth and learn from the fate of disbelievers […].' Allah through his holy Quran encourages humankind to visit the historical place and to learn lessons from the deeds of the previous generation, and He encourages humankind to visit various creatures, landscapes and topographies with the following verse of the Quran. '[…] travel through the earth and see how Allah did originate creation […]' (the holy Quran 29:20). Islam encourages adherents to gain knowledge through the five senses by traveling (Battour & Ismail, 2016; Khan & Callanan, 2017; Samori et al., 2016). This concept has been stated in the Holy Quran, 22:46 as follows: 'Why have they not traveled through the earth so that they should have hearts [minds] that help them understand and ears that can help them hear?'

Allah (SWT) makes tourism among the mandatory duties of adherents though there are some preconditions. Allah in His Holy Quran chapter 22 verse 27 says, '[…] and We [Allah] declare unto humankind to perform the Hajj (pilgrimage). They could use various means of transportation and across valleys, mountains from near and distant locations to perform Hajj.' Again, in *Suratul Al-Bakarah* (the Chapter of the Cow) verse 125 Allah recommends people to perform pilgrimage toward Kaaba and to keep visitor destinations clean as follows: '[…] and We rendered the House [Kaaba in

Saudi Araba, Mecca] a place deserve visitation and a sanctuary for the people, wherein Abraham stood and worship. We [Allah] commanded Abraham and Ishmael to sanitize Kaaba for [the halal visitors] for those who circumambulate it, those who visit it for devotion and those who bow down and prostrate' (the holy Quran 2:125).

In Islam, adherents are encouraged to travel around the world and contemplate by observing the wonders that Allah has created. For example, in Surat Al-An'am, Allah (SWT) orders people to move around the earth and learn the destiny of the previous generations, especially those who denied Allah, and believed in idols, and prostrate for them. The following Quranic verse reinforces the foregoing statement. 'Move through the earth and learn from the fate of those who did deny the truth' (the holy Quran, 6:11); '[…] travel in the land and observe what was the end of idolaters […]' (the holy Quran, 30:42); and '… travel through the earth, and see the fate of disbelievers' (the holy Quran, 3:137).

Muslims also advised visiting destinations for less than a year mainly for four months. According to the definition of tourism, the stay of a tourist in the destination must not exceed one consecutive year, and the following verse of the Quran fits with this definition. In *surah Ate-wbah* verse two Allah says, 'Travel freely through the earth for four months and keep in mind that one cannot be out of the will of God […]' (the holy Quran, 9:2). There are Muslims *Jamaa* known as *Tebligh* who travel for preaching, teaching and spreading Islam accordingly. They mainly traveled for less than four months. The *Tablighi* movement began in the early 20th century in India. In this movement, Muslim men travel and stay in various mosques around the world to meet Muslims and remind them about the spirit and spiritual practices of Islam (Abbasi, 2019; Haq & Wong, 2010). The *Tebligh* crews are said to have been well-educated and professional Muslim men of all ages who travel to visit and stay in various mosques, meet with the local Muslims and non-Muslims, and teach and learn Islam in both theory and practice (Abbasi, 2019). Travelers are also exempt from some religious duties as mentioned in both the Quran and Hadith. 'When you travel through the earth, there is no blame on you if you shorten your prayers […]' (the holy Quran, 4:101). Traveling also receives a due emphasis in the Quran. For instance, the phrase 'go travel around the world,' which commands Muslims to travel, has been repeated six times in the following chapters and verses of the Holy Quran, respectively: the Holy Quran, 2:27; 6:11; 27:69; 29:20; 16:26 and 30:42. Here the imperative verb 'travel on the earth' denotes the necessaries of travel for the Muslims. Muslims are advised to visit cities for pleasure. The following Quranic verse is a typical example of this. 'We had set between them and the cities which we blessed to be attractive for the people […] travel therein either by night or by day […]' (the holy Quran, 34:18).

Islam not only encourages people to travel but those who do not travel have also been condemned in the Quran. The following Quranic verses prove this fact. '[…] why have they not traveled through the earth to realize the fate of those disbelievers, of those who were before them [...]?;Why have they not traveled through the earth so that they should have hearts [minds] that help them understand and ears that can help them hear [...]' (the Holy Quran, 10:109; 35:44; 40:21; 40:82; 47:10). There is no power in the Heavens and on the earth to compete with Allah's might: indeed, Allah is the Omniscient Omnipotent' (the holy Quran, 22:46). The preceding Quranic verse order humankind to partake in tourism with the aim of closing to God. In addition, enjoying oneself by observing the wonders of God without transgressing on Islamic principles is also allowed in Islam.

Tourism from the Perspective of Sunnah

As true in the Quran, people have been encouraged to engage in tourism in Sunnah, too, if activities carried out throughout the transit routes or at the destinations are not transgressors against the Sharia. Several Sunnah deals with tourism, travel and journey (Samori et al., 2016). This implies that travel and tourism have a place in both primary sources of sharia law; this, in turn, has a paramount role in understanding the concept of halal tourism from an Islamic perspective. Moreover, some affirmative actions for travelers imply that travelers have a privilege in Islam. Travelers, for instance, could postpone fasting when traveling during the month of Ramadan, shortening or combining prayers.

Moreover, Muslims could pray while riding on the back of pack animals, or they can face the direction where they are sitting if the situation in traveling is not allowing facing Qibla (Kaaba) (Samori et al., 2016). As cited in Samori et al. (2016), Ibn Abbas narrated and reported that Prophet Muhammad (PBUH) said that until 19 days, travelers could shorten prayers. However, long times travelers should perform the full prayer (Authentic Hadith Bukhari: Vol. 2, Book 20, Hadith 186). There is also another hadith favors to travelers. Prophet Muhammad (PBUH) said that traveler who is traveling could offer prayers on his/her means of transport (camel, cars, airplanes, boats and so on) facing their direction by signals (Al-Bukhari, 1997). The above Hadiths typically exempt travelers from some religious duties while traveling. At the same time, it advises Muslims not to give up religious duties even during visitation. Therefore, for destinations to entice and retain halal-conscious visitors, they have to arrange facilities and services for religious duties. There are also hadiths about hospitality and customer handling. In the Hadith narrated by Abu Shuraih Al-Kaaba, Prophet Mohammad (PBUH) says, 'Whoever believes in Allah and the Last Day should serve his guest generously' (Al-Bukhari, 2009). Prophet Muhammad advises people to provide food, shelter and basic need for guests at least for three days. In Islamic traditions, guests have the right to stay with their host for three days (Al-Bukhari, 2009, Vol. 8, Book 73). Islam also promises privileges for Muslim travelers that the supplication of a parent over his children, the supplication of an oppressed and the supplication of the travelers will be inevitably accepted (At-Tirmidhi, 2007). In another hadith, the Prophet said that when a traveler has finished his job, he should return quickly to his family (Authentic Bukhari: 70/57/5429), demanding Muslim hosts relieve fellow travelers. In another hadith, the Messenger of Allah said that allowing a guest for three nights at one's home is obligatory (Al-Bukhari, 2009).

Despite these facts, some Muslims have tried to misuse the following hadiths out of context to discourage travel and tourism in the name of Islam. Allah's Messenger Prophet Muhammad (PBUH) said, '…traveling is a kind of torture, as it prevents one from sleeping and eating.' There is also another hadith narrated by Abu Said Al Khurdi that one should not travel to any place to visit except the three holy Mosques: Kaaba (Mecca), Masjid al-Nebawi (Medina) and Masjid al Aqsua (Palestine) (Al-Bukhari, 2009). By citing the latter Hadith as a piece of evidence, some Muslims argue that only three holy places, namely the holy Shrine of Mecca, the Prophet Mosque in Medina and Aqsua Mosque in Jerusalem are legitimate destinations for Muslim visitors. However, the above Hadith does not mean that it is prohibited to visit mosques or Islamic heritages to Muslims because visiting them has been unequivocally prescribed in the Quran and Hadith. Several Muslim scholars proved that these mosques had been mentioned only to refer to travel to perform rites and accomplish veneration. As discussed above and elsewhere in this paper, Allah (SWT) encourages Muslims in his Quran to visit his universe to contemplate, learn from historical sites and gain knowledge (The Holy Quran Ali, 2006). Prophet Muhammad (PBUH) did the same as narrated in various Hadith. Some people also argue by mentioning Hadith, 'Traveling is a kind of torture, as it prevents one from sleeping and eating.' Indeed this Hadith has connected travel to the concept of self-punishment and exhausting one's body. However, in the 21st century, modern technology in transportation abolished this negative concept of traveling. In the era of modern aircraft, traveling can no longer be a torturing or exhausting task. Even about three specific leisure activities of tourism, namely swimming, shooting and horseback riding, have been mentioned in the Sunnah (Shakona et al., 2015).

Hajj and Umrah: Pilgrimage to Mecca

The Kingdom of Saudi Arabia (KSA) consists of the two holiest cities of Islam, namely Mecca and Medina. Mecca is a city in Saudi Arabia where Prophet Muhammad (PBUH) was born and received revelations from Allah; obviously, Hajj is primarily gone toward it (Battour et al., 2010; Rinschede, 1992; Utomo et al., 2019). Some scholars believe Mecca to be the navel of the earth. Medina, another holy city of Saudi Arabia, into which Prophet Muhammad (PBUH) and his followers migrated in 622 and where the tomb of Prophet Muhammad (PBUH) is found, is the second destination of pilgrims of Hajj.

In Islam, it is not allowed to travel to venerate a specific place except the three holy mosques (Fahim & Dooty, 2014; Rinschede, 1992). A hadith narrated by Abu Said Al Khurdi stated that one should not travel to any place to venerate except the three holy Mosques: Kaaba (Mecca), Masjid al-Nebawi (Medina) and Masjid Aqsua (Palestine) (Al-Bukhari, 2009). However, it should be noted that the prohibition was only for venerating or worshiping other places. Muslims can still travel anywhere for the sake of spreading their religion, contemplation (*tefekur*) or other self-refreshment worldly purposes.

Hajj is an Islamic pilgrimage to Macca in Saudi Arabia and one of the five pillars of Islam (Fakhrutdinova et al., 2017; Gabdrakhmanov et al., 2016b; Vargas-Sánchez & Moral-Moral, 2019). For any Muslim who can afford to do that financially and physically, Hajj is 'a must-do' religious duty to be performed at least once in a lifetime (Ahmed & AKBABA, 2018; Gabdrakhmanov et al., 2016b; Jafari & Scott, 2014). Performing Hajj more than one time is not only possible, it is very advisable and rewarding according to the teaching of Islam. According to many Islamic sources, a pilgrim in Islam is a person who performs the Hajj to Mecca and Medina. Those who have performed this pilgrimage then could honor the honorary title of 'Hajj' (Gabdrakhmanov et al., 2016a). According to the Hadith reported by Abu Hurairah, while the reward of an *Umrah* is expiation for the sins committed in a year, the reward of an accepted Hajj is only paradise. Hajj is precisely specified in terms of where to go, when to go, how to go and who must go. In terms of when to go, Hajj takes place only during the first ten days of the lunar month of *Zul-Hajjah*, the 12th month of the Islamic calendar. Among these ten days, the ninth *Zul-Hijjah* is known as the Day of Arafah, and this day is called the day of Hajj. Rule and regulations of Hajj are described in the Holy Quran chapter two from verses 196 to 203. Variables of Hajj such as time, place, behaviors and activities of pilgrims and duration are specified and detailed in Hadith. In terms of where to go and where it takes place, it is in Saudi Arabia's holy cities of Mecca and Medina.

Kaaba is a cubical building found in the Masjid al-Haram in Mecca that Muslims revere as the original sanctuary and relic. It has been serving as a point of reference for prayer, and every Muslim must face it while praying (Meri, 2015). Kaaba is believed to have been built by Prophet Abraham (Ibrahim) as a shrine to worship God. However, some people argue that Prophet Adam built Kaaba for the first time, and Prophet Abraham rebuilt it (Meri, 2015). It is believed that the Kaaba had been a center for the veneration of idols until the Prophet Muhammad destroyed them following the conquest of Mecca in 630. Although the Kaaba has been vandalized, damaged and repaired throughout history, Muslims believe the 'Black Stone' is the original cornerstone (Herrmann & Bucksch, 2014). Muslims circumambulate the Kaaba seven times and kiss the Black Stone as part of the rites of the Hajj and Umra (Herrmann & Bucksch, 2014). In Islamic tradition, it is also believed that a black stone, also called 'Heavenly Stone,' was found in Kaaba to have fallen from paradise for Adam and Eve (Hawa) as a guide to constructing an altar (Herrmann & Bucksch, 2014).

Recently Saudi Arabia has paid strong attention to the annual hajj and umrah pilgrimages to attract close to 10 million pilgrims annually and generate over US$8 billion in revenue. The vision of Saudi Arabia is to attract 30 million pilgrims a year for Umrah by 2030 (Dinarstandard, 2019).

Table 2.3 Pilgrims into Mecca and Medina (Saudi Arabia) (2000–2019)

S. No.	Numbers of Pilgrims	Years	
		Islamic (HC)	Gregorian (AD)
1	2,313,278	1430	2009
2	2,789,399	1431	2010
3	2,927,717	1432	2011
4	3,161,573	1433	2013
5	1,980,249	1434	2014
6	2,085,238	1435	2015
7.	1,952,817	1436	2016
8	1,862,909	1437	2017
9	2,352,122	1438	2018
10	2,371,675	1439	2019

Source: General Authority for Statistics [GASTAT], 2019.

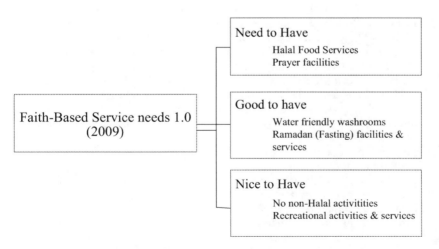

Figure 2.1 Faith-based service needs 1.0 (2009).

Sources by the Author.

70 *Travel, Tourism and Worship*

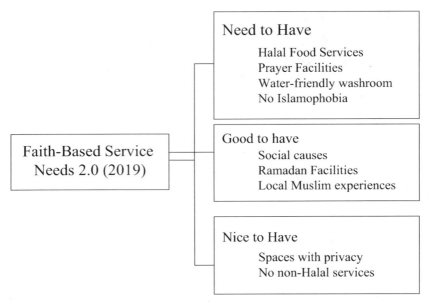

Figure 2.2 Faith-based service needs 2.0 (2019).
Sources prepared by the Authors.

References

Abbasi, A. S. (2019). Tablighi Jamaat: A Multidimensional Movement of Religious Travellers. In A. Jamal, R. Raji, & K. Griffin (Eds.), *Islamic Tourism: Management of Travel Destinations* (pp. 228–243). CABI.

Adie, B. A. (2020). Marketing Europe to Islamic Heritage Tourists. In C. M. Hall & G. Prayag (Eds.), *The Routledge Handbook of Halal Hospitality and Islamic Tourism* (pp. 157–169). Routledge. https://doi.org/10.4324/9781315150604-26

Ahmed, M. J., & Akbaba, A. (2018). The Potential of Halal Tourism in Ethiopia: Opportunities, Challenges and Prospects. *International Journal of Contemporary Tourism Research*, *1*, 13–22. https://doi.org/10.30625/ijctr.397499

Al-Bukhari, M. I. I. (1997). *The Translation of the Meanings of Sahih Al-Bukhari (Voume II)*. Darussalam Publisher & Distributors.

Al-Bukhari, M. I. I. (2009). *English Translation of SAHIH BUKHARI (Volume 1-9)*. DARUSSALAM Publishers & Distributors.

Al-Munajjid, M. S. (2009). *Travel and Tourism (Siyaahah) in Islam – Rulings and Types*. Islamhouse.Com.

Álvarez-García, J., del Río Rama, M., & Gómez-Ullate, M. (2018). *Handbook of Research on Socio-economic Impacts of Religious Tourism and Pilgrimage* (Issue August). https://doi.org/10.4018/978-1-5225-5730-2

Ambrósio, V. (2007). Sacred Pilgrimage and Tourism as Secular Pilgrimage. In Razaq Raj & Nigel D. Morpeth (Eds.), *Religious Tourism And Pilgrimage Festivals Management: An International Perspective* (pp. 78–88). CABI.

At-Tirmidhi, A.-H. (2007). *English Translation of At-Tirmidhi*. Books, Darussalam Global Leader in Islamic.

Battour, M. (2019). *Halal Tourism: Achieving Muslim Tourists' Satisfaction and Loyalty*. Author. https://books.google.com.tr/books?id=Jx-lyAEACAAJ

Battour, M., Hakimian, F., Ismail, M., & Boğan, E. (2018). The Perception of Non-Muslim Tourists towards Halal Tourism: Evidence from Turkey and Malaysia. *Journal of Islamic Marketing*, *9*(4), 823–840. https://doi.org/10.1108/JIMA-07-2017-0072

Battour, M., & Ismail, M. N. (2016). Halal Tourism: Concepts, Practises, Challenges and Future. *Tourism Management Perspectives*, *19*, 150–154. https://doi.org/10.1016/j.tmp.2015.12.008

Battour, M., Ismail, M. N., & Battor, M. (2010). Toward a Halal Tourism Market. *Tourism Analysis*, *15*(4), 461–470. https://doi.org/10.3727/108354210X12864727453304

Battour, M. M. (2016). Muslim Friendly Tourism. July. https://doi.org/10.13140/RG.2.1.4915.6084

Battour, M. M., Battor, M. M., & Ismail, M. (2012). The Mediating Role of Tourist Satisfaction: A Study of Muslim Tourists in Malaysia. *Journal of Travel and Tourism Marketing*, *29*(3), 279–297. https://doi.org/10.1080/10548408.2012.666174

Blackwell, R. (2007). Motivations for Religious Tourism, Pilgrimage, Festivals and Events. In R. Raj & N. D. Morpeth (Eds.), *Religious Tourism and Pilgrimage Festivals Management* (pp. 1–18). CABI

Caidi, N. (2019). Pilgrimage to Hajj: An Information Journey. *The International Journal of Information, Diversity, & Inclusion (IJIDI)*, *3*(1). https://doi.org/10.33137/ijidi.v3i1.32267

Çetin, G., & Dinçer, M. Z. (2016). Muslim Friendly Tourism (MFT): A Discussion. *Journal of Tourismology*, *2*(1), 65–67. https://doi.org/10.26650/jot.2016.2.1.0005

Din, K. H. (1989). Islam and Tourism. Patterns, Issues, and Options. *Annals of Tourism Research*, *16*(4), 542–563. https://doi.org/10.1016/0160-7383(89)90008-X

Dinarstandard. (2019). State of the Global Islamic Economy Report 2019/20. In *Dubai International Financial Centre*. https://haladinar.io/hdn/doc/report2018.pdf

Duman, T. (2020). Attributes of Muslim-Friendly Hospitality Service in a Process-Based Model. In M. Hall & G. Prayag (Eds.), *The Routledge Handbook of Halal Hospitality And Islamic Tourism* (pp. 53–69). Taylor & Francis. https://doi.org/10.4324/9781315150604-3

Durán-Sánchez, A., Álvarez-García, J., del Río-Rama, M. & Oliveira, C. (2018). Religious Tourism and Pilgrimage: Bibliometric Overview. *Religions*, *9*(9), 1–15. https://doi.org/10.3390/rel9090249

Egresi, I., Kara, F., & Bayram, B. (2012). Economic Impact of Religious Tourism in Mardin, Turkey. *Journal of Economics and Business*, *2*, 7–22. http://papers.ssrn.com/sol3/Delivery.cfm?abstractid=2184124#page=7

El-Gohary, H. (2016). Halal Tourism, is it Really Halal? *Tourism Management Perspectives*, *19*, 124–130. https://doi.org/10.1016/j.tmp.2015.12.013

Elseidi, R. I. (2018). Determinants of Halal Purchasing Intentions: Evidences from UK. *Journal of Islamic Marketing*, *9*(1), 167–190. https://doi.org/10.1108/JIMA-02-2016-0013

Fahim, S. T., & Dooty, E. N. (2014). Islamic Tourism: In the Perspective of Bangladesh. *Global Journal of Management and Business Research: Real Estate Event and Tourism Management*, *14*(1), 21–26.

Fakhrutdinova, L. R., Grigorieva, E. V., Gabdrakhmanov, N. K., Eidelman, B. M., & Bunakov, O. A. (2017). Religious Tourism in the Tourism System. *Revista San Gregorio*, *20*(SI), 96–102.

Gabdrakhmanov, N. K., Biktimirov, N. M., Rozhko, M. V., & Khafizova, L. V. (2016a). Problems of Development of Halal Tourism in Russia. *Journal of Organizational Culture, Communications and Conflict, 20*(2), 88–93.

Gabdrakhmanov, N. K., Biktimirov, N. M., Rozhko, M. V., & Mardanshina, R. M. (2016b). Features of Islamic Tourism. *Academy of Marketing Studies Journal, 20*(Special Issue), 45–50.

Gambrell, J. (2015, December 10). *Over 2,400 killed in Saudi hajj stampede, crush.* Associated Press.

Griffin, K. A., & Raj, R. (2017). Editorial: The Importance of Religious Tourism and Pilgrimage: Reflecting on Definitions, Motives and Data. *International Journal of Religious Tourism and Pilgrimage, 5*(3), ii–ix. https://doi.org/10.21427/D7242Z

Hakim, R. (2019). A Review on Halal Tourism: an Analysis on the Parameters. *Jurnal Ilmiah Ekonomi Islam, 5*(3), 166. https://doi.org/10.29040/jiei.v5i3.555

Hall, C. M. (2011). Health and Medical Tourism: A Kill or Cure for Global Public Health? In *Tourism Review.* https://doi.org/10.1108/16605371111127198

Haq, F., & Wong, H. Y. (2010). Is Spiritual Tourism a New Strategy for Marketing Islam? *Journal of Islamic Marketing, 1*(2), 136–148. https://doi.org/10.1108/17590831011055879

Henderson, J. C. (2010). Islam and Tourism: Brunei, Indonesia, Malaysia, and Singapore. *Bridging Tourism Theory and Practice, 2*, 75–89. https://doi.org/10.1108/S2042-1443(2010)0000002009

Henderson, J. C. (2016). Halal Food, Certification and Halal Tourism: Insights from Malaysia and Singapore. *Tourism Management Perspectives, 19*, 160–164. https://doi.org/10.1016/j.tmp.2015.12.006

Herrmann, H., & Bucksch, H. (2014). Black Stone. In *Dictionary Geotechnical Engineering/Wörterbuch GeoTechnik.* Springer Berlin Heidelberg. https://doi.org/10.1007/978-3-642-41714-6_21787

Jafari, J., & Scott, N. (2014). Muslim World and its Tourisms. *Annals of Tourism Research, 44*(1), 1–19. https://doi.org/10.1016/j.annals.2013.08.011

Jamal, A. & El-Bassiouny, N. (2019). Islamic Tourism: The Role of Culture and Religiosity. In Ahmad Jamal, R. Raj, & G. Kevin (Eds.), *IslamIc TourIsm: management of Travel Destinations.* CABI.

Kadhim, M., Monqid, O. Bin, & Baghdadi, A. El. (2008). History of Tourism in Islam: Muslims Knew Tourism since their Early Centuries. *Islamic Tourism, 34*, 54–58.

Khan, F., & Callanan, M. (2017). "The 'Halalification' of Tourism." *The Journal of Islamic Marketing, 8*(4), 558–577.

Lipka, M. (2015, August 9). *Muslims and Islam: Key findings in the U.S. and around the world | Pew Research Center.* http://pewrsr.ch/2s2KmpU

Mastercard-CrescentRating. (2018). Global Muslim Travel Index 2018. In *Mastercard-Crescentrating* (Issue April). https://www.crescentrating.com/download/thankyou.html?file=X7UrOM8Y_GMITI-Report-2018-web-version%281%29.pdf

Meri, Y. (2015). Ka ` aba. *Oxford Bibliographies*, December *2009*, 1–3. https://doi.org/10.1093/OBO/9780195390155 0046

Mujahidin, M. (2020). The Potential of Halal Industry in Indonesia to Support Economic Growth. *Al-Kharaj: Journal of Islamic Economic and Business, 2*(1), 77–90. https://doi.org/10.24256/kharaj.v2i1.1433

Ojo, B., & Busayo, B. (2017). Exploring the Relationship between Religion Tourism and Economic Development of a Host Community. *International Journal of Business and Management Invention, 6*(9), 41–51.

Öter, Z., & Çetinkaya, M. Y. (2016). Interfaith Tourist Behaviour at Religious Heritage Sites: House of the Virgin Mary Case in Turkey. *International Journal of Religious Tourism and Pilgrimage*, 4(4), 1–18. https://arrow.dit.ie/ijrtp/vol4/iss4/2

Pew Research Center. (2011). The Future of the Global Muslim Population. Projections for 2010–2030. *Population Space and Place*, 13(1), 1–221.

Pew Research Center. (2015). *The Future of World Religions: Population Growth Projections, 2010–2050*. 2010–2050. http://www.pewforum.org/2015/04/02/religious-projections-2010-2050/

Rashid, T. (2007). Islamic Pilgrimage and the Market Need for Travel Insurance. In R. Raj & N. D. Morpeth (Eds.), *Religious Tourism and Pilgrimage Festivals Management an International Perspective* (pp. 1–18). CABI.

Reuter, T. (2015). State of the Global Islamic Economy. In *Dubai the Capital of Islamic Economy*.

Rinschede, G. (1992). Forms of Religious Tourism. *Annals of Tourism Research*, 19(1), 51–67. https://doi.org/10.1016/0160-7383(92)90106-Y

Samori, Z., Md Salleh, N. Z., & Khalid, M. M. (2016). Current Trends on Halal Tourism: Cases on Selected Asian Countries. *Tourism Management Perspectives*, 19, 131–136. https://doi.org/10.1016/j.tmp.2015.12.011

Santos, M. (2003) Religious tourism: Contributions towards a clarification of concepts. In Fernandes, C., McGettigan, F. and Edwards J. (Eds), *Religious Tourism and Pilgrimage* (pp. 27–42). Atlas: Special Interest Group (1st Expert Meeting), Tourism board of Leiria/ Fatima, Portugal.

Secinaro, P. P., & Biancone, S. (2019). The Halal Tourism: A Business Model Opportunity. In K. A. Jamal, A. Raj, & R. Griffin (Eds.), *Islamic Tourism: Management of Travel Destinations* (pp. 192–201). CAB. https://doi.org/10.1079/9781786394132.0010

Shackley, M. (2008). Management Challenges for Religion-based Attractions. In *Managing Visitor Attractions*, Second ed. https://doi.org/10.4324/9780080557588

Shakona, M., Backman, K., Backman, S., Norman, W., & Luo, Y. (2015). Understanding the Traveling Behavior of Muslims in the United States. *International Journal of Culture, Tourism, and Hospitality Research*, 9(1), 22–35. https://doi.org/10.1108/IJCTHR-05-2014-0036

Statistical Economic and Social Research and Training Centre for Islamic, & (SESRIC). (2018). *OIC ECONOMIC OUTLOOK 2018: Challenges and Opportunities towards Achieving the OIC-2025*. Organisation of Islamic Cooperation. www.idi.org.il

Tală, M. L., & Pădurean, A. M. (2008). Dimensions of Religious Tourism. *Amfiteatru Economic*, 10(SUPPL. 2), 242–253.

The Holy Quarn (Ali, A. Y.) (2006). The Meaning of The Noble Qur'an. In *Commentary*. www.holybooks.com. http://www.pdf-koran.com/Koran.pdf %5Cn http://www.pdf-koran.com/Koran.zip

Timothy, D. J., & Olsen, D. H. (2006). Tourism, Religion and Spiritual Journeys. *Tourism, Religion and Spiritual Journeys*. https://doi.org/10.4324/9780203001073

University of Venda [UNIVEN]. (2015). *The Socioeconomic impact of religious tourism on local communities in Limpopo: A case study*. University of Venda

Utomo, S. B., Scott, N., & Jin, X. (2019). The Impacts of Hajji Satisfaction on Islamic Religious Commitment: A Theoretical Framework. In A. Jamal, R. Raj, & G. Kevin (Eds.), *Islamic TourIsm: managemenT of Travel DesTInaTIons*. CABI.

Vargas-Sánchez, A., & Moral-Moral, M. (2019). Halal Tourism: Literature Review and Experts' View. *Journal of Islamic Marketing*, 11(3), 549–569. https://doi.org/10.1108/JIMA-04-2017-0039

Zamani-Farahani, H., & Henderson, J. C. (2010). Islamic Tourism and Managing Tourism: Develop. *Inter*, *89*(July 2009), 79–89. https://doi.org/10.1002/jtr.741

Zamani-Farahani, H., & Musa, G. (2012). The Relationship between Islamic Religiosity and Residents' Perceptions of Socio-cultural Impacts of Tourism in Iran: Case Studies of Sare'in and Masooleh. *Tourism Management*, *33*(4). Elsevier. https://doi.org/10.1016/j.tourman.2011.09.003

3 Major Themes and Issues in Halal Tourism Development

Tourism Development

Development has various meanings in different contexts (Abuiyada, 2018; Navarro-Jurado & Gemma, 2016). Gemma and Andreu define development as socio-cultural, economic and political progress (Navarro-Jurado & Gemma, 2016, p. 256). Coccia (2020) defines it as a multidimensional process that gives rise to economic, technological, social and institutional change to support the wealth of countries and the general wellbeing of society. There is only a limited number of works of literature on tourism development. Throughout tourism literature, tourism development has been examined from the geographic, economic and political contexts of locations and the human element perspective in the sense of both the visited destinations and the visitors (Butler, 2008). The development of destinations might be affected not only by unforeseen factors but also by unavoidable factors such as the response of entrepreneurs and initial visitors, the richness of destinations in terms of physical attractions and the unfortunate timing of economic or political events, including market downturns, increases in the price of oil, revolutions or coups (Butler, 2008). Butler further describes that tourism destinations face general and specific economic, socio-cultural and political problems as they develop. Butler (2008) states that a destination may involve tourism for various reasons. In some destinations, the local governors may consider tourism as a means of economic development and a source of employment. In other places, the destination could be selected by entrepreneurs such as tour companies and travel agents as potential tourist destinations and be developed accordingly. In several cases, tourism can be developed in some destinations with little effort due to their suitable location and strategic position for new services from visitors' origin country markets. In the effort to develop halal tourism, Ethiopia could benefit from its geostrategic location to the potential visitors' origin country.

In the early 1960s, tourism development was viewed only positively for its role in economic development, whereas its negative impacts were highly overlooked (Navarro-Jurado & Gemma, 2016; Sharpley & Roberts, 2004). However, since the late 1960s, there has been a growing awareness of tourism's increasing socio-cultural and environmental negative impacts. In the

DOI: 10.4324/9781003355236-4

1980s, the concept of alternative tourism development, at least theoretically, emerged in contrast to mass tourism (Sharpley & Roberts, 2004). Sofronov (2018) argues that the development of the travel and tourism industry is reflected in the increasing demand in the population for an ever-increasing range of consumer goods and services. A study conducted by the Government of the Northwest Territories [GNT] (2019) argues that, like any industry, the tourism industry changes over time and necessitates the development of new niches. One reason for the change is the emerging travel trends and new demand from the customer; destination managers and marketers need to appraise and respond accordingly. For example, halal tourism developers need to be aware of the trends and behaviors of halal-conscious customers, predominantly the characteristics of Muslim customers, because before proceeding into a detailed development analysis, it is critical to determine whom the potential customers are for the planned facility or service (the target market).

World Tourism Organization (UNWTO) states that product development refers to commercial facilities, vacation packages and attractions built and developed. Sometimes product development involves creating a new experience but often expanding or enhancing existing products. A study conducted by the Government of the Northwest Territories [NWT] (2010) points out that to develop tourism in a certain destination, the question of what you want to do, where you want to be and how you are going to get there should be addressed. According to the GNT (2019) study, tourism resource identification, market segmentation, and brand and image development are among the priority areas of tourism development. For instance, to deal with owners of the local attractions, it is necessary to identify in which land claim area the sites are located and approach the concerned aboriginal institutions and peoples to discuss plans for potential tourism development (Government of the NWT, 2010). As the study reveals, in investigating the feasibility of a tourism development project, as with any business, accurate market assessment and the availability of actual visitors' attractions are critical to be considered. In order for a country to enter a new tourism niche, it must assess the emerging trends. The consumer trend and behavior must be researched to ensure the availability of a sufficient number of people interested in the new concept, that they have sufficient money to spend on it, and their willingness to spend their money. Moreover, NWT (2019) recommends the following questions to be considered while developing tourism.

- What kind of tourism do you plan to entice the intended target market?
- What is the trend of the area tourist flow, and what have been the recent trends?
- What competitive amenities and services are there in the market area? Which of these do you consider your primary competitors? What competitive and comparative advantages do you have over your potential competitors, and in the market area, is the project entering a very competitive market with well-established competition?

- What is the development status of the tourism niche that you intend to flourish?
- What market share can you expect to capture, and what market do you hope to attract or create?
- Will the project be the first of its kind in the area? Why do you think it will succeed?
- Does the local community support the project?
- How are accommodation facilities in the area?
- What facilities and services of food and beverage are available and demanded in the area?
- How many of these tourists could potentially use your service or facility?
- If you anticipate a mainly local demand, what is the population's projected growth, average income levels, spending patterns, and demographics (age, sex, marital status)?

According to Gee and Solá (1997), tourism development at any destination bears the following triple objectives: increase the foreign exchange earnings of a nation, designate specific areas for the development of infrastructures and improve local employment through the tourism industry. They also note that the current demand analysis and intended visitor markets of the destination, economic and financial analysis, inventory of existing attractions, and inventory of facilities, services and infrastructure are among the top tasks of tourism development. They also further illustrate that the type and quality of development shall bear fundamental issues in determining how the new development will affect the environment and people of a host community. The authors advise that tourism development should be measured not in terms of the number of visitor arrivals but in terms of potential contributions to the local communities and the environment. Hence, tourism developers must discern methods of analyzing, anticipating and managing the impacts of tourism development. There should be a balance between the current benefits and sustainability over the long term. It must also be noted that tourism development should consider the cultures and religions of visitors. By its very nature, tourism brings people from different places to meet face-to-face, and celebrating others' values must be one tenet of tourism development. Sharpley and Roberts (2004) propose three principles of tourism development.

- Tourism development must consider sustainable economic development options equally with other economic activities when making development decisions.
- There must be a relevant tourism database to permit recognition, analysis and monitoring of the tourism industry concerning other sectors of the economy.
- Tourism development must be carried out in a way that is compatible with the principles of sustainable development (Sharpley, 2018, p. 327).

The Theories of Tourism Development

Abuiyada (2018) defines development theories as 'a hybrid term for myriad strategies adopted for socio-economic and environment transformation from current states to desired ones.' According to Larrain (1989), there are four major theories of development such as modernization, dependency, world-system and globalization. Harrison (2015), on the other hand, mentioned some basic theories of tourism development, such as modernization theory, underdevelopment (dependency), neoliberalism, environmentalism, sustainable development theories and globalization theories. However, among other modernization, dependency and sustainable development theories are the most dominant theories in tourism development (Harrison, 2015; Navarro-Jurado & Gemma, 2016).

Modernization Theory

Modernization theory is ethnocentric because it promotes Western capitalist values and devalues the traditional values of developing nations. It holds that the socio-economic development of a country is an evolutionary process from a traditional to a modern society, from agrarian to industrial. The main premise of modernization is that less developed countries could develop when they leave aside their traditional cultures and adopt Western-style civilization (Britton, 1982; Chaperon, 2014; Harrison, 2015; Navarro-Jurado & Gemma, 2016). Put another way; modernization indirectly forces African and developing countries to adopt the Western style (Sharply, 2018). Modernization theorists argue that underdevelopment is one stage in the development process that developed economies have passed through (Navarro-Jurado & Gemma, 2016). However, proponents of dependency theory argue that underdevelopment is the accumulative outcome of historical processes of domination that yields an undeveloped and developed world and is not a stage that precedes development (Sharply, 2018).

Dependency (Underdevelopment) Theory

Dependency theory, sometimes called underdevelopment theory, emerged in the 1960s to fill the gap in the modernization paradigm (Chaperon, 2014; Navarro-Jurado & Gemma, 2016). The premise of this theory is that the situation of one country affects other countries' development. Put another way, the developed Western nations use their bargaining power to dominate peripheral developing nations (Chaperon, 2014; Harrison, 2015; Sharpley, 2018). Therefore, less developed countries remain dependent on developed ones, and their development depends on the latter's willingness (Chaperon, 2014). Frank (1967) classifies the global economic system as developed (metropolitan center) on one side and underdeveloped (periphery) on the other one. The latter exported raw materials and imported the manufactured form of their raw material, whereas the formers manufactured these raw materials from the periphery and sent them back. In such a way, the periphery remains dependent on the center (cited in Chaperon, 2014). Proponents of the dependency theory claim that external political, institutional and economic structures hold developing economies to have a dependent relationship with developed ones (Navarro-Jurado and Gemma, 2016). According to dependency theory, internal factors and traditions do not cause underdevelopment.

When dependence theory is seen from a tourism development perspective, tourist-generating countries could be considered centers, whereas developing countries as destinations are periphery. The former sends tourists into the latter, but these tourists stay at Western-owned accommodations and use products of developed countries. Their giant companies already dominated the tourism sector, and developing economies either remain only raw material providers or are employed at Western companies with low salaries (Britton, 1982). According to Britton, in dependency theory, products or services are also owned and run by firms of developed nations. Britton confirmed that such tourism development tends to create vulnerability and structural dependency of developing countries on developed countries (Britton, 1982). According to Sharpley (2018), tourism development inevitably adopts the 'center-periphery' dependency development model for the unforeseen future.

The presence of Western tourists could inject hard currency into the local economies of developing countries. However, the dependency theory is claimed to be one-sided in that it considers only the negative part of international tourism, mainly mass tourism, and neglects the role of domestic tourism. Therefore, scholars criticize dependency theory for being pessimistic and extremely abstract (Chaperon, 2014). According to Chaperon, the critics that companies of developed countries controlled almost all tourism accommodations in developing countries do not hold water. He exemplified that the availability of tourism companies is in the hands of locals.

Sustainable Development (Alternative Tourism)

Unlike modernization or dependency theory, sustainable development gives an excellent chance to indigenous societies (Harrison, 2015), so it adopts the 'bottom-up' or grassroots approach. Sustainable development focuses on equity and sustainability than making a financial profit. Sustainable development encompasses alternative tourism.

Harrison (2015) argues that alternative tourism and sustainable tourism development are over-ambitious and impracticable. According to Harrison, the concept of alternative tourism is vague. However, it seems to encompass all forms of tourism except mass tourism, such as nature-based, ecotourism and pro-poor tourism. Furthermore, Harrison criticizes the theory of sustainable tourism development for its idealistic and impractical alternative nature though it bears a golden goal. Harrison (2015) argues that alternative tourism cannot exist without mass tourism because it depends on it. Harrison (2015) concludes that neither sustainable tourism development nor alternative tourism could be a model or theory of tourism development. Though policymakers and governments have rarely taken up dependency or underdevelopment mainly for political correctness, underdevelopment theory coexists with globalization.

Tourism development is almost an under-theorized concept. Strictly speaking, there is no theory or school of theories on halal tourism development in the literature. However, this does not mean that there are no relevant interpretations whereby theorists have sought to engage creatively with it. Some authorities recommend modernization and underdevelopment (dependency) theories for tourism development that could be applied to halal tourism development. Harrison (2015) argues that the underdevelopment (dependency) theory has been criticized as a tool for development; it has been implemented practically. Shapley and Telfer (2008) criticize the underdevelopment theory that when developing countries are taken as destinations, those developed country destinations are advanced in the area and become unequal partners. The developing countries are economically, socially, culturally or politically dependent, and it becomes unequal marriage with their more developed partners, especially transnational companies such as tour operators or hotel groups may have strong bargaining power against their junior partners (Harrison, 2015). Hence, as Harrison concludes, dependency or underdevelopment theory has been utilized in academic literature, but policymakers and governments have rarely adopted it. In most African countries, white tourists served by black people have been presumed to be tourism development. As true for tourism, modernization of culture and lifestyles is criticized as cultural imperialism, demonstration effects and assimilation. Some scholars consider tourism development, for example, in many Island destinations, to be similar to the economic dependency of neo-colonialism, where rich Western societies dominate the tourism industry of underdeveloped destinations by exploiting the resources of 'tourism enclaves.' In developing countries, investment incentives such as tax benefits, repatriation of profits and import allowances have been practiced to attract tourism developers (Stabler et al., 2010).

However, some scholars still propose modernization development strategies for tourism because it generates foreign capital, increases employment and facilitates technology transfer. However, there is serious criticism against this theory, as discussed above (Harrison, 2015). Though criticized for being vague, idealistic and impractical, alternative and sustainable tourism development theories are more appropriate for the study under consideration. Harrison (2015) contends that sustainable tourism development is predominantly found in tourism development plans though its presence is more dominantly rhetoric than in practice. Sharply expressed sustainable tourism development as 'a morally desirable but fundamentally idealistic and impractical alternative' (Harrison, 2015).

Glocal Strategy and Halal Tourism Development

The increased proliferation of globalization cannot abolish the importance of cultural and religious diversities. Rather, the importance of multiculturalism and multi-religion is enhanced now than in the past (Khondker, 2005; Nicholas & Gundala, 2017). As explained by Gobo (2016), the failure of globalization to entertain heterogeneity and the inability of localization to cope with modernization gave rise to the birth of glocalization. The concept of globalization promotes uniform products and services while undermining heterogeneity and discouraging diversity. Companies that belong to global corporations do not cater to various customers' tastes. Rather they try to entertain their customers as a single entity. Such organizations sell products and services in the same way everywhere; they focus on standardization and homogenization of products and services.

Given that tourism customers are heterogeneous, suppliers of tourism products must find an appropriate balance between visitors' secular and sacred needs. Delivering experiences that allow visitors to practice their religion and develop an awareness of one's existence and connection with self and others is the central principle in halal tourism. The experience of halal tourism differs from mainstream tourism in the sense that halal tourism provides unique products and services to cater to the religious needs of Muslims. From such unique characteristics of halal tourism, the researcher proposes a glocal strategy as the best strategy for halal tourism development. The concept of Glocalization is derived from the Japanese word *dochakuka*, which originally meant adapting the farming technique to one's local condition (Khondker, 2005). British-American sociologist Robert Robertson introduced the terminology to academia. The main intention of Glocalization is middling globalization and localization and filling the gaps between the two strategies. The glocalization strategy creates products or services for the global market while customized to suit the local cultures. As Nicholas and Gundala (2017) stated, glocalization is a 'think global, act local' that operates symbiotically with globalization and localization. Global strategies bear a notion of thinking globally, whereas local strategies bind by the principle of acting locally. The glocal strategy, therefore, represents a middle way between the global and the local strategies (Khondker, 2004). Glocalization helps develop products for global markets, but at the same time, it allows the product to be modified to suit the expectations of the individual markets. Glocalization's essence is tailoring global products and services to customers' tastes and preferences. Khondker (2005) conceptualized the glocal strategy as 'the universalization of particularization and the particularization of universalism.'

Some social scientists allege that tourism products and services have been tailored to Western experiences; therefore, when this industry is introduced and transplanted to destinations such as the Middle East and Africa, there is a need for tailoring tourism products and services (Soulard & McGehee, 2017). Glocalization has emerged to minimize the fear that globalization ignores and erases heterogeneities (Khondker, 2005). Glocalization entails how organizations customize their global products to the local customers by culturally adapting their services, communication and marketing strategies to the local context. It increases travelers' loyalty to the organization by considering culturally sensitive services as its binding principle (Soulard & McGehee, 2017). Creating a conducive environment, personalizing experiences and establishing a cultural bridge are strategies for enhancing travelers' loyalty.

To succeed in halal tourism, corporations must apply a glocal strategy, thereby customizing and tailoring global products and experiences per customers' preferences. By so doing, multinational tourism products and services suppliers such as chained international hotels, tour operators and travel agencies should be flexible and apply glocal strategies to cater to the various needs of customers, in this case, cater to the religious needs of halal visitors. Therefore, destinations that envisage flourishing halal tourism must rethink their 'one-size-fits-all' strategy by employing a glocalization strategy.

Phases of Tourism Development

As Weaver and Lawton (2014) presented, in the 1980s Butler proposed the 'S-shaped model' of tourism development, known as the Butler sequence. According to Butler's model, tourist destination development is supposed to pass five distinct development phases: exploration, involvement, development, consolidation and stagnation (Weaver & Lawton, 2014). Based on the responses of destination managers, the stagnation phase tends to decline or rejuvenate.

Phase I: Exploration: According to Butler's tourism development model, exploration is the initial stage in tourism destination development. This stage is characterized by the presence of a few visitors who stay relatively long. No tourist facilities have been established, and services are not offered at this stage. Visitors of this phase are predominantly researchers, adventurous and allocentric types who seek to visit authentic and 'unspoiled' non-commodified cultural and natural attractions (Weaver & Lawton, 2014). They seek to consume and taste local products. Therefore, linkages with the local economy are very high, and the multiplier effect is large. The host-guest relationship is not only positive but also cordial, and the tourists are treated with curiosity as honored guests and receive genuine hospitality. Therefore, the host–guest relationship can be seen as pre-euphoric, so the negative impact of tourism in this stage is negligible or insensible. This phenomenon is expressed as the 'pre-tourism' stage, where special accommodation or meal is unavailable for visitors. Therefore, guests have to share the available services and facilities with residents. According to Humphreys and Holloway (2016), the response of locals to tourists gradually comes down. In the first stage of development, locals are enthusiastic about seeking job opportunities related to economic gains. As the number of visitors increases, the locals tend to be conscious of the negative impacts of tourism.

Phase II: Involvement: In the involvement stage, local entrepreneurs begin to invest in response to the regular appearance of tourists; therefore, visitors start to utilize services and facilities. Like the exploration phase, the number of visitors is very limited and the locals' attitudes toward tourism remain positive. Finally, locals may start to show antagonism toward tourists openly. Therefore, a kind of formal tourism industry starts during the involvement stage.

Phase III: Development: The third development stage is manifested by rapid growth and dramatic changes in all aspects of the tourism sector. The change from involvement to development is mainly marked by the construction of the first mega-resort or a celebrity visit that can act as a catalyst for accelerated change. In this phase, he mass influx of visitors and large-scale tourism development so that the host communities will be overwhelmed by visitors. Tourist facilities and services are transformed into the formal tourism system, and national and transnational companies run tourism facilities. From the visitors' perspective, mid-centric and psychometric visitors start to engage in large. Large multi-purpose resorts replace small hotels and guesthouses; agricultural land is also used for golf courses and theme parks. The attitude of residents toward visitors gradually deteriorates, and locals' complaints against tourists start modestly. However, as tourist numbers continue to increase, both material and non-material cultures become highly commoditized.

Phase V: Consolidation: In the consolidation phase, the inflow of visitors and the total amount of activities continue to rise; however, there is a decline in the growth rate of visitor arrivals and other tourism-related activities. The negative impacts of tourism have become more visible. Tourism products and the subsequent quality of the tourist and resident experience continuously decline, and a psychometric clientele dominates the destination. International hotels and other facility providers control the business, and the locals are pushed out of business, so the leakage and repatriation of profits become very high. Seasonality emerges as a major issue for tourism employees. Host–guest conflict become very high and residents blame tourism for all problems, justifiably or not. Locals start to employ some derogatory terms and insult inbound visitors. Locals are also exploited as 'tourist objects' to suit the interest of tourists.

Phase VI: Stagnation: Tourist traffic reaches its climax, and tourism growth stops. Carrying capacity becomes a serious problem, and tourism products lead to further deterioration. The destination may still have a high profile. Still, the number of visitors does not increase because the location is perceived as 'out of fashion' or otherwise less desirable as a destination, and everything becomes stagnant. The stagnation stage may theoretically continue for an unspecified period but based on the decision of destination managers' three scenarios are possible: Continued stagnation, decline or rejuvenation. If serious amendments are not taken, the decline scenario will be realized, and a good manager may take effective action to help the tourism development rejuvenate.

The construction of halal tourism in Ethiopia seems on the first stage, and only a few sites might be in the second stage. Only a few halal tourists have arrived, mainly from Sudan, Saudi Arabia, Pakistan, Sudan, Eritrea, Djibouti and India. No halal products and services have been established and offered to those tourists. Visitors share the available halal foods, products and services with local Muslims. Therefore, the stage of halal tourism development in Ethiopia is predominantly on exploration. However, a few parts of the countries seem just to be entering the involvement stage.

Needs, Principles and Attributes of Halal Tourism

Faith-Based Service Needs of Halal Tourism

Duman (2020) states that every Muslim's action should theoretically comply with sharia or Islamic principles. It is believed that all aspects of Muslims' life, from womb to tomb, abide by the teachings of Islam. However, just like the adherents of other religions, the strength of the devotion of Muslims varies from individual to individual. Therefore, Muslims have heterogeneous faith-based needs. Considering this fact, Mastercard-CrescentRating (2018, 2019) has proposed three types of faith-based service needs clustered under 'Need to have,' 'Good to have,' and 'Nice to have' (Mastercard-CrescentRating, 2019).

'Need to Have' Faith-Based Services of Halal Tourism

As incorporated in Service Needs 2.0 of Mastercard-CrescentRating (2019), the need to have faith-based service incorporates halal food and beverages, prayer facilities, water-friendly washrooms and no Islamophobia (Mastercard-CrescentRating, 2019). These needs can be seen as 'must-have' products and minimum requirements for the destination to launch halal tourism. Without these products and services, it will no longer be possible for halal tourism to flourish.

Halal food and beverages: Halal food and beverages are the most important services of halal tourism for which halal-conscious travelers are looking. Broadly speaking, all foods and beverages are generally permissible except for those prohibited, such as products and by-products of swine, dogs, feline, predators or carrion and beverages containing alcohol and other harmful or poisonous ingredients. Many Muslims also believe that slaughter must be carried out in the name of God (Evans & Syed, 2015). The Holy Quran states, '[…] foods such as carrion, blood, and any product of swine and flesh that is not slaughtered in the name of Allah are not halal […]' (the Quran, 2:173). The first item that a Muslim traveler looks for when traveling to any destination is halal food and beverages. For many years, the very terminology 'halal' has been used to refer to halal foods and beverages (Battour et al., 2010; Evans & Syed, 2015; Haq & Wong, 2010; Khan & Callanan, 2017). Therefore, halal foods and beverages are among the must-have products of halal tourism (Mastercard-CrescentRating, 2019).

Prayer Facilities: Given prayer is the second of the five pillars of Islam and one of the fundamental tenets of Islamic practice and worship, many Muslims give due attention to prayer. The Holy Quran states, '*…and be* *steadfast in prayer, practice regular charity, and bow down your heads with those who bow down in worship*' (the Holy Quran, 2:43). Wherever they are, Muslims are obliged to perform prayer. Indeed, while traveling, some prayers can be combined and shortened so that the five times per day prayer could turn into three times a day and four *Rakat* can be turned into two (El-Gohary, 2016). Therefore, for a halal destination to satisfy its customers, providing prayer rooms with *Qiblah* directions marked and equipped with ablution (*wudhu*)-friendly washrooms cannot be an option but a must. According to Islam, Muslims worldwide must face Mecca, where the sacred Masjid Al Haram is located, during any prayer. The Holy Qur'an states:

> O Muhammad, We [Allah] have seen you turning your face towards Heaven several times. Now, We [Allah] shall turn you towards the Qibla, which will please you, and you like it best: so turn your face towards the holy Masjid Haram of Mecca where Kaaba is found. From this day forward, turn your face towards it wherever you pray.
>
> (The Holy Quran, 2:44)

This implies that in addition to assigning the place of prayer, the hotel rooms are advised to have indicators of the direction of Mecca for customers who need to pray in their rooms.

Water-Friendly Washrooms: In Islam, both spiritual and physical purity and cleanliness are core aspects of faith, and hygiene matters a lot. Cleaning private parts with water after using the toilet is a usual etiquette for Muslims; even non-Muslims are accustomed to this habit. This implies that the provision of water in the toilets should be compatible with Islamic culture, and due attention must be given while fixing water facilities such as hand showers to ensure they are Muslim friendly and/or bidets should be kept in and around toilets. Providing such facilities helps Muslim travelers to perform ablution easily so that they feel as if they are at home.

No Islamophobia: as will be discussed later in this chapter thoroughly, the proliferation of Islamophobia becomes a barrier to halal tourism development. After the 9/11 incident, severe Islamophobia emerged in the Western World and eventually spread to the rest of the globe, including some Muslim countries. According to Mastercard-Crescentrating (2019) research, Muslim travelers have nullified destinations that are perceived to be unwelcoming and Islamophobic environment destinations from their visitation plan. Therefore, halal destinations are expected to combat prejudice and Islamophobia in all its forms.

'Good to have' Faith-Based Service of Halal Tourism

'Good to have' faith-based service needs 2.0 includes social causes, Ramadan services and local Muslim experiences. The provision of these facilities and services is essential but not very critically essential as 'need to haves' are.

Social Justice: social justice is among the key tenets of Islam. Driven by the teachings of Islam and global tourism trends toward sustainable tourism development, Muslims are becoming more conscious of being socially responsible during their travels (Mastercard-CrescentRating, 2019). Social justice includes being mindful and empathetic toward self, others and the environment (Mastercard-CrescentRating, 2019). Mastercard-CrescentRating (2019) states that in the viewpoint of halal tourism, social just refers to the ability to improve the lives of the host communities, appreciate various green initiatives to protect the environment and support eco-friendly tourism practices.

Ramadan Services: Even though more Muslims tend to fast Ramadan at their home by reciting the Quran, praying additional prayers and supplication, some Muslims also want to spend Ramadan away from home. Furthermore, many Muslims also look for holiday breaks during the two Eids (Mastercard-CrescentRating, 2019). Destinations working to have satisfied Muslim travelers during these periods need to be able to fulfill the special needs of Muslims during Ramadan and festivals.

Local Muslim Experiences: One of the best things visitors need is to spend time with the local people and enjoy a unique experience with the host community. In addition to having experiences with local Muslims, Muslim travelers want to visit Islamic heritage sites and other destinations with a historical or live connection with Islam. Some Muslim travelers also desire to pray in local mosques, attend local people's sermons and enjoy learning about local Muslim's socio-cultural situations. Therefore, arranging this opportunity is very important to satisfy Muslim customers (Mastercard-CrescentRating, 2019).

'Nice to have' Faith-Based Service of Halal Tourism

'Nice to have' faith-based service needs 2.0 are recreational spaces with privacy and no non-halal services. These needs help to excel in halal tourism.

Recreational Spaces with Privacy: Battour et al. (2012) point out that Islam prohibits intermingling, crowding together and the exposure of women to men. It is also stated in the Holy Quran that '[…] when you ask women for something you want, ask them from before a screening curtain: that makes for greater purity for both parties' (The Holy Quran, 33:53). In most cases, Muslims assign a special door to women to enter or leave mosques for the sake of avoiding unnecessary interaction of the opposite sex. Therefore, practicing Muslim travelers prefer male-female separated recreational facilities such as swimming pools and gyms, beaches, spas and beauty salons. To have delighted Muslim customers, the tourism and hospitality industry must welcome their guests by assigning separate male and female facilities such as rooms, gyms, and swimming pools (Battour & Ismail, 2015). Newly emerging halal hotels are considering these issues (Mastercard-CrescentRating, 2019).

No Haram Services: Several Muslims want to stay far away from the haram activities such as gambling, alcoholism, prostitution, voyeurism, nightclub, music, dancing and inappropriate wearing. Therefore, to attract a good number of Muslim tourists, a destination should avoid unIslamic activities discussed above. Mastercard-CrescentRating (2018) jotted down some needs, good to have and nice to have, to the following selected sectors, and I adopted them as follows.

Table 3.1 Summary of Components of Halal Tourism

Sectors	Need to Have:	Good to Have:	Nice to Have:
Airport	• Halal food and beverages in public and transit areas • Prayer rooms in a public area with ablution facilities • Toilets with bidets or hand showers • Trained staffers about the needs and behaviors of Muslims at the airport	• Standard halal restaurants • Prayer rooms in public and transit areas with separate male and female spaces and ablution facilities • Friday prayer services in the public area prayer room	• Souvenir shops (which contain goods that reflect Islamic culture and heritage)
Accommodation services (Hotel, Halal rooms)	• Halal food • Rooms are marked with the *Qiblah* direction • Place of prayer • Water usage-friendly washroom • Quran copy • Alcohol-free beverages in the fridge • Female staff for women • A session for ladies in the swimming pool/gym • Toilets with bidets or hand showers	• Standard halal restaurants • Ability to cater during the month of fasting (Ramadhan) • Prayer mats are available at the request • Prayer timetable • Family-friendly viewing TV • Certified halal food/kitchens • Women-only floor/family-only floor • Ramadan services and facilities	• No non-halal activities in the hotel (no alcohol, discotheques or casino) • Swimming pools and gyms: either segregated or provide different timings for males and females • Gender-separate resorts • Well-trained staff to satisfy Muslims
Restaurants	• Halal restaurant • Toilets with bidets or hand showers	• Properly dressed and well-trained staff to satisfy Muslims • Visitor attractions and location maps	• A prayer room with ablution facilities • Restaurant not serving alcohol

(*Continued*)

Table 3.1 (Continued)

Sectors	Need to Have:	Good to Have:	Nice to Have:
Shopping	• Availability of halal food outlets • Halal meal and prayer place indicators • A prayer room with ablution facilities • Staff at the information counters are trained on the Muslim traveler's needs and can answer their information requests • Toilets with bidets or hand showers, water jug or bottle	• A prayer room with separate male and female spaces with ablution facilities • Halal restaurants	• Family-friendly recreational facilities • Museums
Visitor Information Centers	• Staff at the information counters are trained on the Muslim travelers' needs and able to answer their information requests	• Muslim visitor guides can be given to the visitors	• Staff who speak more than one international language, such as English and Arabic
Travel agents/ Tour operators	• The availability of staffers to care for Muslim customers • Tour packages comply with Sharia	• Well-trained Muslim staff and tour guides	• Staff who speak more than one international language, such as English and Arabic
Tour Guides	• Trained about the behaviors of Muslim visitors • Understanding of Islamic etiquette	• Understanding of Islamic history • Accredited by CrescentRating	• Staff who speak more than one international language, such as English and Arabic

(*Continued*)

Table 3.1 (Continued)

Sectors	Need to Have:	Good to Have:	Nice to Have:
Attractions	• Availability of halal food outlets • A prayer room with ablution facilities • Staffers who are aware of the needs of Muslim visitors • Toilets with water jug or bottle	• Standard halal restaurants • A prayer room with separate male and female spaces with ablution facilities • Toilets with bidets or hand showers	• Souvenir shops that have Islamic heritages, headscarf
Conference & Event Venues	• Halal food availability • Ability to provide a temporary prayer room with wudu facilities • Toilets with water jug or bottle	• Standard halal restaurants • A prayer room with separate male and female spaces with ablution facilities • Toilets with bidets or hand showers	• Museums, souvenir shops
Spas & Wellness centers	• Separate facilities for males and females • Female staffs assist female customers & males to males • Private treatment rooms/spaces • Toilets with water jug or bottle	• Muslim-friendly dress code for staff • Halal-certified products (as far as possible) • Toilets with bidets or hand showers	• Alternative halal game centers such as volleyball and handball
HealthCare centers	• Prayer rooms • Rooms marked with the Qibla direction • Water-friendly toilets	• Availability of halal food • Male doctors and nurses for male patients and females for females	• Halal medications (as far as possible) • Halal pharmaceuticals and sanitary materials • Mosque

Source: Modified and Adapted from CrescentRating, 2018.

Samori et al. (2016) also classify the service needs of halal tourism into three groups. The first is basic service needs, including halal food and beverages, Qibla signage, prayer mat, bidet in the room, no alcohol, gambling and nightclub. They designate the second service needs of halal tourism as intermediate. This includes services such as separate recreation facilities for males and females, a prayer mat, no voyeurism entertainment, prayer time and a Mosque location. The third one, known as extensive service, includes a Zakat counter, Islamic-related brochure, classes, and Azan at floor level and Islamic tourism packages.

Principles of Halal Tourism

Razalli et al. (2012) identify fundamental principles of halal tourism, such as halal food, halal transportation, halal hotel, halal logistics, Islamic finance, Islamic travel packages and halal spa. Fakir and Erraoui (2019); Shakona et al. (2015) suggest five pillars of halal tourism. These are nonalcoholic drinks, halal food, separation of men and women, place of worship and appropriate dress code.

Battour (2019) identified the following principles of halal tourism

- No alcoholic beverage is to be served
- No unIslamic entertainment, such as nightclubs and gambling
- Halal food shall be served, and no pork and its derivatives
- Gender segregation in the prayer room
- Male staff for a man and female staff for women and families
- In-house religious figures and schedules depicting prayer time and preaching sessions
- Indicators of *Qibla* (direction of Mecca)
- Staff to be predominately Muslims or trained in such away
- Separate wellness facilities such as gyms
- Islamic or conservative TV channels
- A toilet not facing *Qibla*
- Images or pictures should not depict the human form
- Copy of the Holy Quran, prayer mat (Modified and adapted from Battour, 2019a, p. 66).

El-Gohary (2016, p. 127) proposes the following principles of halal tourism

- No alcohol, no nightclubs and gambling, pork or similar products to be served
- Halal food and beverage must be served
- Male staff for single male floors, female staff for women and families and female staff for single female floors
- In-house religious figures and conservative TV channels (appropriate entertainment)
- Sharia-friendly female staffer uniforms (non-see-through garments, untighten and not half-naked)

- Copies of the Quran and prayer mats in each room
- Markers indicating the direction of Mecca
- Women-only gyms and swimming pools
- Gender-segregated prayer rooms
- Art should not depict the human form
- Bidets in the bathrooms

Attributes of Halal Tourism

Battour (2019); Othman and Jamal (2017) identify two broad areas of halal tourism attributes: tangible and intangible. The former incorporates prayer facilities and halal food and beverages, while the latter includes halal entertainment, no alcoholic drinks, an Islamic dress code and observation of Islamic codes of morality. Easy access to places of worship (Masjid/prayer room), access to a halal meal and availability of a copy of the Quran are the major attributes of halal tourism. A study by Battour indicates that Muslim-friendly toilet services and halal entertainment were highly prioritized attributes. Battour (2019, p. 154) lists the following five attributes of halal tourism: (1) provision of maps to indicate locations, facilities and services such as mosques, prayer facilities, tourism information centers, airports, hotels, and parks; (2) providing various schedule and prayer timetables at various touchpoints; (3) availability of taxis with female drivers' service for female passengers; (4) no alcoholic beverages stored in the hotel room refrigerator, and (5) banning of pictures of inadequately dressed women on billboards/outdoor advertisements by the authority.

Battour et al. (2013) identify the following attributes of halal tourism

- Availability of Mosque (Masjid)
- Availability of prayer facilities and *Qibla* direction at various touchpoints
- The availability of Quran in bedrooms
- Availability of water supply in toilets at various touchpoints
- Availability of halal food and beverages at various touchpoints
- Availability of separated halal utensils in hotels and restaurants
- Availability of segregated areas at beaches, swimming pools and gymnasiums for men and women
- The banning of prostitution and sex channels on the hotel entertainment system
- Banning of alcoholic drinks by the authority at various touchpoints
- Banning of gambling activities by the authority at various touchpoints
- Banning voyeurism and sexual permissiveness

Characteristics and Motivations of Halal-Conscious Visitors

Characteristics of Halal-Conscious Visitors

The awareness of halal-conscious tourists' characteristics in the context of halal tourism is very important to stakeholders such as marketers and policymakers to develop appropriate halal tourism infrastructure and facilities, halal travel packages, halal travel activities and design specific means of marketing (Battour et al., 2013; Çetin & Dinçer, 2016; Duman, 2020). Islam suggests what to do and what not to do in all walks of Muslim life, including tourism choices, so that Muslim's behavior is shaped by the principles of their religions (El-Gohary, 2016; Evans & Syed, 2015). As noted by Battour (2019); Duman (2020), religion highly affects customers' behavior. For instance, fashion styles, foods and drinking, cosmetics usage, social and political visions, and sexual behavior of customers have been highly influenced by customers' religions.

Mastercard-CrescentRating (2018) proposes three types of segmentation of halal tourism based on the level of the needs of halal-conscious travelers. *Segment A*: this segment consists of conservative or strictly practicing Muslims. These travelers are likely to be very strict in adherence to all faith-based needs wherever they are. Therefore, they choose only those services that provide a strictly sharia-compliant environment while traveling. For instance, they look for hotels that do not have non-halal activities, products and services. They also look for halal food that concerned authorities have assured be halal. *Segment B*: these are mildly practicing Muslims. These Muslims generally do not compromise some of their needs and will be comfortable with some alternatives. Their religious needs are limited to the availability of halal meals, ablution facilities and space for prayers. They would, however, still prefer Muslim-friendly service to less Muslim-friendly service. *Segment C*: this category includes non-practicing Muslims. Muslim travelers of this segment are indifferent to religious needs when choosing destinations. However, they may look for halal or pork-free food and products.

A study conducted by Mastercard-CrescentRating (2019) shows that Muslim travelers are mainly enticed by faith-based services and facilities and the availability of other Muslim-related heritage sites and prices. Halal-conscious customers, mainly Muslims, have peculiar destination and site selection behaviors. For instance, a study by Adie reveals that Muslim visitors prefer Islamic historical, religious and cultural sites to Western-culture-loaded ones (Adie, 2020). Regarding marketing halal tourism, scholars such as Adie (2020) proposed utilizing the 'think halal, act local' approach. He states that products should be communicated without exaggeration within ethical boundaries, and customers must not be deceived. Honesty, transparency and clarity have high value in marketing halal products. For a marketer to attract sharia-conscious customers using a Western-style promotion, for instance, stereotyping and exploiting women as objects to lure and attract customers is not advisable (Adie, 2020).

Motivations of Halal-Conscious Visitors

Blackwell (2007) defines motivation as a driving force that inspires people to engage in some action. Investigating why people like to travel and engage in tourism remains the main issue for tourism stakeholders. Addressing questions such as what motivates halal-conscious tourists to travel to a certain destination, what motivates them to engage in specific tourism activities, and to choose one destination over another is a very important concern for destination marketers (Camilleri, 2018b, 2018a). Scholars classify the motivational factors of tourists into intrinsic and extrinsic, push and pull or internal and external (Battour, 2019). Convinced by either internal and/or external factors, people might decide to travel to a destination. According to Battour (2019), the push-pull theory assumes that people are first pushed to travel by internal desires or emotional factors. Then they are pulled by external or tangible factors known as destination attributes. Push factors motivate visitors to get away from the mundane environment by traveling and selecting one destination over another, whereas pull factors attract those motivated visitors toward a certain destination. Destinations that can offer Islamic attributes could easily capture the demand of halal-conscious visitors. The push and pull factors are interdependent and interconnected. Jamal and El-Bassiouny (2019) state that push factors are the internal motivations that goad visitors to tourism.

In contrast, full factors are external factors in the attractions that entice visitors toward them. Battour (2019) employed push and pull theories of tourist motivation while studying the motivational factors of Muslim tourists. Battour argues that push factors refer to the internal stimulations that click the people's minds to decide to travel. In contrast, pull factors are an external force that enables tourists to decide where to go and take a vacation. Put another way, push factors are psychological motivations, such as escape from the mundane environment, seeking pleasure, and enjoying with families and friends.

Push factors are a response to why questions and are intangible, intrinsic desires of the individual traveler. In contrast, pull factors enable individuals to choose suitable destinations once the travelers have decided to go based on the push factors and rarely will the reverse also happen. That means some extraordinary attractions of a destination may cause internal motivation. As Battour explains, their own desires, coupled with the external factors of a destination's attributes, make tourists decide to travel. As stated by Jamal and El-Bassiouny (2019), the motivation for halal tourism can be purely religious, a mixture of religious and non-religious. Without appropriate motivation, tourists would not be able to visit a destination. Several theories of motivation have been drawn from studies of workplace motivation. Battour (2019) also proposes that the expectancy theory of motivation is one of the popular motivation theories employed in halal tourism (Camilleri, 2018b, p. 4).

Battour again mentioned Crompton's (1979) theory, which could be conceptualized as halal tourism (Battour, 2019b). Crompton has identified seven social-psychological motives for travel: escape from a perceived mundane environment, exploration, relaxation, prestige, enhancement of relationships and creating social interaction (cited in Battour, 2019, p. 14).

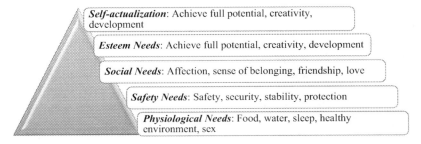

Figure 3.1 Maslow's hierarchy of needs.
Source: Adapted from Blackwell, 2007.

Barriers to Halal Tourism Development

There is no doubt that halal tourism has been blossoming. However, the rapid development of halal tourism is not without obstacles. Complex challenges beset halal tourism development. The constraints of halal tourism development could vary from place to place. This study identifies the following major constraints of halal tourism development through a rigorous literature review.

Lack of Awareness

In the context of halal tourism, awareness means having knowledge and experience of halal tourism and being well-informed about what is happening now regarding halal tourism development and growth (Ambali & Bakar, 2014). The previous studies' findings show that there are vast misunderstandings, misconceptions and confusions regarding halal tourism concepts and practices. As noted by Bilim et al. (2019), not only among non-Muslims but also a misperception of halal tourism exists among some Muslims. According to the same authors, some perceived tourism activities such as voyeurism, sexual permissiveness, consumption of pork and alcohol, gambling and naked clothing that contradict the Islamic rules and law give tourism a negative image from the perspective of Muslims. Though tourism naturally is not anti-Islam, such undesired touristic activities made some pious Muslims tourismophobes. Such things cause to exist a paradoxical relationship between tourism and Islam. Non-Muslims, on the other hand, consider halal products and services as the manifestation of Islamism and radicalism. For instance, in Ethiopia, it is common to see a Muslim being described as acquiring 'radical Islamic color' for obeying the sharia rules and principles.

The Prevalence of Islamophobia and Xenophobia

It is often difficult, if not impossible, to trace the origin of concepts of Islamophobia. No matter who coined it first, it is clear that the term consists of two words 'Islamo' & 'Phobia.' The former refers to Islam, while the latter is derived from the Greek term 'phobia,' which means 'fear of' (Mohideen & Mohideen, 2008). The simplest definition of Islamophobia is 'the fear of Islam' (Çaki & Gülada, 2018). According to Mohideen and Mohideen, Islamophobia refers to unjustifiable fear and hatred of Islam and Muslims or prejudices against Islam and Muslims. It manifests in physical, political, cultural, linguistic and other forms of attack. Beydoun (2018) define Islamophobia as an "'irrational fear' of Muslims. Islamophobia dates back to the Crusades and the inquisition in Spain but has rapidly mounted in the past two decades (Bahdi & Kanji, 2018, p. 325). Mohideen and Mohideen identified 18 derogatory terminologies of Islamophobia employed mainly by the Western Media, namely Islamic terrorism, Muslim terrorist, Islamic fanatics, political Islam, radical Islam, Islamic fundamentalism, Islamic extremists, Islamic radicals, radical Muslims, Islamic fascists, Islamic fundamentalism, Islamists, jihadist, Islamism, militant Islam, militant-Muslim, fanatical Islam and militant-Muslims (Mohideen & Mohideen, 2008, p. 57). These terminologies have been used derogatorily to humiliate Muslims psychologically. The terrorist act of September 11, 2001, against the US Twin Towers caused Islamophobia to be more severe than ever before (Bahdi & Kanji, 2018; Çaki & Gülada, 2018; Mohideen & Mohideen, 2008), but the origin of Islamophobia traced back to the conquest of Spain (Andalus) by Muslims in 711 (Çaki & Gülada, 2018). The inflow of immigrants toward Europe following the Arab Spring adds xenophobia to Islamophobia (Çaki & Gülada, 2018). The Western media seriously engaged in proliferating negative propaganda myths against Islam and Muslims in the aftermath of the terror. They calculatedly associated terrorism with Islam. The 9//11 attack, therefore, has made Muslims scapegoats and caused a devastative socio-economic and political impact on the Muslim world (Mohideen & Mohideen, 2008). Discrimination against Muslims and othering of their religious and cultural manifestation has been experienced in many non-Muslim countries and organizations, and Islamophobia today takes multiple forms. Mohideen and Mohideen (2008) note that even supposedly Christian evangelists insult Islam as 'a bloody, brutal type of religion.' As Mohideen and Mohideen (2008) noted, Muslims are described as 'terrorists' and 'women repressors' in many Western magazines and newspapers. The negative representation of Muslims by world powers in the press has caused a negative perception of the masses toward Muslims (Çaki & Gülada, 2018). The recent Arab Spring that began in 2010 left millions of Muslims homeless and refugees in Europe. This exacerbates the preexisting Islamophobia. Nowadays, Muslim travelers and visitors have been demonized and dehumanized, especially in Western countries, recently in China and India. As noted by Mohideen and Mohideen (2008), Islam does not inspire, nor does it aspire to terrorism, radicalism and militancy, but unfortunately, it has been associated with these terminologies. Gradually, demonizing Islam and dehumanizing Muslims became almost normal, especially for Western elites and politicians. As noted by Çaki and Gülada

(2018), even some Muslim scholars have become Islamophobes in intellectual discourse. In countries with shared common values, such as the United States, Canada, Europe and Australia, Islamophobic activities are mainly state-driven and perpetuate with defining institutional culture.

According to Çaki and Gülada (2018), Islamophobia, orientalist perspectives, ethnic hatred, xenophobia and intolerance significantly affect tourism experiences. Today, due to the prevalence of Islamophobia and xenophobia, Muslim visitors have been attacked on the street, in the bus, on the plane, in their places of worship and at their accommodations (Bahdi & Kanji, 2018; Mohideen & Mohideen, 2008). According to the Directorate of Youth and Sport of the Council of Europe (2004), Muslim travelers in Western countries are experiencing an increasingly hostile environment, such as suspicion, deep-rooted prejudice, and ignorance, physical and verbal harassment (cited in Ramberg, 2004). The report describes Islamophobia as a violation of human rights and a threat to social cohesion.

The Perceived Paradox of Islam and Tourism

Though the very principles of Islam and tourism do not contradict each other (Henderson, 2010a, 2010b; Zamani-Farahani & Musa, 2012), some Muslims perceive that the very objective of tourism is against the principles of Islam. As discussed throughout the study under consideration, many Quranic verses and hadiths encourage Muslims to travel. Din (1989) finds that many Muslim countries do not promote tourism because they consider it unethical and unIslamic. Indeed, some unIslamic touristic activities mainly inherited from the Western culture, such as alcoholism, voyeurism and sexual permissiveness, made Muslims develop a negative attitude toward tourism. To clarify this confusion and misunderstanding, it is very important to see the history of tourism development and assess the very aim of tourism. The history of tourism reveals that tourism was started to free oneself from alcoholism and gambling.

> Thomas Cook, also known as 'the father of modern tourism,' has broadly been associated with the emergence of tourism in a modern way in the 1840s though mass tourism was yet to start 150 years later on a global scale. As complained by Baptist preachers concerned with the declining morals of the English working-class increase, Cook arranged a trip at cheap fares to take workers to temperance (i.e., anti-alcohol) meetings and bible camps in the rural areas and got the working class of English free from alcohol drinking. The first excursion of this kind was conducted as a day trip from Leicester to Loughborough on July 5, 1841, mainly for spiritual purposes. This episode is sometimes denoted as the beginning of the contemporary era of tourism. Gradually, these trips developed in terms of both the purpose of visitation and destination so that excursions expanded in the number of participants and the variety of destinations. Concurrently,

the purpose of the trip also shifted from spiritual to sightseeing and pleasure. In 1845, Cook established the first 'Thomas Cook & Son' tour operator and gave service between Leicester and London. In the 1870s, 60 Thomas Cook & Son tour operators' offices operated worldwide.

(Weaver & Lawton, 2014, p. 57)

Therefore, the raison d'être of tourism during the early period was temperance. However, it has gradually deviated from its very purpose. Even though halal tourism is believed to be a mediator of body and soul needs, there is a widely held misconception and misunderstanding of the very concept of halal tourism. As El-Gohary (2016) states, some people still doubt and question the halalness of halal tourism. Referring to some hadiths such as 'traveling is a kind of torture for it prevents one from sleeping and eating' and 'journey may not be made for a visit except to the three mosques: Masjedel Haram, Masjidel Nabawiand Masjid el Aqsua' out of context, some people consider tourism as anti-Islam. However, many Muslim scholars have proved that these places have been mentioned only to venerate and perform ritual activities. Islam apparently encourages Muslims to visit the universe, contemplate, learn from historical sites, and gain knowledge. Traveling for leisure and reaction is also not forbidden in Islam (Battour et al., 2010).

Lack of Basic Halal Tourism Infrastructure and Superstructure

As studied by Han et al. (2019), Muslim travelers prefer to visit a tourist destination where Islamic attributes and halal infrastructure are available because the presence of halal attributes and infrastructure allows observant Muslim visitors to practice their religious duty while visiting. Given that halal tourism is a recent phenomenon (Battour et al., 2010), the existing tourism infrastructures have been built to suit the Western style so that most destinations fail to fulfill halal infrastructure, superstructure and halal attributes. Therefore, halal-conscious travelers often experience inconveniences while visiting such destinations (Han et al., 2019). The extant inconveniences arising from the unavailability of halal infrastructures and superstructures adversely affect halal tourism development. Álvarez-García et al. (2018); Bilim et al. (2019); Secinaro and Biancone (2019) argue that tourism has not been given due attention in many Muslim nations, and Muslims have abstained from joining tourism, leisure and recreational activities despite the fact that Islam encourages travel. Nurdiansyah (2018) argues that today, halal-conscious visitors remain relatively under-served mainly due to the unavailability of established infrastructure and superstructure of halal tourism. Particularly those located outside of Muslim-majority localities cannot cater to the needs of halal-conscious visitors due to the unpreparedness of suppliers. In other words, given that halal tourism is a new business, most destinations are not ready to offer halal products and services for halal-conscious visitors (Bilim et al., 2019). As the relationship between tourism and Islam was largely distorted for many years, the tourism industry did not consider the needs of Muslims. A study conducted by Han et al. (2019) reveals that the post-purchase decision-making of visitors has been affected by the conveniences and inconveniences of specific products and services. Khoiriati et al. (2018) claim that most non-Muslim countries do not even afford minimal facilities to Muslim travelers.

Furthermore, the availability of alcohol is considered one criterion for rating and ranking international hotels and such a Western tradition has its share in hampering halal tourism development by default (COMCEC, 2016). In the hotel industry, investors fear losing revenue in food and beverage if they invest in halal hotels, the so-called dry hotels. Therefore, the reluctance of investors to finance the development of halal tourism products and services will continue to be a big challenge to halal tourism development (COMCEC, 2016).

Unavailability of Halal Standardization and Certification

A study by the Committee for Economic and Commercial Cooperation of the Organization of the Islamic Cooperation (COMCEC) (2016) proves that the unavailability of a universal halal certification system, Muslim-friendly measurement, and wide variations in halal policies and procedures have adversely affected halal tourism development. The existence of various certification bodies in different countries causes disagreements over types of animals, slaughtering methods, packaging, logistics and other issues; this, in turn, confuses customers of halal tourism. According to Halim and Salleh (2012), the absence of uniform halal standardization and certification affects demands for halal products worldwide and thereby affects the fast growth of halal tourism. Although uniformity and consensus on halal standards and certification are undoubtedly important to ensure halal tourism's development and growth, there has been no universal standardization and certification thus far. The halal industry has prioritized the need to establish one global halal standardization and certification (Halim & Salleh, 2012). However, due to the prevalence of various schools of thought within Islam and cultural differences among countries, it is very challenging to have a worldwide universal standardization and certification system for halal. As of 2012, there were about 122 recognized active certifying bodies comprising government, non-government, mosques and other Islamic organizations worldwide. In a country where state religion exists, every food that circulates within the country is presumed to be halal by default. The issue of halal is not a great deal in these countries because the authorities are expected to ensure that all products produced and/or entered into these countries are halal. Saudi Arabia can be mentioned as the best example in this regard. However, in non-Muslim countries or secular states, obtaining genuinely halal products and services remains challenging (Nurdiansyah, 2018).

Identified Research Gaps and Conceptual Framework

Identified Research Gaps in the Existing Literature

An extensive literature review that deals with the halal tourism fields were performed. As stated by Vargas-Sánchez and Moral-Moral (2019), the literature review has at least dual aims in halal tourism studies: first, to identify past trends, evaluate current patterns and summarize existing research and, second, to identify conceptual frameworks and the existing gaps in the literature. Studies have been conducted on Islamic tourism for at least the past three decades, starting from 1989, when Din published the first article on Islamic tourism. Din published a journal article entitled 'Islam and Tourism: Patterns, Issues, and Options' in *Annals of Tourism Research*. This article has served as an eye-breaker and benchmark for the subsequent studies of sharia-compliant tourism and has become one of the most referenced papers in the field. After two decades, Battour, Ismail and Battor coined the term 'halal tourism' in 2010 (Battour et al., 2010). They published an article entitled 'Towards Halal Tourism Marketing.' In the past couple of years, several articles, conference proceedings, book chapters and books have been published in academic journals. Geographically, these studies have been confined predominantly to South East Asia, such as Malaysia, Indonesia and Turkiye. The contents of the literature can be classified into two major categories. First, the authors focus on concepts and definitions to create common terminology, scope and boundaries. However, a universal consensus over definitions and concepts are not achieved yet. Second, the authors conducted empirical research on tourist behavior, satisfaction, and infrastructure of halal tourism.

Generally, the existing literature on halal tourism has the following limitations. First, most studies did not differentiate the basic concepts and terminologies of sharia-compliant tourism, such as Islamic tourism and halal tourism. These two terminologies have been used interchangeably throughout literature, but there is a clear distinction between these terminologies. The former focuses on religious traveling, whereas the latter is open to everyone, and both are sharia complaints. Of course, a few authors, such as El-Gohary (2016), have tried to differentiate such terminologies. Second, in the bulk of academic journals and literature, halal tourism has been seen as a 'Muslim for Muslims' type of tourism in that destination marketers promote and market halal tourism as 'Muslim customers to Islamic destinations,' which is fatal to the development of halal tourism. Some authors have seen customers of halal tourism Muslims. Only a few authors have tried to see halal tourism as a secular business that invites both Muslims and non-Muslims (Ahmed & AKBABA, 2018; El-Gohary, 2016; Jaelani, 2017).

To sum up, there is confusion, misconception and misunderstanding in the existing literature regarding the terminologies such as halal tourism and Islamic tourism. Only a few researchers have tried to differentiate these terminologies. Regarding research approaches, qualitative, quantitative and mixed methods have been used, and we have learned that qualitative methodology is more appropriate for the present type of study. Therefore, a qualitative method was chosen to conduct this study.

Conceptual Framework of the Research

This subsection is born out of reflections on the critical engagements in halal tourism literature and scholarship in recent years about tourism's disciplinary nature and industrial framework. Is the vast body of existing literature suggestive of the maturing of halal tourism as a sub-discipline of tourism? How far have these contributed to establishing a strong scientific foundation to understand halal tourism's disciplinary and industrial characteristics? What future direction would these debates take halal tourism? Many scholars argue that tourism in general, halal tourism in particular, lacks the theoretical underpinning that would allow us to solve such issues. Though the proliferation of academic journals devoted to halal tourism has been recently seen, it remains un-theorized and disparate. Nor is the paradoxical nature of halal tourism knowledge fixed. Indeed, scientific understanding of halal tourism until the 2010s was somewhat limited. Many scholars agree that the literature on halal tourism remains comparatively scant rather than impressionistic or trade, and the conceptual tools brought to bear on it were blunt. However, in response to the fast growth in sharia-compliant tourism, academic interventions have been gaining momentum, particularly since the late 2010s, and critics have begun to challenge the wisdom of many established ideological and philosophical positions on halal tourism. In addition to publications in core tourism entitled books and journals, there have been plenty of scholarly research articles on tourism and related themes, which appeared regularly in various other disciplinary and/or interdisciplinary journals/books. Needless to state, a sizable portion of this burgeoning literature on halal tourism does not address development theories, processes and outcomes, with a seemingly more intense focus on terminologies, theoretical concepts and the potential of tourism development. Halal tourism development, like the domain of tourism itself, is still at an early stage of theoretical development. The cause of tourism development is vast because it encompasses destinations, origins, motivations, impacts, and the complex linkages between all the people and institutions of that interlocking, global supply and demand system (Babu et al., 2008).

According to Butler (2008), though tourism literature has been mushrooming in the past few decades, it has been based on a shallow theoretical foundation, and tourism development has received little attention. As far as halal tourism is concerned, it is not fair to criticize the policymakers and practitioners alone for being insufficiently proactive toward the ever-expanding halal tourism theoreticians must be criticized. Though the proliferation of academic journals devoted to halal tourism has been burgeoning, the paradoxical nature of halal tourism knowledge is not fixed yet.

After a thorough review of related literature, the researchers under consideration try to draw a theoretical research framework. The factors that affect

Major Themes and Issues in Halal Tourism Development 101

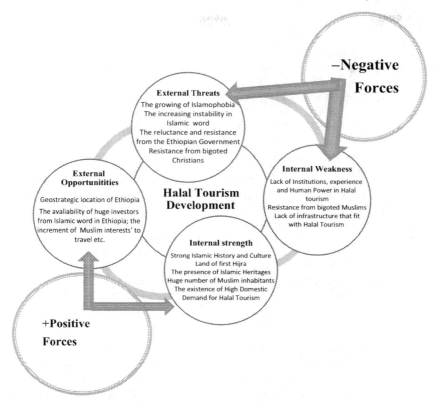

Figure 3.2 Conceptual framework of the research.
Source: The Authors, 2020.

tourism development are broadly classified into two major groups, namely positive forces and negative forces. Positive forces include external opportunities and internal strength. External opportunities such as the strategic geopolitical location of Ethiopia, the presence of huge investors from the Islamic world in Ethiopia, the rise of Muslim communities' interest to travel, Muslim communities' habit of traveling with family and the ever-increasing of Muslims globally. Internal strength includes strong Islamic history and culture, being the land of the first Hijra, the abundance of Islamic heritage and the existence of vast domestic demand for halal tourism. Negative forces are external threats and internal weaknesses. External threats are the prevalence of Islamophobia, the increasing instability in the Islamic world, the reluctance and resistance from the Ethiopian government, and the resistance of bigoted Christians. Internal weakness factors include a lack of institutions, experience and human power in halal tourism, resistance from bigoted Muslims and lack of infrastructure and superstructure that fit with halal tourism.

References

Abuiyada, D. R. (2018). Traditional Development Theories Have Failed to Address the Needs of the Majority of People at Grassroots Levels with Reference to GAD. *International Journal of Business and Social Science*, 9(9), 115–119. https://doi.org/10.30845/ijbss.v9n9p12

Adie, B. A. (2020). Marketing Europe to Islamic Heritage Tourists. In C. M. Hall & G. Prayag (Eds.), *The Routledge Handbook of Halal Hospitality and Islamic Tourism* (pp. 157–169). Routledge. https://doi.org/10.4324/9781315150604-26

Ahmed, M. J., & Akbaba, A. (2018). The Potential of Halal Tourism in Ethiopia: Opportunities, Challenges and Prospects. *International Journal of Contemporary Tourism Research*, 1, 13–22. https://doi.org/10.30625/ijctr.397499

Álvarez-García, J., del Río Rama, M., & Gómez-Ullate, M. (2018). *Handbook of Research on Socio-economic Impacts of Religious Tourism and Pilgrimage* (Issue August). https://doi.org/10.4018/978-1-5225-5730-2

Ambali, A. R., & Bakar, A. N. (2014). People's Awareness on Halal Foods and Products: Potential Issues for Policymakers. *Procedia – Social and Behavioral Sciences*, 121(October), 3–25. https://doi.org/10.1016/j.sbspro.2014.01.1104

Babu, S., Mishra, S., & Parida, B. B. (2008). Tourism Development Revisited: Concepts, Issues and Paradigms. In S. Babu, S. Mishra, & B. B. Parida (Eds.), *Tourism Development Revisited: Concepts, Issues and Paradigms*. SAGE Publications Ltd. https://doi.org/10.4135/9788132100058

Bahdi, R., & Kanji, A. (2018). What is Islamophobia? *University of New Brunswick Law Journal*, 69, 325–363.

Battour, M. (2018). Muslim Travel Behavior in Halal Tourism. In L. Butowski (Ed.), *Mobilities, Tourism and Travel Behavior – Contexts and Boundaries* (Issue October 2017, pp. 1–16). Intechopen. https://doi.org/10.5772/intechopen.70370

Battour, M. (2019a). *Halal Tourism: Achieving Muslim Tourists' Satisfaction and Loyalty* (Vol. 2, Issue August). Author.

Battour, M. (2019b). *Halal Tourism: Achieving Muslim Tourists' Satisfaction and Loyalty*. Author. https://books.google.com.tr/books?id=Jx-lyAEACAAJ

Battour, M., Battor, M., & Bhatti, M. A. (2013). Islamic Attributes of Destination: Construct Development and Measurement Validation, and their Impact on Tourist Satisfaction. *International Journal of Tourism Research*, 16(6), 556–564. https://doi.org/10.1002/jtr.1947

Battour, M., & Ismail, M. N. (2015). Halal Tourism: Concepts, Practises, Challenges and Future. *Tourism Management Perspectives*, 9(May), 150–154. https://doi.org/10.1016/j.tmp.2015.12.008

Battour, M., Ismail, M. N., & Battor, M. (2010). Toward a Halal Tourism Market. *Tourism Analysis*, 15(4), 461–470. https://doi.org/10.3727/108354210X12864727453304

Battour, M. M., Battor, M. M., & Ismail, M. (2012). The Mediating Role of Tourist Satisfaction: A Study of Muslim Tourists in Malaysia. *Journal of Travel and Tourism Marketing*, 29(3), 279–297. https://doi.org/10.1080/10548408.2012.666174

Bilim, Y., Bişkin, F., & Kaynak, İ. H. (2019). Islamic Tourism: Management of Travel Destinations 38. In A. Jamal, R. Raj, & K. Griffin (Eds.), *Islamic Tourism: Management of Travel Destinations* (Vol. 38, p. 2019). CABI.

Blackwell, R. (2007). Motivations for Religious Tourism, Pilgrimage, Festivals and Events. In R. Raj & N. D. Morpeth (Eds.), *Religious Tourism and Pilgrimage Festivals Management* (pp. 1–18). CABI.

Beydoun, K. (2018). *American Islamophobia: Understanding the Roots and Rise of Fear*. University of California Press.
Britton, S. (1982). The Political Economy of Tourism in the Third World. *Annals of Tourism Research, 9*, 331–358. https://doi.org/10.1016/0160-7383(82)90018-4
Butler, R. (2008). Butler Tourism Development Revisited. In S. Babu, S. Mishra, & B. B. Parida (Eds.), *Tourism Development Revisited: Concepts, Issues and ParadigmsIssues and Paradigms* (pp. 55–64). SAGE Publications Ltd.
Çaki, C., & Gülada, M. O. (2018). The Representation of Muslims in Public Spot Advertisements Against Islamophobia: The Case of USA, Canada and the Netherlands. *Journal of Media and Religious Studies 1*(2), 243–254.
Camilleri, M. A. (2018a). Chapter 1 The Planning and Development of the Tourism Product. In *Tourism Planning and Destination Marketing* (Issue November). https://doi.org/10.1108/978-1-78756-291-220181001
Camilleri, M. A. (2018b). The Tourism Industry. In *Travel Marketing, Tourism Economics and the Airline Product* (Issue October, pp. 3–27). Springer Nature. https://doi.org/10.1007/978-3-319-49849-2
Çetin, G., & Dinçer, M. Z. (2016). Muslim Friendly Tourism (MFT): A Discussion. *Journal of Tourismology, 2*(1), 65–67. https://doi.org/10.26650/jot.2016.2.1.0005
Chaperon, S. (2014). Dependency Theory: Tourism. In J. Jafari & H. Xiao (Eds.), *Encyclopedia of Tourism* (Issue July, pp. 237–240). SpringerReference. https://doi.org/10.1007/978-3-319-01669-6
Coccia, M. (2020). Global Encyclopedia of Public Administration, Public Policy, and Governance. June. https://doi.org/10.1007/978-3-319-31816-5
COMCEC. (2016). Muslim Friendly Tourism: Developing and Marketing MFT Products and Services In the OIC Member Countries. *Standing Committee for Economic and Commercial Cooperation of the Organization of Islamic Cooperation (COMCEC)*, August, 148. www.comcec.org
Din, K. H. (1989). Islam and tourism: Patterns, issues, and options. *Annals of Tourism Research, 16*(4), 542–563.
Duman, T. (2020). Attributes of Muslim-Friendly Hospitality Service in a Process-Based Model. In M. Hall & G. Prayag (Eds.), *The Routledge Handbook of Halal Hospitality AND Islamic Tourism* (pp. 53–69). Taylor & Francis. https://doi.org/10.4324/9781315150604-3
El-Gohary, H. (2016). Halal Tourism, is it Really Halal? *Tourism Management Perspectives, 19*, 124–130. https://doi.org/10.1016/j.tmp.2015.12.013
Evans, A., & Syed, S. (2015). Halal Goes Global. In *International Trade Centre*. International Trade Centre. http://search.proquest.com.ezaccess.library.uitm.edu.my/docview/224324915?accountid=42518
Fakir, F., & Erraoui, E. (2019). Moroccan Tourist's Perceptions Toward Halal Tourism. *2nd International Halal Tourism Congress/04-06 April 2019/Anatalya-Turkey*, November, 1–13.
Frank, G. (1967). *Capitalism and Underdevelopment in Latin America*. New York: Monthly Review Press.
Gee, C. Y., & Solá, E. F. (1997). *International Tourism: A Global Perspective*. WTO Tourism Education and Training Series. WTO box of Camelia.
Gobo, G. (2016). Glocalization: A Critical Introduction Glocalization. *European Journal of Cultural And Political Sociology*, 1–5. https://doi.org/10.1080/23254823.2016.1209886
Government of the NWT. (2010). *Tourism Handbook for the Development Northwest Territories*. Government of the NWT.

Halim, M. A. A., & Salleh, M. M. (2012). The Possibility of Uniformity on Halal Standards in Organization of Islamic Countries (OIC) Country. *World Applied Sciences Journal*, *17*, 6–10.

Han, H., Al-Ansi, A., & Kim, H. C. (2019). Perceived Inconveniences and Muslim Travelers' Loyalty to non-Muslim Destinations. *Sustainability (Switzerland)*, *11*(17), 1–14. https://doi.org/10.3390/su11174600

Haq, F., & Wong, H. Y. (2010). Is Spiritual Tourism a New Strategy for Marketing Islam? *Journal of Islamic Marketing*, *1*(2), 136–148. https://doi.org/10.1108/17590831011055879

Harrison, D. (2015). Development Theory and Tourism in Developing Countries. *International Journal of Asia Pacific Studies*, *11*(S1), 53–82.

Henderson, J. C. (2010a). Islam and Tourism: Brunei, Indonesia, Malaysia, and Singapore. *Bridging Tourism Theory and Practice*, *2*, 75–89. https://doi.org/10.1108/S2042-1443(2010)0000002009

Henderson, J. C. (2010b). Islam and Tourism. In N. Scott & J. Jafari (Eds.), *Tourism in the Muslim World: Bridging Tourism Theory and Practice* (pp. 75–89). https://doi.org/10.1108/s2042-1443(2010)0000002009

Humphreys, C., & Holloway, J. C. (2016). *Business of Tourism* (10th ed.). Pearson Education Limited.

Jaelani, A. (2017). Halal Tourism Industry in Indonesia: Potential and Prospects. *SSRN Electronic Journal*. https://doi.org/10.2139/ssrn.2899864

Jamal, A., & El-Bassiouny, N. (2019). Islamic Tourism: The Role of Culture and Religiosity. In Ahmad Jamal, R. Raj, & G. Kevin (Eds.), *Islamic Tourism: Management of Travel Destinations*. CABI.

Khan, F., & Callanan, M. (2017). "The 'Halalification' of Tourism." *Journal of Islamic Marketing The*, *8*(4), 558–577.

Khoiriati, S. D. S., Krisnajaya, I. M., & Dinarto, D. (2018). Debating Halal Tourism Between Values and Branding: A Case Study of Lombok, Indonesia. *KnE Social Sciences*, *3*(5), 494–515. https://doi.org/10.18502/kss.v3i5.2352

Khondker, H. (2004). Glocalization as Globalization: Evolution of a Sociological Concept. *Bangladesh E-Journal of Sociology*, *1*(2), 1–9.

Khondker, H. H. (2005). Globalisation to Glocalisation: A Conceptual Exploration. *Intellectual Discourse*, *13*(2), 181–199.

Larrain, J. (1989). *Theories of Development* (Issue 12). Polity Press in Association with Basil Blackwell Editorial. https://doi.org/10.1093/oxfordjournals.jhered.a103703

Mastercard-CrescentRating. (2018). Global Muslim Travel Index 2018. In *Mastercard-Crescentrating* (Issue April). https://www.crescentrating.com/download/thankyou.html?file=X7UrOM8Y_GMITI-Report-2018-web-version%281%29.pdf

Mastercard-CrescentRating. (2019). *Global Muslim Travel Index 2019* (Issue April).

Mohideen, H., & Mohideen, S. (2008). The Language of Islamophobia in Internet Articles. *Intellectual Discourse*, *16*(1), 73–87.

Navarro-Jurado, E., & Gemma, M. (2016). Development. In J. Jafari & H. Xiao (Eds.), *Encyclopedia of Tourism* (pp. 254–257). SpringerReference. https://doi.org/10.1016/s0160-7383(02)00009-9

Nicholas, F., & Gundala, R. R. (2017). Glocalization of Consumers in the Caribbean: A Case Study of Trinidad and Tobago. *Global Observations of the Influence of Culture on Consumer Buying Behavior*, 94–107. https://doi.org/10.4018/978-1-5225-2727-5.ch006

Nurdiansyah, A. (2018). Halal Certification and Its Impact on Tourism in Southeast Asia: A Case Study Halal Tourism in Thailand. *KnE Social Sciences*, *3*(5), 26–43. https://doi.org/10.18502/kss.v3i5.2323

Othman, N. A., & Jamal, A. S. (2017). Innovative System Indicators for Islamic Tourism Using C-PEST Factors. *Journal of Tourism & Hospitality*, *6*(4). https://doi.org/10.4172/2167-0269.1000298

Ramberg, I. (2004). Islamophobia *and its consequences on Young People Seminar report* (Issue June). Directorate of Youth and Sport of the Council of Europe.

Razalli, M. R., Abdullah, S., & Hassan, M. G. (2012, June 20-30). *Developing a Model for Islamic Hotels: Evaluating Opportunities and Challenges.* Paper presented at the International Conference on Knowledge, Culture and Society, Jeju Island, South Korea.

Samori, Z., Md Salleh, N. Z., & Khalid, M. M. (2016). Current Trends on Halal Tourism: Cases on Selected Asian Countries. *Tourism Management Perspectives*, *19*, 131–136. https://doi.org/10.1016/j.tmp.2015.12.011

Secinaro, P. Pietro, & Biancone, S. (2019). The Halal Tourism: A Business Model Opportunity. In K. A. Jamal, A. Raj, & R. Griffin (Ed.), *Islamic Tourism: Management of Travel Destinations.* (pp. 192–201). CAB. https://doi.org/10.1079/9781786394132.0010

Shakona, M., Backman, K., Backman, S., Norman, W., & Luo, Y. (2015). Understanding the Traveling Behavior of Muslims in the United States. *International Journal of Culture, Tourism, and Hospitality Research*, *9*(1), 22–35. https://doi.org/10.1108/IJCTHR-05-2014-0036

Sharply, R. (2018). Development Theories and Tourism Theories. In R. Shapley & D. J. Telfer (Eds.), *Tourism and Development: Concepts and Issues* (pp. 1–10). Channel View Publications.

Shapley, R., & Telfer, J. (2008). *Tourism and Development in Developing Worlds.* Routledge.

Sharpley, R., & Roberts, L. (2004). Rural Tourism: An Introduction. *International Journal of Tourism Research Int.*, *6*, 119–124. https://doi.org/10.1002/jtr.478

Sofronov, B. (2018). the Development of the Travel and Tourism Industry in the world. *Annals of Spiru Haret University. Economic Series*, *18*(4), 123–137. https://doi.org/10.26458/1847

Soulard, J., & McGehee, N. (2017). Glocalization Management Strategies of NGOs Engaged in Transformative Tourism. *Tourism Travel and Research Association: Advancing Tourism Research Globally*, 0–8. http://scholarworks.umass.edu/ttra/2017/Academic_Papers_Visual/5/

Stabler, M. J., Papatheodorou, A., & Sinclair, T. M. (2010). *The Economics of Tourism* (3rd ed.). Routledge.

Vargas-Sánchez, A., & Moral-Moral, M. (2019). Halal Tourism: Literature Review and Experts' View. *Journal of Islamic Marketing*, *11*(3), 549–569. https://doi.org/10.1108/JIMA-04-2017-0039

Weaver, D., & Lawton, L. (2014). *Tourism Management* (5th ed.). Wiley & Sons.

Zamani-Farahani, H., & Musa, G. (2012). The Relationship between Islamic Religiosity and Residents' Perceptions of Socio-cultural Impacts of Tourism in Iran: Case Studies of Sare'in and Masooleh. *Tourism Management*, *33*(4). Elsevier. https://doi.org/10.1016/j.tourman.2011.09.003

4 Ethiopia and Its Tourism Potential

Located in the horn of Africa and bordered by six countries, namely Djibouti, Eritrea, Kenya, Somalia, South Sudan and Sudan, Ethiopia is one of the oldest countries in Africa that has never been colonized by foreigners except the five years of occupation by Italy from 1936 to 1941. It is the seat of continental and international organizations such as the African Union (AU) and the United Nations Economic Commission for Africa (UNECA). It was in 1900, during the reign of Emperor Menelik II, that Ethiopia held its current map and shape. Ethiopia is a heterogenic country with a rich diversity of culture, religion and customs of more than 80 ethnic groups, languages and religions. To express this diversity, Rossini calls Ethiopia 'un Museo Popoli' (the Museum of the Peoples) (Rossini, 1937, cited in Gudina, 2003, p. 141). The country is endowed with rich and varied historical, natural and cultural resources. United Nations Educational, Scientific and Cultural Organization (UNESCO) has registered about 12 of its heritages as world heritages. It has very different cultural and historical products. Its history and traditions date back to 3,000 years. The ancient Axumite civilizations and the ancient walled city of Harar, with its seven gates, considered the fourth holiest city in Islam, are among the historic pioneer cities of Ethiopia. These ancient cities are great assets to the country's tourism development. Ethiopia is also believed to be a cradle of human beings, with fossilized evidence of the ancestors of Homo sapiens as old as 4.4 million years B.C., such as the famous *Dinknesh*, commonly called Lucy.

Regarding physiography, Ethiopia is full of contrasts and extremes, from the cool Semen Mountains peaking at over 4,600 m to the low-lying Danakil Afar depression 120 m below sea level, one of the hottest places on earth. The country comprises unique species of flora and fauna. Among others, 31 mammals, 17 birds, 14 reptiles, 30 amphibians, 40 fish and about 1,000 plant species are endemic in Ethiopia. There are 24 national parks, 2 wildlife sanctuaries, 5 wildlife reserves and 21 controlled hunting areas in the country (Federal Ministry of Culture & Tourism, 2016). Ethiopia comprises various religions, including Christianity, Islam, Judaism and diverse African traditional beliefs. Therefore, Ethiopia can offer not only the usual African game and safari experiences to visitors but also a rich array of historical and cultural sites that set it apart from most of its neighbors (World Bank, 2006b).

DOI: 10.4324/9781003355236-5

Moreover, Ethiopia is the origin of Coffee Arabica (Tucker, 2011) and the source of the Blue Nile, the longest river in the world. In 2009, it adopted a national tourism policy to use the sector as one pillar of socio-economic development. It has also adopted a motto of tourism entitled 'the land of origins' (ምድረ-ቀደምት). Ethiopia is a holy place from the perspective of religion. Its name has been mentioned both in the Bible and in hadiths.

Currently, only a few visitors have visited restricted tourist sites. These sites include the capital city (Addis Ababa), the historic northern route (Axum and the rock-hewn churches of Lalibela, the castles of Gondar and the Bahr Dar monasteries and Lake Tana), the southern pastoralist, mainly the rift valley lakes and the indigenous communities keep their unpolluted cultures such as Hamar and Omo and Gambella basins. In addition to these, national parks and, to some extent, the Walled City of Harar have been visited by inbound visitors.

An Overview of Ethiopian History

Under this subtopic, Ethiopian history will be highlighted. In the study under consideration, the researchers shall not be concerned about the detailed history of Ethiopia but focuses only on the part of it that affects the current study in one way or another. The aim is, therefore, to give a general picture of Ethiopian history on related themes.

Before briefing the history of Ethiopia, it is imperative to explain the etymological origins of the nomenclatures Habesha, Habeshistan, Abyssinia and Ethiopia. Most Arab countries have known Ethiopia by the name 'Habesha,' while the Turks employ the term *Habeshistan* and *Abyssinia* employed by the Westerners. The name 'Habesha' has been used to denote the concept of 'mixture' or of 'mixed blood' (Trimingham, 1952). The term is believed to have been derived from the name of South Arabian or *Sabaean* tribes known as *Habashat* (Ahmed, 2013). According to Trimingham, *Habashat* was among the Semitic immigrants from the Sahartan province of Yemen in the 7th century B.C. Ottoman Turks deployed the names such as *Habeshistan* to their African coastlands of the Red Sea and neighboring lowland possession that was constituted into a separate province, the *Pashalik* of Habesha or *Habeshistan*. Abyssinia and Abyssinians are the European equivalents of the Arabic terms *Habesha* and *Habash*. The terms *Abyssinia* and *Habesha* have an etymological connection. It is believed that the term Abyssinia itself is the derivative of the term *Habesha*. The name *Abyssinia* is derived from Habesha as of European languages' pronunciation. The Portuguese term *Abassia* came from the Arabic Habasha (Ahmed, 2013; Trimingham, 1952), which eventually was modified into Abyssinia. The Christian Kingdom of the Amhara and Tigreans of Ethiopia's northern and central highlands mainly connote Abyssinia. Even these days, only northerners (Amharas and Tigrians) have accepted the names *Habesha* and Abyssinia. For its historical relation with Islam, Muslims also accept and utilize the term *Habesha*. Traditionally, the Amharas and the Tigreans of the northern and central highlands have identified themselves as the 'true' Ethiopians or the 'Abyssinians proper.' Other 'Southern Ethiopians', such as Oromo, Somali, and Cushitic speakers, dislike both terminologies. For instance, Ethiopian Somali use the term *Habesha* for all Ethiopians other than the Somalis. The Oromo elites also use the terms *Habesha* and *Abyssinia* to refer to the Christian Kingdom, the Amharas and Tigreans of the northern and central highlands.

After the First World War, the name 'Ethiopia' was adopted as the country's official name. This name was recognized by the League of Nations in 1932. Etymologically, the term 'Ethiopia' is said to have derived from the Greek term 'Aithiopes,' consisting of two words: Opis, which means 'face' and Aieth, meaning 'burnt,' that is, literally 'burnt faces' (Ahmed, 2013). Many historians define Ethiopia as the land or country of dark-skinned peoples. The Hebrew Bible used the term 'Cush' instead of Ethiopia. However, the Hebrew name 'Cush' was translated into Greek as 'Ethiopia' (Ahmed, 2013).

The Legend of Queen of Sheba and King Solomon

The myth of the Queen of Sheba and King Solomon has a visible impact on the current image of Ethiopia. Therefore, it is essential to highlight the brief stories of the Queen of Sheba and King Solomon and Ethiopia's subsequent Solomonic dynasty that lasted until 1974. Sheba, also called Saba, is a kingdom mentioned in the Old Testament and the Quran. Sheba has been known in Jewish, Muslim and Christian, particularly Ethiopian Christian traditions. It was the home of the biblical 'Queen of Sheba,' left unnamed in the Bible but named Makeda by Ethiopians and Bilqis in Arabic literature (Jeenah, 2004). The Queen of Sheba, popularly known in Muslim tradition as Bilqis and Makeda by Ethiopians, is presented in the Quran (Jeenah, 2004). The story of the Queen of Sheba was narrated in the story of the Prophet Suleiman and exists in Surah Al-Naml (the Ants), verses 15–44. Though her name is not specifically mentioned in the Quran, Muslim scholars claimed the said Queen in these Quranic verses to be Bilqis (Queen) Sheba of Yemen. According to Muslim traditions, a famous Queen named Bilqis ruled the kingdom of Sheba in Yemen during the reign of Prophet Suleiman. Prophet Suleiman is believed to have been an extraordinary man who could communicate with animals, including birds and ants. According to the Islamic tradition, hoopoe or Hubhub (bird) had told him about the existence of the Queen of Sheba named Bilqis and then Suleiman sent letter to the queen. The queen seemed to have learned about the story of King Solomon from the letter dropped by hoopoe to invite the queen to the court (Adamu, 2009). According to legend, the queen first sent precious gifts to Suleiman, but she herself visited him after Suleiman rejected the gifts. Muslims believe that, ultimately, she embraced Islam, married him, and gave birth to a boy named Ibnu Malik.

According to Ethiopian Christians' document named the Kebra Negast (the Glory of Kings), which was written in the 14th century (Budge, 2000) and draws largely from regional oral histories as well as Jewish and Islamic traditions, Queen of Sheba is considered to be the queen of Ethiopia and named as *Makeda* (Adamu, 2009; Kurt, 2013; Ramos, 2003). According to the Christian tradition, the Queen of Sheba slept with King Solomon, got pregnant for Solomon as a result, and gave birth to a male child named Menelik some months after her return to Ethiopia. When Menelik became an adolescent, he was sent to Jerusalem to meet his father (Ramos, 2005). It is said that King Solomon was thrilled and invited the boy to be his heir, but Menelik refused and backed his country. Then, King Solomon declared his son Menelik to be the future king of Ethiopia. The King assigned some advisers to accompany him and assist him in his rule. These people are said to have brought the 'Ark of the Covenant,' on which the Ten Commandments given to Moses by God were kept, to Ethiopia. Ethiopian Orthodox Church believes the 'Ark of the Covenant' is still kept at the Saint Mary's Church of Zion at Aksum in northern Ethiopia. However, the Ark is said to have been kept at the Cathedral of Saint Mary's Church of Zion, and only one guardian monk is allowed to enter a special sanctuary. No other person has ever been allowed to see the Ark where it has been kept for centuries. Therefore, the Ark's presence cannot be proven beyond the rumor (Adamu, 2009).

According to the tradition of (mainly Ethiopian Christians), on the death of Queen Makeda in the mid of 10th century B.C., Menelik established a dynasty named 'The Solomonic dynasty' and assumed power as Emperor Menelik I. This dynasty is believed to have lasted until Haile Selassie I was overthrown in 1974. Emperor Haile Selassie I, who ruled the country for about half a century, constitutionalized the legend of the Solomonic Dynasty. In his constitution, Haile Selassie declared that only people from the Solomonic dynasty (the 'Solomonic' lineage) and members of Ethiopian Orthodox Tewahdo could assume power in Ethiopia. Hence, according to the tradition of the Solomonic dynasty, only anointed priest-kings of the Solomonic lineage would rule Ethiopia. The Solomonic Dynasty kings were considered to have divine power and were elected by God; therefore, no one dared to revolt against them or question their authority.

The Solomonic legend was constitutionally guaranteed during the reign of Haile Selassie I. According to the constitution of Haile Selassie I, the imperial dignity of Ethiopia was permanently guaranteed to the descendants of King Sahle-Selassie. He is believed to have been a descendant of Menelik I, Queen of Sheba and King Solomon of Israel. His constitution proclaims that the Solomonic dynasty has ruled Ethiopia for centuries and would continue. The infinity and the divine power of Haile Selassie-I are marked in article 4 of the constitution. This article declares that power shall be held only by blood and anointment. The article further states the absolute, inviolable and indisputable power of Haile Selassie I. The article also states that any activity against the power of Haile Selassie I is punishable (Ethiopian Constitution, 1955; Steen & Constitution, 1936).

110 *Ethiopia and Its Tourism Potential*

The official title of Haile Selassie I, the last king of the Solomonic dynasty who ruled Ethiopia from 1930 to 1974, was 'His Imperial Majesty Ras Tafari Makonnen Haile Selassie I, Emperor of Ethiopia, Elect of God, King of Kings, and Lion of Judah.' It is claimed that except for sporadic interruptions such as by Imam Ahmed (the Sultanate of Adal 1527–1543) in the 16th century, the Solomonic dynasty ruled Ethiopia from the last quarter of the 13th century until the last quarter of the 20th century, although the claim is mainly ahistorical. Therefore, even though there was some interruption for some limited periods, the priest-kings of the Solomonic dynasty ruled Ethiopia until 1974, and the country's image has been drafted accordingly. In 1974, the Solomonic dynasty was demised and superseded by Derg's military regime. *Derg* ruled Ethiopia from 1974 to 1991 and was replaced by Ethiopian Peoples' Revolutionary Democratic Front (EPRDF). EPRDF was a coalition of four political parties, namely Tigray's People Liberation Front (TPLF), Amhara Democratic Party (ADP), Oromo Democratic Party (ODP) and Southern Ethiopian People's Democratic Movement (SEPDM). Following public resistance and disobedience in the last eight years (2012–2020), Abiy Ahmed disbanded EPRDF in November 2019 and replaced it with Prosperity Party (PP). Chaired by Abiy Ahmed Ali, PP was officially founded on 1 December 2019, and now (2022) PP is the country's ruling party. Presently Abiy Ahmed Ali is the president of PP and the prime minister of Ethiopia.

The Introduction of Religions in Ethiopia

Even though it is not the scope of the study under consideration, highlighting the history and the status of religions in Ethiopia is vital for halal tourism development because religions have direct and indirect impacts on the development of halal tourism.

Ethiopia welcomed the three great Abrahamic religions, namely Judaism, Christianity and Islam, at a very early point (Erlich, 2009). Ethiopia accepted Christianity as early as Armenia, Egypt and Syria, and it welcomed Islam even before Medina did. As noted by the author, in Ethiopia, the three Abrahamic religions grew side by side, intertwined in many ways, and existed harmoniously in most cases (Hussien, 2001). Having the age of 1,700 and 1,400 years, respectively, Christianity and Islam have co-existed for the past 1,400 years in Ethiopia though sporadic conflicts and polemics among their elites are undeniable.

The Introduction of Christianity in Ethiopia

Ethiopia adopted Christianity from the Middle East in c. 350 AD during the reign of King Ezana (Erlich, 2009; Trimingham, 1952). The two brothers, Frumentius and Aedesius, from the town of Tyre (Syria), introduced Christianity to Ethiopia (Desplat & Østebø, 2013). Christianity was first introduced to the royal court of Aksum. Then, supported by royal houses and state institutions, Christianity in Ethiopia spread rapidly. The coming of the nine saints to Ethiopia from the Oriental world played an important role in expanding Christianity out of the royal circles. This event further strengthens the relationship between the Oriental world and Ethiopia.

During the reign of Kaleb, one of his generals, known as Abraha had built churches in Sana'a, Yemen. Equipped with elephants, he was to invade Mecca in 570 to destroy Ka'ba. This event is remembered as 'the year of the Elephant or Amul-Fill.' It was during this particular period that Prophet Muhammad (PBUH) was born. Until 1959, Ethiopia used to get its patriarch appointed from Alexandria of Egypt; until 1974, Orthodox Christianity was the official state religion of Ethiopia. Ethiopia stopped receiving Bishop from Egypt only in 1959 when Abuna Basilios appointed as the first Ethiopian Patriarch of Ethiopia (Erlich, 2009). There is also other denomination of Christianity in Ethiopia, such as protestant and Catholic.

Ethiopia and Islam

Many authors have agreed that Islam in Ethiopia is as old as Islam itself (Erlich, 2009; Hussien, 2001; Trimingham, 1952). Islam's first arrival in Ethiopia was traced back to the beginning of the 7th century A.D. when a group of persecuted Muslims fled to Habesha in 615 from Arabia (Erlich, 2009). Ethiopia is the second country in the world to accept Islam, and as an individual, an Ethiopian Bilal Ibn Rabah is the third Sahaba to embrace Islam. Therefore, Ethiopia and Ethiopians have been among the pioneers to accept Islam and have a special place in Islamic history. Prophet Mohammed himself has given the following testimonies about Ethiopia and its people.

> [...] oh, my people flee to Habesha! There you will live under the protection of the King of Habesha. Under his realm, no one faces persecution. It is a land of righteousness where God will give you relief from what you are suffering. Leave Al-Habash in peace as long as they do not take the offensive.
>
> (Trimingham, 1952, p. 44)

Bilal, Emu Ayman (Baraka) and Nejashi were the three prominent Ethiopian Muslims who tied up Ethiopia with Islam. Bilal bin Rabah, believed to have been the first Muazzin of Islam, was an Ethiopian. Bilal was serving as a slave to his enslaver Umayah Ibn Kalaf. Bilal ibn Rabah is said to have been naturally talented and gifted with a deep, melodious and resonant voice. He was one of the most beloved and loyal Sahabah by the Prophet. When Prophet Muhammad announced his prophethood and began to call to Islam, Bilal immediately renounced idol worship to embrace Islam. He is said to have been the third individual to accept Islam after Khadija and Abubakr. However, Bilal faced serious persecution from his enslaver, Umayyah ibn Khalaf and Abu Jahl. Umayah is said to have tortured Bilal to force him to denounce Islam. However, Bilal refused to renounce Islam and instead said, 'Ahadun Ahad' God is one. Irritated by Bilal's firm stance, Umayah persecuted and tortured him inhumanly. Prophet Muhammad (PUBH) heard about the story of Bilal and sent Abubakr to emancipate Bilal. Then Abubakr emancipated him (Erlich, 1994). As Erlich explained, it is commonly said that the Khalifa shall be for Quraysh, Call players (Azan) to behold by Ethiopians. Later, Bilal rose to prominence in the Islamic State of Medina. In addition to serving as Muazzin, Prophet Muhammad appointed him minister of the Bayt al-mal (treasury or finance). Bilal later died in Damascus and was buried there.

Ethiopia and Its Muslim Sultanates

Muslims controlled Ethiopia's port Adulis in 702. Following the occupation of the Dahlak Islands and Adulis in 702, Ethiopia lost its historic port; thereupon, Muslim sultanates began to rise in Ethiopia and the horn (Erlich, 1994). While the Christian kingdom controlled Northern Ethiopia, the Muslim Sultanates controlled East and Southeastern Ethiopia (Cerulli, 1971). According to Trimingham (1952), the Muslim Kingdoms began in the 9th century when the first Muslim sultanate of Shewa was founded in 896 and continued until the 20th century when the last Muslim sultanate of Harar collapsed in 1887. From 896 to 1887, four notable sultanates, namely the Sultanate of Shewa (896–1285), Sultanate of Ifat (1286–1415), Sultanate of Adal (1415–1557) and the Emirate of Harar (1647–1887) existed one after another in Ethiopia (Cerulli, 1971; Trimingham, 1952).

The Sultanate of Shewa, founded by the Makhzumi Dynasty, is the oldest Muslim Kingdom in Ethiopia (Trimingham, 1952). Its capital was Walale, situated in East Showa. The Sultanate of Shewa is said to have survived for about three centuries, from 896 to 1285 (Cerulli, 1971). According to Trimingham (1952), founded by the Walasma dynasty, Ifat Sultanate succeeded the Shewa sultanate in 1285. Recently, archaeologists have discovered remnants of the Ifat sultanate, such as Mosques and palaces in the present-day North Shewa (Khalaf & Insoll, 2019). Ifat was once the easternmost district of Shewa Sultanate. It lasted from 1286 to 1415. Adal Sultanate replaced the Sultanate of Ifat in 1415 with its center Dakar. It lasted until 1520. The capital of the Sultanate of Adal shifted to Harar in 1520. Harar city was the capital of the Adal sultanate and later Harar Emirate. It served as the learning center of Islam in the Horn of Africa (Ahmed, 2015; Insoll, 2017). The city is considered the fourth holiest city of Muslims worldwide (Ahmed, 2015). The great wall, as a trench, has encircled the historic part of the city. Amir Nur Mujahid constructed the trench Wall of Harar, also known as Jugol, in 1552–1555 (Trimingham, 1952). The fortified wall of Harar that encircles the historic city is still standing and was registered by UNESCO in 2006. Harar fell under Egyptian control for a decade (1875–1884). The walled city of Harar consists of 99 mosques and 5 gates, where 99 represent the 99 names of Allah and the five gates represent the five prayers of a day. Emirate of Harar died in 1887 following the conquest of Menelik II. Besides these four reckon Muslim kingdoms, other Sultanates existed in the medieval period, such as Dawaro, Bali, Mara, Hadiya, Dara, Aussa and Sharka (Cerulli, 1971; Trimingham, 1952).

Muslim sultanates competed with the Christian kingdom of the North, and when they were subdued, they were required to pay tributes to the Christian highland kingdom. They controlled trade routes so that almost all caravan routes from the Christian kingdom to the coast passed through some of the Muslim states, and the maintenance of peaceful relations between the Christians and the Muslims was of great importance for both groups. These days, archaeologists have discovered remnants of these Muslim sultanates in many parts of Ethiopia. Therefore, if well developed, the archaeological sites of these sultanates will become important attractions for halal visitors.

Ethiopia and the Ottoman Turk

Turkey is among the potential senders of halal visitors to Ethiopia. Hence, it would be vital to highlighting the historical ties between Ethiopia and the Turk. After 1517, the Ottoman Turk replaced the Arab as a caliphate and solidified its position at the Red Sea (Cerulli, 1971). The Ottoman Turk called the region 'Habashistan.' During that time, there was conflict and rivalry between Ethiopian Christians and Ethiopian Muslims. A notable leader named Imam Ahmed Ibrahim, the contemporaneous of Suleiman the Magnificent (1520–1556) of the Ottoman Turk, has led Ethiopian Muslims. While the Portuguese supported the Christians, Imam Ahmed appealed to Suleiman of the Ottoman Turk. He gave nine hundred trained warriors of Turk, Albanian and Arabs as well as ten cannons (Erlich, 1994). Earlier than Turk, four hundred well-trained Portuguese troops led by De Dagama had arrived in Ethiopia via Massawa to help the Christians' war. In the battle in 1542, the force of Dagama was defeated, and Dagama himself was captured and killed. Imam Ahmed sent the Ottoman contingent and Dagama's head to Yemen Pasha while the Portuguese troops worked with the Christian forces. By so doing, Imam Ahmed committed a fatal mistake. A few months later, Imam Ahmed himself was killed at the battle of Woina Dega in 1543. From 1543 to 1855, Ottoman Turk controlled the Red sea area. Ethiopia has no way to exercise its politics in the area. The Ottomans called the region 'Eyalet of Habash.' There Turkey has strong historical and actual ties with Ethiopia. In addition to having Embassy at Aldiss Ababa, Turkey has a consulate in the historic city of Harar. It also has various investment projects in Ethiopia.

The First Hijra toward Ethiopia and the Image of Ethiopia in Islamic Eyes

Ethiopia is considered an extension of the Oriental World (Erlich, 1994). The author notes that waves of immigrants from the southern Arabian Peninsula have imported their Semitic language and cultures since the 7th century B.C. Because of these immigrants and the results of intermingling with local culture, Ethiopians now have a peculiar culture and skin color that lies between Arab and Black Africans.

Ethiopia welcomed and sheltered Muslim immigrants when they faced persecution from their tribe Quraysh in the early 7th century (Trimingham, 1952). In Islamic history, this historic emigration toward Ethiopia has been known as 'the First Hijra.' It is one of the famous episodes repeatedly mentioned in the works of Arab and Ethiopian historians. In 615, when Prophet Mohammed began to preach Islam openly, he faced serious resistance from the Meccan Quraysh nobility. When the persecution against him and his followers intensified, Prophet Muhammad ordered his followers to immigrate to Aksum, Ethiopia, the Habesha. The Prophet orders his followers, '[...] oh my people flee to Habesha! There you will live under the protection of the King of Habesha. Habesha is the land of righteousness where God will give you relief from what you are suffering' (Trimingham, 1952). Following this prophetic speech and advice, about 17 Sahabas (companions of Prophet Muhammed), including his daughter Rukya and his son-in-law Osman bin Affan immigrated to Aksum (Erlich, 1994). The then ruler of Habesha Nejashi warmly welcomed them. Nejashi is known in various literature by names such as Armah, Ella Saham, As-Hama, and As-ham bin Abjar (Erlich, 1994; Trimingham, 1952). After three months, the refugees turned to Mecca because of a false rumor that the persecutors accepted and were no more a threat. However, they learned that the persecution was rather intensified. Following this episode, an additional 616 refugees, including Ja'afar bin Abu Talib have taken asylum in Ethiopia (Erlich, 1994).

The Quraysh nobilities heard the news and sent envoys to the Nejashi to ask if the refugees might be handed over to them (Trimingham, 1952). The envoys tried to convince the king by offering a precious gift so that he would hand over the refugees to them. A Meccan emissary led by Amru bin al-As, known to have been Ethiopian, had come to Aksum and given gifts for nobilities and clergies of Aksum. He asked Nejashi to hand over the Muslim refugees to the Meccan emissary. He also tried to convince the king by giving wrong information about the tenet of Islam. He said to the king,

> '[...] only some foolish people from us follow them, they denied our religion and not accepted yours as well, but they have come up with an invented religion which you nor we know nothing about it [...] so handover them to us and do not speak anything with them.'
>
> (Desplat & Østebø, 2013)

It was a vital question its answer determine Ethiopia's future relationship with Islam. If Nejashi had handed over these refugees to the Meccan nobilities, the relationship between Ethiopia and Islam would have been distorted. However, Nejashi did not accept the claim of the Quraysh nobilities. Rather he has allowed the refugees to respond so that he would able to triangulate the claim. Accordingly, the refugees were asked whether they had denied the faith of their ancestors. Ja'afar responded, on the one hand, by explaining how much those Arab pagans were primitive, cruel and ruthless and how Prophet Muhammed brought about the light and progress of monotheism. He said that he orders them to worship one God, associates no one with him, offers prayer, gives alms and fasts. On the other hand, he explained Jesus Christ by reciting from the Quran. Ja'afar has recited (the Holy Quran, 4:149):

> 'Verily Christ Jesus, the son of Virgin Mary, is the apostle of God and his word, which he conveyed into Marry spirit proceeding from him.' Ja'afar read the sura 19:16-34 about Marry: '[...] and my spirit hath rejoiced in God and my savior.' By reciting these important verses from the holy Quran, Ja'afar was able to convince King Nejashi that Nejash granted the refugees to take asylum. The king rejected the gifts of the Quraish, and he sent them back to Mecca.
>
> (Desplat & Østebø, 2013; Trimingham, 1952)

The decision of King Nejashi in favor of the Muslim refugees has been remembered in history as a moment of importance regarding the relationship between Ethiopia and Islam. According to Islamic sources, Amru bin al-As later converted to Islam and became an influential general during the occupation of Egypt in 640 (Erlich, 1994). Until they went back in 631, about six had already returned in 622, the Sahabas had lived in Ethiopia harmoniously, and about 20 Sahabas are said to have been buried in Ethiopia. They intermarried and intermingled with local people. Even one Sahaba named Ubaydalla bin Jahsh is said to have embraced Christianity and thereupon divorced his wife Umm Habiba, who later married the Prophet. In 628, the Prophet sent emissaries to the then world powers when Nejashi was one of these powers to invite them to accept Islam. These powers include Chosroes of Persia, Heraclius of Byzantium, and Nejashi of Ethiopia (Erlich, 1994). According to Erlich, Amru bin Umayah al-Damari was the envoy to Ethiopia.

The letter sent to Nejash from the Prophet Muhammed read as follows:

> To the Ahl al-Kitāb [people of the scripture]
> To request to reexamine the status of Jesus [Prophet Isa] and to Embrace Islam. I start with the Name of Allah; he is the Most Gracious and the Most Merciful. Muhammed, the apostle of God to Nejashi Ashama, King of Habesha. Greetings [...], I testify that Jesus, the son of Marry, is the spirit and the word of God and that he sent him down to Marry, the blessed, immaculate virgin, and she conceived. He created Jesus of his spirit and made him live by His breath. I summoned thee to worship in one God. Accept my message, follow me, and be one of my companions. For I am the apostle of God... set aside the pride of the sovereignty.
>
> (Erlich, 1994, p. 11)

Following this message, Nejash converted to Islam, replied to the following letter to the Prophet, and changed his name to Ahmed al-Nejashi.

> In the Name of God [...] to Muhammad, the apostle of God [...]. There is no God but Allah has brought me to Islam [...]; what you said about Jesus is the right belief. I bear a witness that now onwards I am a slave of the God, and I have sworn this in the presence of Ja'afar, and I have accepted Islam before him...
>
> (Erlich, 1994, p. 11)

This event left a legacy of the important message that tied up Islam and Ethiopia. However, it was said that Nejashi did not publicize his conversion out of fear it would cause riots from his generals and clergies. Upon his death, Prophet Muhammad performed a mourning prayer (Salatel-Gha'eb) in absentia. For all contributions of Ethiopia, Prophet Muhammad has declared the following notable and privileged Hadith in favor of Habesha (Ethiopia). 'Leave the Abyssinians alone as long as they do not take the offensive.' Thereupon, the image of Ethiopian and Ethiopia in the eyes of Islam remained positive. According to Erlich (1994), more than 20 Ethiopian Sahabas have been close companions of the Prophet. The grandmother of the second Caliph Umar is also believed to have been Ethiopian. Ethiopian Fatih Ata bin Rabah also has been a mufti during the time of Umayyad Khalif. Due to these historical ties, the image of Ethiopia in Islamic eyes as a historical, touristic and respected nation remains important. Prominent Muslim scholars such as Ibn Hawqal (10th C), Ibn Khaldun (14th C), and Ibn Battuta (1304–1369) have written about the land of Habesha, Ethiopia. During the expansion of Islamic states worldwide, Ethiopia was treated as a land of neutrality (*dar al hiyad*). Ethiopia's position has been unique in Islam. Ethiopia is also considered the ultimate model of righteousness and justice.

The Image of Ethiopia in the Eyes of Outsiders

Destination image and tourism development are closely entwined entities that destination image profoundly influences tourism development. Therefore, it is imperative to assess the possible impact of the current image of Ethiopia as a destination in the course of halal tourism development. Different scholars have defined destination image differently. For instance, Barich and Kotler (1991, p. 95) define the country image as 'the overall beliefs, attitudes, and impressions of a person or group of persons have toward a country or destination.' Tasci (2009) defines the destination image as a mental picture of a destination composed of how people visualize, think, and feel toward the destination. People's cognitive representations (images) affect their decisions and actions toward these destinations (Buhmann, 2015). The author adds that a destination's positive image and reputation have become more imperative than access and resources in the era of globalization and medialization. Images can be ideal or naïve images. People will have such kind of image because of promotion by destination or word of mouth and other informal sources. Benjamin et al. (2020) contend that historically or politically marginalized groups are not well represented in travel brochures and images. A country's image, legend, history and perception significantly impact tourism development, especially in the current time (Selamawit, 2013; Shanka & Frost, 1999). Image refers to a collection of information, facts, legends and myths about a certain destination for a relatively long period. Country image is, therefore, an idea, value, judgment and perceptions individuals hold about a specific country or destination based on the current or perceived information aired through different media. The country's image greatly impacts the country's foreign relations and tourism promotion, either positively or negatively (Shanka & Frost, 1999).

Although Ethiopia has great tourism potential to be the best destination, at least in Africa, its current image has affected its tourism development (Shanka & Frost, 1999). Given that the media about Ethiopia covers mainly wars and famines experienced for years, the world has known the country with plights. The image of Ethiopia has been shaped based on the old legends, stories and recent events of droughts. Shanka and Frost (1999) allege that promoting Ethiopia as a tourist destination is an uphill struggle. Even though Ethiopia is rich in history, culture, flora, fauna, and other tourist attractions, it has been perceived as a famine-stricken, war-ravaged and politically unstable destination (Shanka & Frost, 1999). Under such conditions, it has faced serious challenges to enter into the tourism market.

The Western and Eastern words have developed various perceptions of the image of Ethiopia. Religious and cultural sameness and otherness in Ethiopia cause different outlooks of Western and Eastern camps over Ethiopia. Christianity and its associated privileges remain deeply rooted in the established bedrock of the country's image, legends, landscapes, promotional materials and travel brochures. In the eyes of Westerners and Christian Europe, Ethiopia is considered the center of Christianity, known as the Christian Island, whereas, in the eyes of Middle Eastern, Arab and Muslims, Ethiopia is remembered as the land of the first Hijra, the land of Justice and the savior of Islam. As noted by Desplat and Østebø (2013), Westerners have considered Ethiopia as the 'Christian Island in a sea of Muslims,' though half of the population is Muslim (Gnamo, 2002). This reveals how much simplistic thinking about the image of Ethiopia has been produced and reproduced even by some scholars. For Westerners, Ethiopia is commonly assumed to have been a shelter of Christianity in the continent and a loyal ally of Europe in the horn of Africa in the war against Islam and Arabs since the rise of Islam (Desplat & Østebø, 2013). As discussed earlier, King Nejashi has been placed in the history of Arab and Muslims of the world, and the image of the country has been shaped accordingly. The Muslim images of Ethiopia and Ethiopians have played a significant role in determining the relations of the Islamic world with the country. In addition to the Nejashi narration, the traditional biographies of the Prophet have a strong connection with Ethiopian Sahaba Bilal Ibn Rabah, the second male convert to Islam after Abu Baker, as well as the first Muezzin (caller for prayer) in Islam (Erlich, 1994). Furthermore, Non-Arab Muslim countries such as Turkey hold a positive outlook on Ethiopia because of Ethiopia's historical connection with Islam.

The image of Ethiopia from the perspective of the Westerns is connected with the Solomonic myth and the legend of King Prester John (Erlich, 1994). At the same time, Arabs and Muslims have tried to connect their relation with Ethiopia with the Nejashi narration traced back to the 7th century. The Westerners have built up a new Legend of King Prester John in the 14th on the Solomonic myth. In the 14th century, a new legend was grafted onto the old legend of the Queen of Sheba. According to Western tradition, by 1350, Ethiopia was referred to as a country of Prester John. It was believed that the king of Abyssinia had political and religious authority in Ethiopia (Morrison, 1971). Therefore, Christian Europe believed that there was a priest-king named Prester John in the medieval period who protected Christianity and blocked the expansion of Islam in the region. They thought that this legendary king had lived in Ethiopia and wanted diplomatic relations with King John. Prester John is believed to have been a priest-king who ruled Ethiopia and its environs. He was known to be a rich and powerful Christian savior-sovereign beyond the Muslim Middle East (Kurt, 2013). According to Kurt, John is believed to have originally come from India, so sometimes, the term 'Indies' was suffixed onto his name. Europeans believed that the king of Abyssinia was extremely powerful and a Christian who would be a good ally of Europe.

Rubenson (2009) argues that the image of Ethiopia as an isolated Christian region was primarily an elusive European idea because there is little proof that Ethiopia needed to perceive Islam as a threat. However, the concept of a 'Christian Island' has not been merely a European idea. The Ethiopian rulers and Christian elites have also perceived the Muslims as a real threat to the country. Accordingly, in the eyes of Europe, Ethiopia is a strongly Christian country in Africa that blocked the expansion of Islam toward the continent. In contrast, Arabs and Muslims consider Ethiopia a historic country that saved Islam and whose king Nejashi embraced Islam earlier than any king in the world.

For Africans, Ethiopia symbolizes freedom and liberty (Shanka & Frost, 1999). It is the only independent country on the continent because of its resistance movement. Ethiopia defeated the imperialist force of Italy at the Battle of Adwa in 1996 and aborted the imperialistic ambition of Italy over Ethiopia. This victory has been recorded as 'the first black victory over whites' in human history. Therefore, African freedom fighters of the colonial era, such as Kwame Nkrumah of Ghana, Nnamdi Azikiwe of Nigeria and Jomo Kenyatta of Kenya, have used the rhetoric of independent Ethiopia to be a powerful symbol and a source of inspiration for the attainment of independence and self-determination for their colonized countries (Ahmed, 2013). Haile Selassie I's role in forming the Organization of African Unity, now the African Union, in 1963 and the serving of Addis Ababa as the Administrative Capital of the Union are also favorites of Ethiopia for Africa. For its historical role during the formation of the African Union, some called Ethiopia 'a mother of African countries.' However, others still claim Ethiopia could not be said to be 'a proper Africa.' They argue that even the term *Habesha*, one of the former names of Ethiopia, signifies the impurity of Ethiopians' race roots. Some scholars, such as Erlich (1994), consider Ethiopia an extension of the Oriental World.

On the other way round, the image of Ethiopia as famine-stricken, war-ravaged and politically unstable (Shanka & Frost, 1999) and an underdeveloped country is usually presented in the writings of economists and political scientists. The countryside of Ethiopia has been almost totally ignored to represent the image of the country, though it is where the majority of the people have lived; thereupon, the main culture has manifested and has been practiced, and the majority of tourist attractions have been located.

Generally, there has been a tendency by the Christian elites to brand, advocate and promote Ethiopia as a Christian state to outsiders. However, this book challenges the dominant idea of a Christian Ethiopia and advocates that Ethiopia is just as much Muslim as it is Christian. Both religions have a parallel history and role in Ethiopia, both in the past and now. Both left important heritages, and they have an important live culture that made up the dominant culture of Ethiopia. Therefore, any attempt to magnify the role of one over others in the making of Ethiopia's image is myopia and unadvisable.

To conclude, Islam and Muslims have been disregarded from the country's image and/or negatively characterized both in modern politics and throughout history. Artworks, various words and symbols were deployed as psychological weapons to destroy numerous reputations of Ethiopian Muslim icons and elites. Many factors contributed to the exclusion of Muslims and their manifestations from the image of Ethiopia. First, Ethiopia's very state formation favored Christianity, while Muslims were considered aliens and newcomers until the end of the last century. There was also 'character assassination' against Ethiopian Muslims, their institutions and elites. The Muslim elite's role and histories were not only excluded from Ethiopian history, but also Ethiopian writers considered Muslim elites such as Imam Ahmed Ibrahim al-Ghazi as invaders. In such a way, some Ethiopian elites negatively affected Ethiopia's Muslim image mainly through character assassination. Character assassination has been achieved by eliminating collective memory through history distortion and silencing Muslims' roles, merits or professional achievements in the country's public sphere. These factors cause Ethiopia as the destination to be perceived as a 'Christian Island.' This, in turn, could become one major obstacle to build halal tourism in Ethiopia. In reality, Ethiopia is a multiethnic, multilingual and multi-religion country. For most potential visitors, this naive image as a Christian island might constitute the basis for the decision; most visitors expected to investigate and incorporate it into their plan's planning and marketing activities based on the reevaluated images. Therefore, Ethiopia should be promoted in a way that reflects its identity as a multiethnic, multilingual and multi-religion country. Representation matters a lot in promoting national treasures, and it is imperative to represent the diverse and inclusive tourism resources Ethiopia has while designing tourism advertisements and promotional materials.

An Overview of Tourism Development in Ethiopia

Ethiopia was not late to begin the tourism industry, but the growth pace has been very slow. The beginning of modern tourism as an important official economic sector in the country can be traced back to the imperial regime of the 1960s (Getahun, 2016; Sisay, 2009). According to the country's ministry of culture and tourism (2009), tourism has been considered an important development tool since 1965. The first official national tourism office, the Ethiopian Tourist Organization (ETO), was established in 1961 (Sisay, 2009). Therefore, Ethiopia is one of the first African countries to establish a tourism industry. During the imperial regime, which lasted until 1974, there was appreciative progress in tourism development. According to Sisay (2009), the then government of Ethiopia gave due attention to tourism development and activities were carried out to flourish the tourism industry in the early 1960s. For instance, by the invitation of the Ethiopian government, international consulting companies and individuals such as C. Angeline and S. Moudine from UNESCO, the Italian Tourism Consultancy Firm (IANUS), and Arthur d. Little ltd studied the potential of Ethiopia's tourism (Sisay, 2009). A study entitled 'Proposals for the Development of Sites and Monuments in Ethiopia as a Contribution to the Growth of Tourism' has been conducted by UNESCO. The study identifies the potentiality of historical sites in northern Ethiopia for tourism development. IANUS identified six major potential tourism sites: Addis Ababa, Lake Tana, Massawa and the Dahlak Islands, Harar, Dire Dawa, and Arbaminch. At the end of the decade, Arthur D. Little ltd also proposed important potential areas such as Addis Ababa, and the Historic Route includes Bahir Dar, Gondar semen mountains national park, Lalibela, Aksum and the Rift Valley. Tourism infrastructures, and main hotels, have been built by the government. For instance, hotels such as Wabe Shebelle (1968), D' Afrique (1966), Blue Nile (1968), Ethiopia Hotel (1963) and Hilton Hotel (1969) were built (Birtukan, 2018). Ethiopia attracted 19,215 and 73,662 inbound tourists in 1963 and 1973, respectively. From 1970 to 1973, the average annual income from tourism was about 10.2 million dollars (Sisay, 2009). The country's tourism infrastructure has been underdeveloped compared with neighboring countries such as Kenya, Tanzania and Uganda (Kidane-Mariam, 2015). During the Derg regime (1974–1991), tourism development declined. This was because of the recurrent civil war and drought, weak diplomatic relationships with tourist-generating regions, and entry restrictions (Getahun, 2016).

In 1991, the military government of Derge toppled down and was superseded by the Federal Democratic Republic of Ethiopia (FDRE). FDRE has given due attention to the sector and established the ministry of culture and tourism. The Ministry of Culture and Tourism of Ethiopia is responsible for formulating national policies and programs for developing and promoting domestic and international tourism in collaboration with other stakeholders, including various central ministries, regional governments, and associations and the representatives of the private sectors (Getahun, 2016). According to data obtained from the ministry, the ministry's policy planning, evaluation and monitoring directorate statistics division is responsible for compiling, tabulating, and disseminating information on various aspects of tourism in Ethiopia. Even though never commensurate with its potential, the influx of inbound tourists and annual revenue from tourism began to increase in 1991. According to the FRDE Ministry of Culture and Tourism (2009), the average annual inbound tourist arrivals from 2005 to 2008 was about 324,664, and the average annual revenue was about 167 million dollars. Ethiopia's tourism had shown a relatively good record in 2015 when 863742 inbound tourists visited the country and generated about 3,233,850,048 USD. The number of tourists increased by 12.1% over the same period in 2014. The international visitor arrivals to Ethiopia in 2013 and 2014 also showed a steady increase, with 681,249 and 770,428 international visitors, respectively (Federal Ministry of Culture & Tourism, 2013, 2016). In terms of generating regions for 2012–2015, Africa, America, Europe, East Asia, the Pacific, the Middle East and South Asia sent many tourists. Regarding revenue generation, the United States of America, the United Kingdom, China, Germany, Italy, Kenya, India and Saudi Arabia spent a high amount of dollars as their order of importance.

Business, conferences, leisure and holidays, transit and visiting relatives and friends are the purposes of their visitation. In terms of seasonality, spring, specifically November and December, are peak seasons, whereas summer, mainly July and August, have been registered as a low season (Federal Ministry of Culture & Tourism, 2013, 2016). Based on the five years statistics (2007–2011), tourism comprised 1% of GDP and 10% of the country's exports. As seen from Table 4.1, the number of inbound tourist arrivals fluctuated year after year. The growth rate has decreased and entered negative in the past few years. This was because of the recurrent political turmoil, public disobedience and civil wars that the country experienced in the past five years.

According to the Ministry of Culture and Tourism (2016), there were about 164 star-rated hotels as of 2015. Of them, 79 are located in the capital city, Addis Ababa, 30 in Oromia Regional State, 20 in Southern Nations, Nationalities and Peoples Regional State (SNNPR), and 19 in Amhara regional state, 11 in Tigray regional state, and 5 in Dire Dawa and Harar. Moreover, there were also 22 lodges distributed throughout Ethiopia as of 2015.

122 Ethiopia and Its Tourism Potential

Table 4.1 Inbound Visitors Arrivals and Tourism Receipt (2000–2018)

Year	Numbers of Arrivals	Growth (%)	Receipts in USD	Growth (%)
2000	135,954	18.2	68,000,000	102.4
2001	148,438	9.2	73,808,411	8.5
2002	156,327	5.3	77,100,000	4.5
2003	179,910	15.1	89,946,355	16.7
2004	184,078	2.3	114,627,850	27.4
2005	227,398	23.5	138,599,940	20.9
2006	330,026	45.1	169,975,086	22.6
2007	357,841	8.4	213,936,063	25.9
2008	383,399	7.1	204,855,489	−4.2
2009	427,286	11.4	246,415,374	20.3
2010	468,305	9.6	333,352,000	35.3
2011	523,438	12	411,638,987	23.5
2012	596,341	13.9	333,236,539	−19.05
2013	681,249	14.2	2,550,596,256	665.4
2014	770,428	13.09	2,884,482,432	13
2015	863,742	12.1	3,233,850,048	12
2016	870,597	0.7936	3,259,515,168	0.7936
2017	933,344	0.07207	3,494,439,936	0.07207
2018	849,122	−0.09	3,179,112,768	−0.099

Source: Federal Ministry of Culture & Tourism, 2013, 2016.

Religious Tourism in Ethiopia

In Ethiopia, more than 98% of the population is believed to be religious, no matter which religion they follow. About half of the population is believed to be Muslims. Indeed, there is a disagreement regarding the number of Muslims in the Country. Ethiopian Muslims claim about 65% of the population to be Muslims, whereas the government has reduced this to 34%. Most of the country's heritage is affiliated with either Christianity or Islam. Hence, it is expected that religious travel and tourism are not uncommon in Ethiopia. Religious tourism has been practiced in Ethiopia for a long period (Bayih & Tola, 2017; Daricha & Weldesenbet, 2019). However, only limited literature exists about religious tourism in Ethiopia.

Most of the literature on Ethiopian religious tourism gives due attention to Christian religious tourism in general and Ethiopian Orthodox Christian churches and monasteries in particular. UNESCO has registered two religious festivals, 'finding of True Cross' (*Meskel*) and Epiphany (*Timket*), as supernatural world heritages of Ethiopia. Most of the domestic customers of these heritages are pilgrims from Ethiopian Orthodox church members. Moreover, Rock-hewn churches in the Tigray and Amhara regions, which are among the top destinations of domestic visitors, are affiliated to the Ethiopian Orthodox Church. On top of that, the beautiful Islands of Lake Tana and the Rock-hewn churches of Lalibela, the top visitor attractions in Ethiopia, are also affiliated to the Ethiopian Orthodox Church (EOC). UNESCO registered the rock-Hewn church of Lalibela in 1978 as a world heritage.

Table 4.2 Top Ten Arrivals by Country of Origin (2012–2015)

Rank	2012 Country	No of Arrival	%	2013 Country	No of Arrival	%	2014 Country	No of Arrival	%	2015 Country	No of Arrival	%
1	The USA	9,642	16.71	The USA	108,089	15.87	USA	124,105	16.11	The USA	139,136	16.11
2	China	5,383	.93	The UK	36,980	5.43	UK	41,629	5.40	The UK	46,671	5.40
3	UK	31,606	5.3	China	31,688	4.65	China	37,157	4.82	China	41,660	4.82
4	Germany	29,918	5.02	Germany	29,286	4.30	Germany	34778	4.51	Germany	38,990	4.51
5	Italy	22,623	3.79	Italy	24,213	3.55	Italy	27999	3.63	Italy	31,390	3.63
6	France	20,972	3.52	Kenya	23,520	3.45	Kenya	26822	3.48	Kenya	30,070	3.48
7	Kenya	20,276	3.4	India	21,789	3.20	India	25606	3.32	India	28,706	3.32
8	India	19,211	3.22	Sudan	20,312	2.98	Saudi Arabia	24181	3.14	Saudi Arabia	27,109	3.14
9	Saudi A.	8,556	3.11	France	20,289	2.98	France	23780	3.09	France	26,660	3.09
10	Sudan	6,816	2.82	Saudi A.	19,494	2.86	Sudan	103	3.00	Sudan	25,901	3.00

Source: Federal Ministry of Culture & Tourism, 2016.

Most religious tourism studies concentrated on this site (Daricha & Weldesenbet, 2019). Rock-Hewn Churches of Lalibela contain 11 medieval cave churches believed to have been carved from a single rock in the 13th century. Daricha and Weldesenbet (2019) find that orthodox Christians' religious tourism constitutes the biggest share of Ethiopian domestic tourism.

Neima (2018) conducted her Master thesis entitled 'Assessment of Religious Tourism in and around the al-Nejashi Religious Site in Tigray Regional State, Ethiopia.' Her thesis focuses on Islamic tourism toward al-Najash religious sites. She tried to assess the challenges and opportunities for Islamic tourism development toward Nejashi Mosque. Her study concludes that there is actual and potential demand for Islamic tourism toward Al-Najashi historical mosques. At the same time, she identified some factors that affected Islamic tourism in Ethiopia and forwarded her recommendations. According to her findings, many Muslims maneuver during Ashura toward Nejashi of Northern Ethiopia and the historic city of Harar. Some others also travel in the congregation to different holy places, shrines, mosques, Islamic heritage and historical sites. There is also strong evidence that halal-conscious millennial and centennial Muslims travel to secular tourism sites and reaction centers for hedonistic leisure purposes. These groups, however, do not want to compromise the Sharia and Islamic values. They visit for both spiritual development purposes and worldly pleasure. Therefore, establishing a Muslim-friendly environment at touch points will increase both the flow toward and duration of stay at a tourist destination. Ahmed and AKBABA (2018) have also highlighted the status of religious tourism in Ethiopia in their journal article entitled 'The Potential of Halal Tourism in Ethiopia: Opportunities, Challenges, and Prospects.' Their paper can be considered a pilot study of the present work.

In Ethiopia, Christian pilgrimage sites are centered in churches and pilgrimage is conducted mainly on the annual holidays of the EOC (Desplat & Østebø, 2013). As stated by the same authors, St. Gabriel Church of Qulubi, St. Giyorgis Church of Lalibela, Tsion Mariam Church of Axum and St. Mariam Monastery of Gishen are among notable pilgrimage sites of the Ethiopian Orthodox Church that attract thousands of pilgrims from all over Ethiopia. At the same time, ceremonies of other churches are attended mainly by residents.

Muslim pilgrimage centers are generally saintly shrines or places related to saintly persons that have been criticized for being against the principles of Islam. As discussed in the later chapters of this book, Dire Sheik Hussein is Ethiopia's most famous Muslim pilgrimage center (Braukämper, 2006). The shrines of saintly persons like Tirusina, Jama Nigus, Dager in Kelala Woreda (South Wollo), and Seid Bushra at Gata Wollo (Braukämper, 2006; Hussien, 2001) are also well-known Muslim pilgrimage centers. Pilgrimages to these saintly Muslim shrines are customarily conducted on Muslim holidays according to the Hijra calendar (Desplat & Østebø, 2013).

Generally, pilgrimage is conducted along religious lines. Muslims travel to Christian holy sites and saints and vice versa. However, in Ethiopia, trans-religious pilgrimage is also not uncommon. Interestingly, Desplat and Østebø

(2013) explain the trans-religious feature of Ethiopia's pilgrimage, which emerged by mixing elements of several religious traditions.

The State of Halal Tourism Development in Ethiopia

The potential of the halal tourism industry in Ethiopia is superior to other similar countries. Although Ethiopia is rich in Islamic heritage and other halal attractions, it has not benefited from the segment's burgeoning potential. Halal tourism is a very significant but missed opportunity in the country. In Ethiopia, the Islamic heritages and attractions are uncharted territory. Ethiopia could have positioned itself as a popular halal tourism destination by offering its rich Islamic values in the bigger picture of most tourism supplies, products, and services. Ahmed and AKBABA (2018) have overviewed Ethiopia's barriers and enablers of halal tourism development. According to these authors, even though there are favorable situations for flourishing halal tourism in Ethiopia, there are also obstacles that could negatively affect halal tourism development in the country. A study of Ahmed and Akbaba is a pilot study for this book. As stated by Rao (2012), the flow of inbound visitors is affected by three factors, namely (a) distance between countries (the greater the distance, the smaller the volume); (b) international connectivity (shared business and cultural values); and (c) general attraction of one country for another (tourism bubble or orientalism). From the perspective of halal tourism, Ethiopia fulfills these triple enabling conditions.

Inventory and Descriptions of Halal Visitor Attractions in Ethiopia

This section will discuss the availability and viability of halal tourism resources and routes in Ethiopia. Tourism development requires detailed information about potential tourism resources that help developers and decision-makers. Accordingly, inventorying the existing, actual, and potential tourism resources must be the first step in assessing the tourism potential of a destination. The main aim of this section is to identify and discuss cultural and natural visitor attractions that will entice halal conscious visiotors. Geographic Information System (GIS) and Geographic Positioning System (GPS) technology were also widely used to identify, locate visitor attractions and plot the spatial interconnection between these attractions. Inventorying the existing and potential tourism resources must be the first step in assessing the tourism potential of a destination. Moreover, this section is also expected to answer the following questions: where are the visitor attractions that suit halal tourism development? What are the suitable and feasible routes to access these attractions?

Attractions are the core elements in tourism development. Unfortunately, the unavailability of data and material has been challenging to research visitor attractions (Fyall et al., 2012). Inventorying and identifying the available visitor attractions are the main tasks in tourism development. Ethiopia, also called the jewelry of the African continent (World Bank, 2006b), is endowed with various natural, cultural and archaeological visitor attractions. This paper seeks to present halal visitor attractions of Ethiopia. The attractions were identified based on personal observation, FGD and interviews with various stakeholders.

Indeed, halal-conscious visitors may be interested in any attraction as far as that attraction is not in a position to transgress sharia laws and halal services and ancillaries are available around that site. However, there are specific products that halal-conscious visitors could specifically prefer. In the current book, the researchers have tried to identify only the major attractions that probably fit the interest of halal-conscious visitors and have been marginalized by tourism developers. Ethiopia's actual and potential halal tourism resources were identified and classified into five clusters: the North, Northeast, East, South East and Southwest, based on geographical zone and location. These clusters include natural resources such as topography and landform, water, the area's geological formation, natural beauty and flora. Tangible cultural resources include archaeological sites, heritage buildings, handicraft products and intangible cultural heritages such as oral traditions, performing arts, social practices, rituals and festive events (Munzuma, Sufi Dances traditions, Islamic festivals such as *Mawlid, Eid Al Fatir* and *Eid Al Adha*).

The North Cluster

Islamic Archaeological Sites of North Showa

Ethiopia is the second country to accept Islam next to Saudi Arabia and is highly attached to Islamic history, heritage and identity (Erlich, 2009; Hussien, 2001; Trimingham, 1952). North Showa is among the historic areas of Ethiopia where Islam left its footprints (Khalaf & Insoll, 2019). It is rich with Islamic archeological remnants, including ruins of Islamic sultanates such as Showa and Ifat. Unfortunately, these beautiful visitor attractions are not promoted and introduced to visitors. Recently archeologists unveiled the ruins of Ifat sultanate towns. French archaeologists unearthed three medieval towns of Ifat Sultanates, namely Asbari, Nora and Mesal, in 2007 (Khalaf & Insoll, 2019). The ruins of mosques and graveyards are discovered. Among others, the remnant of the great mosque of Nora, located at (Nora 09° 50'52.81" N, 40° 3'05.27" E), attracted the attention of archaeologists (Fauvelle-Aymar et al., 2006; Khalaf & Insoll, 2019; Fauvelle-Aymar et al., 2006).

Nora site is found in Kewet Woreda of Northeast Showa in Shewa Robot near the village of Wässiso, about 300 km north of Addis Ababa (Fauvelle-Aymar et al., 2006). The mosque's ruins reveal features of Ethiopia's medieval Islamic civilization. Walls 5 m high surround the remnants of the city's main mosque (Fauvelle-Aymar et al., 2006). It is unprecedented that one door of the wooden mosque has remained standing for centuries (Khalaf & Insoll, 2019).

Recent excavations indicate that Nora is believed to have been the ancient city of Muslims as old as Axum, Al-Nejashi. As noted by Khalaf and Insoll

(2019), the abandoned Islamic town of Nora was the seat of the Ifat Kingdom. Archeologists have verified that Nora was a center of Red sea trade networks and related to the northern Tigray as far as Dahlak Islands. Recently archaeologists have discovered mosques, mausoleums, cemeteries and other heritages (Khalaf & Insoll, 2019; Fauvelle-Aymar et al., 2006). According to key informants, even there is a strong argument that the first Hijra of Muslims of the 615 was conducted toward Showa, not Axum. The researcher interviewed an archeologist who works in the area at Addis Ababa University. He highlighted the potential of Nora archaeological sets for the development of halal tourism. He alleges that North Showa is rich in antique Islamic heritages and a hub of Islamic archaeological sites.

In addition to interviews, a group discussion was held with tourism industry stakeholders to identify the potential of the area. The conclusion of the discussion reveals that in addition to the Nora Islamic archaeological site, there are also several Islamic heritages such as ancient education centers and Mosques. The discussants also allege the availability of ancient manuscripts, including secular and religious documents, in mosques and in the hand of individuals. This indigenous literature is believed to be another asset to attract halal-conscious visitors and researchers.

The Ancient Mosque and Residential Complex of Shonke

The Wollo area is believed to have been Ethiopia's Islamic learning and culture hub. To denote its role as a center of Islamic education and research center, some people call Wollo '*Azharul Habesha*.' Mainly it was from this area that Islamic education and culture spread to different parts of Ethiopia. Nowadays, there are several ancient Islamic education centers and Mosques in Wollo. There are also 'literacy heritages' of old-aged manuscripts, intangible heritage and performing arts such as Islamic Menzuma and Neshida. Some of these heritages are still intact and active, whereas the rests are available only with their remnants and ruins. As one participant speaks, '[…] among the ancient religious sites and *Sufi*-order centers of Wollo, Shonke, Turusina, Gata, JamaNigus, Deger, and Debat are notable ones.'

Shonke is a historic village located 23 km from Kemissie town, in Jirota kebele of the Amhara region. This site has been Islamic education and *Sufi*-order center where notable *Sufi* saint-scholars like Sheikh Jawhar Haydar Ali (1837–1937) permanently taught and produced many Muslim scholars (Ahmed, 2004; Eyassu et al., 2019). The village flourished 900 years ago on the top of a plateau as a residential complex and an Islamic education center. The village has served over 20 generations (Eyassu et al., 2019). Argoba people are believed to have constructed Shonke mosque and village nine hundred years ago (Eyassu et al., 2019). Argoba people are adherents of Islam and have a tradition of constructing mosques and villages from stone, wood and mud. It must be noted that the Argoba people also built Nora mosque (Ahmed, 2004). They constructed the most known Shonke village and mosque in the 12th century. The ancient mosque and village of Shonke are built in a breathtaking mountainous area. Situated with breathtaking views, the historical and religious sites of Shonke consist of residential houses and mosques to draw visitors' attention. According to local tour operators, the ancient villages and building heritages of Shonke are among Ethiopia's underutilized Islamic Heritages.

Shonke is proposed to be among the major node of the proposed Al-Nejash Historic Route. Tour operators and tourism experts allege that the area has a huge potential for halal tourism development. In addition to its location being near the historic sites of the sultanate of Ifat, there are several Islamic heritages and Islamic archaeological sites around Shonke. This important Islamic heritage should be preserved and transmitted from generation to generation.

Al-Nejashi Religious and Historical sites

Ethiopia is the first country in the world to welcome Islam in the early 7th century. The Prophet got his companions to migrate to Habesha when they encountered brutalities and persecutions from the Quraysh of Mecca (Erlich, 1994). Therefore, Ethiopia is a holy country chosen by the Prophet Mohammed (PBUH) to save his companions. Al-Nejashi (As-ham), the then king of Habesha, gladly received the Sahabas and allowed them to live peacefully. Consequently, the Prophet designated Ethiopia as the land of peace and its king Al-Nejashi as an example of justice (Erlich, 1994, 2009).

Al-Nejashi Site, also called Negashi Amedin Mesgid is found in the Tigray regional state of Wuqro town, 790 km north of Addis Ababa. Al-Nejashi mosque is believed to have been the first mosque in Africa, if not in the world. It is named after Nejashi, the Ethiopian king who welcomed companions of the Prophet Muhammed and ultimately converted to Islam (Cerulli, 1971; Erlich, 1994, Trimingham, 1952). Hence, Nejashi village is where the first Muslim settlement flourished in Africa. The Turkish Coordination and Cooperation Agency (TİKA) have recently renewed the mosque. The mosque was built in a historical place where 15 tombs of the prophet's companions are found. It is one of the most visited religious sites by halal-conscious visitors interested in Islamic history and culture.

A respondent from the federal Mejilis highlighted the role of Nejashi as follows:

> Al-Nejashi is not only playing a great role in Islamic history but also serves as an everlasting reminder of the warm welcome extended to the first Muslims by the Habesha king of the time. Therefore, it could be said that Nejash was the best diplomat, hospitable and the one who initiated halal tourism-like activity. It is denoted that Ethiopia is the first country to embrace Islam before Africa and the world except for Mecca, and it is privileged to host halal tourism. Al-Nejashi mosque is a historical and touristic place for anyone who wants to learn about the glorious history of the early Muslim civilizations.

Attractions of Al-Nejashi Religious and Historic Sites

After having interviews with tourism officials, residents and visitors, sub-attractions of Al-Nejashi religious and historic sites were identified and discussed as follows. Most of them have been attracting domestic and international visitors to Al-Nejashi.

The Story of the Sahabas

The first attraction that lures halal-conscious visitors is the story and the legend of the *Sahabas* (Companions of Prophet Muhammad). Most visitors prefer to visit Al-Nejashi to learn about the story of *Sahaba*, who immigrated to Axum, Ethiopia, during the era of Prophet Muhammad C. 615. As discussed earlier, hundreds of *Sahabas* migrated toward Axum, Ethiopia. Most visitors are enthusiastic to hear about the story of those *Sahabas* from the local religious leaders by personally appearing at that historic site. As the Imam states, 'in addition to the story of the *Sahabas*, both domestic and international visitors are interested to hear the story of King Al- Nejashi.' King Al-Nejashi is believed to have been the first King in the world to embrace Islam. Therefore, he has an undeniable place in Islamic history, and many Muslims envision visiting his mosque and hearing about his rich story. Therefore, histories, legends and stories of the Sahaba and king Al-Nejashi served as sub-attractions of Al-Nejashi religious and historic sites.

Shrine and Mausoleums

Shrines and Mausoleums were important attractions in the Nejashi religious site complex. As the Imam of Nejashi mosque cites, there are mausoleums of the *Sahabas* and King Nejash within the compound of Al-Najashi religious and historic sites. According to Neima, the mausoleum of King Al-Nejashi and 15 *Sahabas* (10 males and 5 females) were found in the compound (Neima, 2018). The pilgrims pay due attention to visiting these tombs.

Neima (2018) states that the graveyards of the 12 Sahabas and King Negashi were found in the mausoleum. The other three Sahabas are Udey bin Nedila, Abdela bin Al Haris (Sherif Abdilah), and Musa Bin Al Haris found outside of the Shrine and Mausoleums.

Ashura Ceremony in Al-Nejashi

As the root word of Ashura, '*Ashir*,' indicates, Ashura is the 10th of Muharram, the first month in the Islamic or lunar calendar. *Some Muslims celebrate Ashura*. For instance, according to key informants (religious leaders), Ashura is celebrated in Harar and at Al-Nejashi Wukro. According to one religious leader, many visitors visited Al-Nejashi during the festivity of Ashura. Both domestic and international visitors visited Al-Nejash during Ashura. For instance, there were visitors from Sudan and Eritrea during Ashura, and domestic visitors traveled to Al-Nejashi Wukro from all corners of Ethiopia to celebrate Ashura there, at Al-Nejashi. During Ashura, various performing arts, such as colorful religious songs and dances, exist. There are also souvenirs offered for visitors.

Remnants of the First Al-Nejashi Mosque and Sahaba Houses built by the Suhabas are other important attractions. The Imam of the mosque explains the history of Al-Nejashi mosque as follows:

> The first Mosque of al-Nejashi is different from the modern Al-Nejashi Mosque. There is a misunderstanding among the visitors and media personnel to differentiate between the Al-Nejashi mosque and Al-Nejashi cemetery. Most of the time, the visitors visit the Al-Nejashi cemetery, but they assume it as if it was the Mosque. Al-Nejashi cemetery was constructed during the time of Sahabas, in the 7th century. These days we find only the ruins of the Al-Nejashi Mosque.

The Northwest Cluster

Northeast Ethiopia, mainly the Afar region, is rich in geological, geomorphological and archaeological visitor attractions. This region possesses a huge potential to develop geotourism in Ethiopia. Afar region is internationally known for its geological formation, such as Erta Ale and archaeological sites, such as Hadar (Cavalazzi et al., 2019; Cieśluk et al., 2014). Geologists and archaeologists widely visit the area. Therefore, the Afar region has a great asset to flourish halal tourism in Ethiopia.

Afar holds an important place in the East African Rift System (EARS). Passing through Ethiopia, Kenya, Uganda and Tanzania, EARS is one of the geologic formations wonders of the world. The Afar Triangle is a triple junction zone where the Red Sea, the Gulf of Aden and Ethiopian rifts intersect at the central Afar depression. The Danakil depression is among the lowest and hottest places on earth in the East African Rift valley system. Afar regional state of Ethiopia is rich in both archaeological sites and unique natural resources such as active volcanoes. Having archaeological sites and active volcanos, Afar is one of the most beautiful landscapes to visit (Cieśluk et al., 2014). Though its temperature reaches up to 50% and it seems an inhospitable place, the Danakil depression is still interesting and worth visiting. For 100 years, the Afar Areas have been known for active volcanic and tectonic activities (Cavalazzi et al., 2019; Cieśluk et al., 2014).

Dallol

Located in the northern part of the Triangle (Danakil Depression) in Northern Ethiopia at the Ethio-Eritrea border, Dallol Volcano is an important visitor attraction (Cavalazzi et al., 2019; Cieśluk et al., 2014). With an elevation of about 130 m below sea level, it is one of the planet's hottest places throughout the year. Due to the extremely low elevation, Dallol has become one of the hottest places on earth (Cavalazzi et al., 2019). Though not famous as that Erta Ale, Dallol is also an active volcano located in the lowest place. It is believed that the landscape of the Afar depression was cut off from the sea, and over time, the Danakil Depression lost its water because of desert evaporation. Dallol is found in the depression of 126 m below sea level. Lying 118 m below sea level, there is also a salty lake of Afrera (Cieśluk et al., 2014).

Erta Ale

The term 'Erta Ale' is derived from the Afar language to mean 'Smoking Mountain' (Cieśluk et al., 2014). Erta Ale is an active volcano found between Dalol and Africa, more than 100 m below sea level (Cieśluk et al., 2014). In the Afar Triangle, there are about 34 volcanoes. Of them, five are active, and Erta Ale is the biggest one. Erta Ale is a rarely found volcano for it is liquid lava in its crater. As Cieśluk et al. (2014) state, Erta Ale remained active for at least 100 years, and it is the most visited volcano in the Afar region.

The Hadar Archaeological Site

Not only known for active volcanoes, but also the Afar region is a hub of archaeological sites where the oldest and the most famous archaeological finding of Australopithecus remains, such as Lucy were discovered. Afar has diverse archaeological and paleontological heritage resources. Hadar is the known archaeological site of the Lower Awash of Ethiopia. It is one of the most prolific hominid archaeological sites in the world. During the survey conducted in the 1970s, about 240 hominids were unearthed, and today about 400 specimens of Australopithecus Afarnes are uncovered in Afar (Cieśluk et al., 2014). Of them, Lucy was the most famous one. The Hadar archaeological site is located in the Afar depression, west-central Afar Triangle, about 300 km from Addis Ababa. Lucy (ድንቅነሽ) (Australopithecus Afarnes) is an almost complete skeleton of the first primitive man, which was estimated at 3.2 million years. Lucy was discovered in 1974 at Hadar, a site in the Awash Valley of the Afar Triangle in Ethiopia, by paleoanthropologist Donald Johanson (Cieśluk et al., 2014).

The Eastern Cluster Attractions

The Ancient Walled City of Harar

Harar is a historic walled city in Eastern Ethiopia. It was established in the 7th century (Ahmed, 2015). Located 500 km east of Addis Ababa, Harar serves as the capital city of the Harari region (Bank, 2006a). Harar is believed to have been the seat of the Islamic Kingdom of Adal from 1520 to 1557 (Insoll, 2017). Harar is the fourth holiest city of Islam in the world. It has been serving as a center of Islamic education and learning.

132 *Ethiopia and Its Tourism Potential*

Figure 4.1 The Jugol Wall of Harar & its main gate.
Source: Photo by data collectors.

Harar was a base of Imam Ahmed Ibrahim, who defeated the Christian kingdom of the north and ruled Ethiopia for a decade and a half (1527–1543). His successor Amir Nur Mujahid constructed the wall of Harar in 1552–1555 and encircled the historic city with a wall. The wall is 4 m high and has five gates (Ahmed, 2015). The wall surrounding the historic city is called the 'Jugol Wall,' which is still intact as a symbol of Harar city.

One participant from the Harari culture and tourism Bureau alleges,

> [...] Harar city has been known for its values of the coexistence of multiple religions and cultures and its historic wall of Jugol. Furthermore, Harar comprises a variety of cultural and historical attractions. Having such multiple attractions together, Harar city is referred to as an 'Open Museum' of the east.

Figure 4.2 Hyena feeding man in Harar.
Source: Photo by the researcher.

According to a local guide, a long-standing tradition of feeding meat to hyenas evolved during the 1960s into an impressive night show for visitors. As proved by personal observation of the researcher, in Harar, there is a tradition of 'Hyena Feeding Ceremony' every evening that attracts many visitors. According to tour guides, there are more than three spotted hyena-feeding sites on the outskirt of Harar city.

Tour operators often promote Harar as 'an open museum' to refer to Harar as a cultural mosaic that emerges not only from various cultures and traditions, but it connects the traditions with modem practices (Asante, 2009). In addition to being a mosaic per se, Harar city comprises four Museums that display the past and the living heritage of the people of Harar city. These Museums are Harar Regional Museum, Rimbaud's Heritage Building and Museum, Ada Gar (Harari Culture House) and Sherif Private Museum. The curators of these museums in Harar were interviewed. They have highlighted the role of these Museums in halal tourism development. One curator alleges:

> [...] most of the collections in our museum reflect the past civilization of the Harari, Somali, Oromo and other peoples in general, traditional Harari architecture and material culture in particular. The Harari culture is a duplication of Muslim culture. Hence, these collections could attract Muslim visitors who are mainly halal-conscious. In this Museum, one can observe the ancient civilization, culture and history of Islam and Muslims. For instance, one can see ancient coins, antique Arabic manuscripts and the lists of *Amirs* that ruled Harar city from the 11th Century until the 19th Century. Hence, the Museums of Harar are important attractions for Muslim visitors who are enthusiastic about visiting Islamic history and culture [...].

Ada Gar is a museum where visitors enjoy viewing the architecture and house design of the Harari people. The building itself is designed in a way that reflects the internal architecture and house design of the Harari people. Of the four Museums, Rimbaud's Museum was established recently in the Heritage buildings of Rimbaud. The Museum is called Rimbaud after his name. Before he departed Harar city in 1891, French poet Arthur Rimbaud used to live at Rimbaud's Building. In 2000, the house was transformed into a museum (Asante, 2009).

Basketry and Handicraft Products

Although there are problems in production and marketing, handicraft products in the historic city of Harar are another cultural attraction. Harar city is known for basketry. Some respondents referred to the availability of cultural basket-making traditions and the number of women interested in training and production as one of the site's strengths. During the discussion regarding Harar city's handcraft, one participant said the following: 'the handicraft center is a strong point to showcase local traditional products and culture.

134 *Ethiopia and Its Tourism Potential*

Figure 4.3 Colorful basket collections at Harar Museums.
Source: Photo by the researcher.

Women from different parts of Ethiopia have taken basketry training.' Other women allege numerous problems regarding the utility of the handicraft village by the local tourism officer.

> The tourism industry players of Harar city do not fully understand what tourism products and visitor attractions mean. They do not consider these beautiful handcrafts as visitor attractions. They do not know how to sell or promote the products of Harar city.

During the field trip for data collection, the researcher personally observed beautiful basket products of different forms. He has seen women from different parts of Ethiopia taking basket-making training. Besides being and becoming a visitor attraction, these handicrafts products could be offered for visitors as souvenirs.

Heritage Buildings

The existence of unique medieval period buildings is another important element of cultural and heritage attractions in Harar city. Most interviewees believe these buildings could be used for halal tourism development. A tourism officer alleges the following:

> […] the walled city of Harar has old heritage buildings that would contribute to the development of halal tourism. Most of the buildings of the walled city of Harar, such as mosques, were medieval period buildings that reflect the Islamic architecture styles and Islamic civilization of the medieval period so that halal-conscious visitors could prefer them.

A local officer claims:

> Heritage buildings, including about 80 mosques and other ancient buildings located within the walled city of Harar, have been registered as

world heritage. These buildings reflect Harar's Islamic civilization (Asante, 2009). Therefore, these are assets for halal tourism development in the country.

The Abandoned Islamic City of Harlaa

Harlaa, an abandoned Islamic city, signals Islamic civilization in East Africa. Harlaa is believed to be an ethnic group of Eastern Ethiopia from which the terms 'Harar' and 'Harari' stemmed (Ahmed, 2015). It is located between Harar city and Dire Dawa City Administration (see Eastern Route below). Harlaa served as the capital city of Muslim sultanates. Nowadays, archaeologists unearth mosques and other Islamic heritage at Harlaa archaeological sites (Insoll et al., 2017). Recently they found a 12th-century mosque similar to those found in Tanzania and Somaliland. This shows the linkage of Ethiopian Muslim civilization with other African fellows. In addition to mosques and other Islamic heritage ruins, archaeologists unveiled artifacts from Egypt, India and China (Khalaf & Insoll, 2019). This proves that in addition to being the capital city of Islamic kingdoms, Harlaa was a cosmopolitan city where multicultural societies lived together. The discovery of jewelry and other artifacts from Madagascar, the Maldives, Yemen and China proved that Harlaa was a trade center (Insoll, 2017). Archaeologist Professor Insoll has proved that foreigners also used to live in Harlaa city, and trade exchanges were conducted as far as Arabian Gulf, the Red Sea and the Indian Ocean. There is also a remarkable and unguessed thing that huge stone blocks that people's power cannot normally lift were used in construction (Insoll et al., 2017; Khalaf & Insoll, 2019).

The Daketa Rocks in Babile

The Daketa rocks are found 5 km away from the tiny town of Babile, 40 km far from the ancient city of Harar and 560 km from the capital city of the country Addis Ababa (Ahmed, 2012). The majority of the rocks here are extremely endowed with unique natural fascinations. Astonishingly, it is common to find unique ones over overlapped rocks within a few intervals. The number of rocks positioned one over another rock's head sometimes goes up to two to three. It seems like great technological results have been applied in arranging the rocks. With the great scenic beauty of the landscape, the Daketa rocks are a major natural attraction in Babile Woreda. As the researcher's observation and word of mouth of residents, there are also white baboons and various reptiles at Daketa rocks.

Prison House of Lij Eyasu on the Gara Mulleta Mountains

The prison house of Lij Iyasu is found 581 km far away east of Addis Ababa and 76 km west of Harar. According to an unpublished source of Eastern Harerge Zonal department for culture and information bureau, Yemeni architect, by order of Haile Selassie, built the prison house of Lij Iyau in 1931. As the name indicates, it was a prison where an Ethiopian king, Iyasu Michael (Iyasu Mohammed Ali before he was baptized), who ruled the country from 1913 to 1916, was detained (Ahmed, 2012). He was imprisoned after the political intrigue between the Shoan Nobilities to which Haile Selassie I belonged and the Wollo local rulers from which Iyasu had his origin and Haile Selassie I had overthrown him. Therefore, this prison represents one of the historical sites of Eastern Ethiopia and the country. Besides the historical value, the architecture of the prison and the scenic landscape of the Gara Mulata Mountain could be other supplementary visitor attractions of the area.

The Live Culture and Traditional Cottage of Pastoralists

Besides its other cultural and natural attractions, eastern Ethiopia comprises unspoiled and original live cultural attractions. According to one international visitor whom the researcher has interviewed in Harar, the visitors traveling to Daketa valley enjoy not only viewing the unique rocks of the area but also watching and appreciating the very traditional cottage of the local pastoral communities, their camel and their way of life and their unspoiled culture as well. Therefore, the living style of pastoralist and their traditional cottage would become supplementary attractions for Daketa rocks.

Southeast Cluster: Halal Tourism Resources of Bale Zone

Bale is located 430 km away from Addis Ababa in southeastern Ethiopia of Oromia Regional State. This area is endowed with diversified tourism resources of natural, anthropogenic and manmade attractions. Local communities, tourism experts from the culture and tourism offices of Bale Zone and *woredas*, tour guides and visitors were interviewed to identify halal tourism resources in the area. Bale has three major attractions that could attract halal-conscious visitors: the Bale Mountains National Park, Sof Omar Cave System and Dire Sheik Hussein historical and religious sites.

Bale Mountains National Park (BMNP)

Bale Mountains National Park (BMNP) is a semi-developed visitor destination. In addition to being the largest African Afro-Alpine Habitat Park, the park sheltered several endemic animals. According to the local guide, visitors to BMNP could enjoy watching over 46 mammals, more than 200 bird species and the vegetation of an unspoiled wonderland. The park consists of endemic mammals such as the Ethiopian wolf, Bale Monkey, Mountain Nyala and Menelik's Bushbuck (Aynalem et al., 2015). The park is 400 km southeast of Addis Ababa and covers an area of 2,000 km2 (Bayih & Tola, 2017). Both interviewees and focus group discussants confirm that Bale Mountains National Park is the preferable attraction for halal-conscious visitors. The religious leader also alleges that Islam encourages visiting natural attractions to admire what Allah creates

Religious and Historical sites of Dire Sheikh Hussein

Located 620 km southeast of Addis Ababa in Oromia, Ethiopia, Dire Sheikh Hussein is an important historical and cultural heritage of the Bale area. It is one of the oldest surviving Islamic education and cultural center in Ethiopia. The site's history can be traced back to the late 12th century (Semu, 2016). A holy man named Sheikh Nur Hussein Melka founded the shrine 900 years ago (Tola, 2009).

The Shrine is named after this popular religious teacher and leader. The term 'Dire' is derived from *Afan* Oromo words, meaning a plain. According to the local elders, he has known for his high devotion and miraculous deeds. According to local key informants, he was born 950 years ago to his father Melka or Sheik Ibrahim and his mother, Shamsiyya (Semu, 2016). According to legend, Sheikh Hussein lived for 250 years on earth and devoted most of these years to praying and *dhikr*. According to key informants, he is said to have a blood relation with Prophet Mohammed and is credited for Islamizing Bale and its environs. Sheik Hussein is one of the most respected figures among Sufi Muslims. Sufi Muslims throughout Ethiopia venerate Sheikh Nur Hussein as a saint, spiritual leader and Holy man. As noted by respondents [of Sufi religious leaders], the Dire Sheikh Hussein shrine is one of the most visited sites by local pilgrims. People, mainly Sufi Muslims, make pilgrimages toward Dire Sheik Hussein to seek good health, fertility, and material well-being and remedy all their difficulties. The site of Dire Sheik Hussein shrines consists of magnificent groups of building heritages and courts representing the early medieval period of Islamic civilization, mausoleum architecture, historic settlement and beautiful landscape. The site is a huge countryside religious settlement portraying the past's living culture that continued for nearly 1,000 years.

According to respondents, people make a pilgrimage to Dire Sheikh Hussein twice a year. The major pilgrimage is carried out during Sheikh Hussein's birthday festival, mainly fixed in the first week of August. The second one is during the feast of *id 'al-Kabir,'* the great feast at the end of the *Zul Hija* (Semu, 2016). This one is the month of the pilgrimage to Mecca and the last month of the Islamic calendar. The key informant (Sufi-Muslim) alleges, 'The poor people who cannot afford the pilgrimage to Mecca, the pilgrimage to Sheikh Hussein could substitute it.' According to participants, Sufi Muslims consider Dire Sheik Hussein as 'the little Mecca' for Ethiopian Muslims, as Lalibela is considered 'the Little Jerusalem' for the Ethiopian Christian community (Semu, 2016).

Religious performance arts and the practice of pilgrims are living heritages. Visitors across ethnic and political boundaries, sometimes across religious boundaries, enjoy the festivals, melodious religious songs and dances. Pilgrims and local visitors allege, 'The building of the site is aesthetically and architecturally attractive.' Dire Sheikh Hussein's site has comparative location advantages over other similar sites. Located between the peaks and the plains, in the eastern foothill of the Bale Mountains range and the Sof Omar Cave System, Dire Sheikh Hussein can add value to the visitors' experience.

The Sof Omar Cave System

The Sof Omar cave system, also known as Holqa Sof Omar, is one of Africa's most spectacular and longest underground caverns (Aynalem et al., 2015). Sof Omar Cave is a giant underground cave formed by the cavernous Weib River that passes through limestone foothills. The Sof Omar cave system is a mixture of cultural heritages. Sheik Sof Omar used to pray within it for many years, and the cave is an extraordinary natural phenomenon of breathtaking beauty and amazing geological formation (Aynalem et al., 2015). The cave is not only a natural heritage but also an important Islamic shrine named after the saintly Sheik Sof Omar Ahmed, who used to pray there in the early 12th century AD. Sof Omar is claimed to have been the favorite disciple and a close relative of Sheik Hussein. He was Sufi Muslims' most celebrated spiritual father next to Sheikh Hussein (Participants, 2019). Therefore, the cave has a religious history that predates the arrival of the Muslims into Bale.

Sof Omar Cave System is 16 km long and has about 40 entrances and exits. To travel throughout the cave system, the travelers are advised to have a hand light because the inside part of the cavern is too dark. The researcher has traveled through the caves and proved that the inside part of the cave is very dark and crosses the Weib River many times. The researcher has also seen a marvel of architecture, stone pillars and a flock of bats. According to local tour operators and elders, the cavern has different parts based on what was used by Sheik Sof Omar. There are parts of the cavern used for prayer and a living room, and there are rooms that were used as a court where justice was given and criminals were jailed. In addition to being a well-preserved sacred place of worship, Sof Omar cave has an indirect role in protecting the environment. It causes the preservation of indigenous forests and the natural

Figure 4.4 The researcher during data collection at Sof Omar Cave.
Source: Photo by data collectors.

habitat of wildlife resources. Around this historic cave, one finds wild animals such as the ape, monkeys, rock hyrax, giant tortoises and lizards, and more than a hundred species of birds (Researcher Personal Observation, 2019). The Cavern of Sof Omar is a unique geological process of limestone landforms and the most significant geological and geomorphological formations. A local government official said:

> Registered in the tentative list of UNESCO, the cave has outstanding universal natural heritage values. For instance, on one side, the Sof Omar cave system contains unique geological and geomorphological formations or areas of exceptional natural beauty and natural aesthetic significance. The outstanding cultural landscape reveals incomparable geological and natural phenomena. This might inspire geologists and archaeologists to study the cave systems' formation over hundreds of millions of years and helps probe the story of in-cave dwelling. On the other side, a cavern is a sacred place for Sufi Muslims, and it has a role as an important cultural heritage. The cave is a palace where saint sheik Sof Omar used to pray day and night. The cave can also be considered an archaeological site and is open to archaeologists.

There are also folktales that the local people believe the cave is mysterious, where the ancestral cult of Sheik Sof Omar Ahmad, his families and descendants observed and practiced their religion annually (Aynalem et al., 2015). Even these days, each cave structure has been assigned and designated to different ritual practices. According to local informants, annual religious (Islamic) festivals and events also occur in the cave shrines and mosques of these underground karstic limestone caverns. Therefore, Sof Omar cave still provides ecclesiastical services to the community because it has exceptional cultural significance to the spiritual life of the Sufi Muslims.

Therefore, as a natural heritage, the cave reveals exceptional physiographic formational. As cultural heritage, it is a typical testimony of human usage of cave shelters for religious purposes and continuation. Thus, it is crucial to utilize this exceptionally beautiful and inspirational combined value and a double feature of the cave system as a visitor destination.

Southwestern Clusters: Jimma and Its Environs

Southwestern Ethiopia is endowed with rich historical, cultural and natural tourism resources that could attract halal-conscious visitors. The Jimma area is blessed with numerous potential cultural, historical and natural halal tourism resources. Among others, the palace of Aba Jifar II, the wild coffee forest and the unspoiled culture of indigenous peoples are the main visitor attraction in this region (Labouisse et al., 2008). According to tour operator interviewees, researchers and domestic visitors have recently been flowing toward Jimma to visit the historic site of Jimma Aba Jifar and the nearby natural attractions. The number of visitors interested in visiting the forest coffee of western Ethiopia has also been increasing. As will be discussed below, Ethiopia is the origin of coffee Arabica, and it was in the Southwestern part of Ethiopia that coffee Arabica was first domesticated (Tucker, 2011). In addition to being the origin of coffee Arabica, one still finds wild coffee in the area these days. Hence, the visitor could enjoy observing wild coffee forests and consuming organic coffee. Moreover, most Ethiopian forest resources are concentrated in this region.

The Palace of Aba Jifar II

The palace of Aba Jifar II is one the oldest, largest and surviving traditional wooden architecture palaces in Ethiopia (Aman, 2019). Aba Jifar I is said to have established the most powerful Kingdom, Jimma, in the 1830s. His relative and successor, Mohammed Dawud, better known as Aba Jifar II, emerged as the most powerful King and built the historic palace of Aba Jifar in the 1880s, 7 km in the outskirt of Jimma city. It is believed Aba Jifar I chose the area for a strategic purpose. The palace's architectural style and design depict the cultural and historical aspects of the Oromo people. One participant speaks as follows:

> The palace of Aba Jifar encompasses the residence of Aba Jifar, the mosque of Aba Jifar and the residence of his grandsons Aba Jobir and Aba Dula. The palace was constructed at the strategic site at the hilltop against enemies. The palace of Aba Jifar is believed to have been built with tonnes of eggs, olive tree wood and selected stones. After the lapse of a century, the palace is still intact. These days, however, some parts of the palace are on the brink of falling.

While visiting Jimma and its vicinity, visitors deepen their expertise and acquire intercultural experiences.

In addition to having the historic Aba Jifar palace, wild coffee trees and rich forest resources, the Jimma area is endowed with material culture and living heritage. Jimma is branded nationally in coffee and living heritages of wood products such as artifacts, handicrafts, statuettes and furniture. The area is known for its quality cultural wood products and furniture, such as beds, tables, stools, bowls, statuettes, Ethiopian Coffee tables *(Rekebot)*, and woody Cushion *(Brkuma)*. Besides being the birthplace of coffee, Jimma is also known for the coffee ceremony.

Islamic Intangible Living Heritages

Ethiopia is rich with varied intangible living heritage resources. These Islamic intangible cultural heritages are available in all parts of Ethiopia. Oral traditions, performing arts, social practices, rituals and festive events are major Islamic intangible heritages. Participants from different parts of Ethiopia cite intangible cultural heritage resources. One participant from North Ethiopia, Dessie, expresses his opinion as follows:

> [...] Wollo is a source of Islam's authentic intangible cultural heritages. In Wollo, one can listen to various traditional *Menzuma* mainly chanted by Sufi Muslims and watch Sufi dance. These are among the intangible heritages of Ethiopian society, which we do not want to change. They could be presented to the visitors as it is because it represents the local community.

Most Islamic intangible heritages are performance arts that could attract visitors looking for new experiences. A respondent from the Federal Mejlis also stated:

> [...] Ethiopian Muslims have much more intangible heritages. These intangible heritages include Islamic songs (*Menzuma*) and Islamic dance. These heritages are indigenous to Ethiopia, and Sufi Muslims still maintain those inherited habits from their ancestors, which could be transformed into products for tourists.

There are also various Islamic festivals, such as Mawlid of Prophet Muhammad (PBUH), *Ashura, Eid al Fatir* and *Eidel Adha*, where Islamic songs and dances are performed, and cultural-religious dressing systems are displayed. These intangible Islamic heritages may retain halal visitors and make them spend more if they participate in activities derived from the local culture. Another participant from the federal tourism office suggests the following:

> [...] these intangible Islamic heritages could be incorporated into cultural tourism in the area that would, in turn, motivate more halal visitors to visit. Moreover, if halal activities representing local culture and customs were organized, more halal visitors would join the tourism sector. Also, the local community could develop many halal tourism-related activities that represent their local culture, providing economic returns for a large segment of the community [...]

References

Adamu, M. M. (2009). The Legend of Queen Sheba, the Solomonic Dynasty and Ethiopian History: An Analysis. *African Research Review*, 3(1), 468–482. https://doi.org/10.4314/afrrev.v3i1.43592

Ahmed, E. A. A. K. (2013). Habasha, Abyssinia and Ethiopia: Some Notes Concerning a Country's Names and Images. *University of Khartoum Conference of Postgraduate Studies and Scientific Research: Humanities and Educational Studies*, February, 399–415.

Ahmed, M. J. (2012). *Barriers of Tourism Development and Tourists' Flow in Eastern Ethiopia: The Case of Babile and Its Environs*. Master's Thesis, Addis Ababa University.

Ahmed, H. (2004). Shaykh Jawhar b. Haydar b. ʿAlī: A mystic and scholar of Shonkē, southeast Wallo, Ethiopia. *Annales d'Ethiopie*, *20*(1), 47–56. https://doi.org/10.3406/ethio.2004.1069

Ahmed, M. J., & Akbaba, A. (2018). The Potential of Halal Tourism in Ethiopia: Opportunities, Challenges and Prospects. *International Journal of Contemporary Tourism Research*, *1*, 13–22. https://doi.org/10.30625/ijctr.397499

Ahmed, W. M. (2015). *History of Harar and the Hararis* (Issue October). Harari People Regional State Culture, Heritage and Tourism Bureau, October.

Aman, A. (2019). Identification and Documentation of Potential Tourism Resources: Its Management Practice in Focus in Jimma Town and its Vicinity, Southwestern Ethiopia. *J Tourism Hospit*, 1–8. https://doi.org/10.35248/2167-0269.19.8.418

Asante, B. (2009). Merging Past and Present: Local Level Conservation of Material Culture in the Museums of Harar, Ethiopia. *Nilo-Ethiopian Studies*, *13*, 1–16.

Aynalem, S., Akele, B., Alemayehu, H., & Molla, G. (2015). Assessment and Identification of the Tourism Resources of Bale Zone, Ethiopia. *Journal of Tourism & Hospitality*, *4*(4). https://doi.org/10.4172/2167-0269.1000176

Barich, H., & Kotler, P. (1991). A Framework for Marketing Image Management. *Sloan Management Review*, 32(2), 94–104.

Battour, M., Ismail, M. N., & Battor, M. (2010). Toward a Halal Tourism Market. *Tourism Analysis*, 15(4), 461–470. https://doi.org/10.3727/108354210X12864727453304

Bayih, B. E., & Tola, M. W. (2017). Practices and Challenges of Promoting Major Tourism Destinations of Bale Zone for Sustainable Tourism Development in Ethiopia. *African Journal of Hospitality, Tourism and Leisure*, *6*(2), 1–19

Benjamin, S., Bottone, E., & Lee, M. (2020). Beyond Accessibility: Exploring the Representation of People with Disabilities in Tourism Promotional Materials. *Journal of Sustainable Tourism*, *29*(2–3), 295–313. https://doi.org/10.1080/09669582.2020.1755295

Budge, S. E. A. W. (2000). *The Queen of Sheba and Her Only Son Menyelek (Këbra Nagast)*. Cambridge Ontario: Paranthesis Publication Ethiopian Ser.

Braukämper, U. (2006). Islamic History and Culture in Southern Ethiopia. Collected Essays. Cahiers d'études africaines (9). http://journals.openedition.org/etudesafricaines/5892 DOI: 10.4000/etudesafricaines.5892

Buhmann, A. (2015). Measuring Country Image: Theory, Method, and Effects. In *Measuring Country Image*. Springer VS. https://doi.org/10.1007/978-3-658-15407-3

Cavalazzi, B., Barbieri, R., Gómez, F., Capaccioni, B., Olsson-Francis, K., Pondrelli, M., Rossi, A. P., Hickman-Lewis, K., Agangi, A., Gasparotto, G., Glamoclija, M., Ori, G. G., Rodriguez, N., & Hagos, M. (2019). The Dallol Geothermal Area, Northern Afar (Ethiopia) – An Exceptional Planetary Field Analog on Earth. *Astrobiology*, *19*(4), 553–578. https://doi.org/10.1089/ast.2018.1926

Cerulli, E. (1971). *The Most Salient Parts, Mainly Focused on Ethiopia: Islam Yesterday and Today*. Roma Istituto Per'Oriente.

Cieśluk, K., Karasiewicz, M., & Preisner, Z. (2014). Geotouristic Attractions of the Danakil Depression. *Geotourism/Geoturystyka*, *1*((36)), 33. https://doi.org/10.7494/geotour.2014.36.33

Desplat, P., & Østebø, T. (2013). *Muslims in Ethiopia: The Christian Legacy, Identity Politics, and Islamic Reformism* (P. Desplat & T. Østebø, Eds.; Vol. 4, Issue 1). Palgrave Macmillan.

Daricha, D.N. & Weldesenbet, G.E. (2019). Religious Tourism Development in Ethiopia: Challenges and Opportunities at Adyame Yordanos Wonkshet St. Gabriel Monastery. *Journal of Tourism, Hospitality and Sports*, *40*, 2312–5179. https://doi.org/10.7176/JTH

Erlich, H. (1994). *Ethiopia and the Middle East*. Lynne Rienner Published Ltd.

Erlich, H. (2009). Islam, Christianity, Judaism, and Ethiopia: The Messages of Religions. *The Nehemia Levtzion Center for Islamic Studies*, 1–19.

Ethiopian Consititution. (1955). The 1955 *Constitution of Ethiopia'* www.abyssinialaw.com.

Eyassu, A. W., Chekole, Y. A., & Tadesse, G. T. (2019). Tourism Development Potentials and Challenges in Shonke Village, Ethiopia. *African Journal of Hospitality, Tourism and Leisure*, *8*(5), 1–16.

Fauvelle-Aymar, F.-X., Bruxelles, L., Amélie Chekroun, R. M., Olivier Onézime, A. W., Deresse Ayenatchew, H. Z., Hirsch, B., & Mohamed, A. (2006). A Topographic Survey and Some Soundings at Nora, an Ancient Muslim Town of Ethiopia. *Journal of Ethiopian Studies*, *39*(1/2), 1–11.

Federal Ministry of Culture and Tourism (2009). *Tourism Development Policy*, Federal Democratic Republic of Ethiopia, Ministry of Culture and Tourism, Addis Ababa.

Federal Ministry of Culture & Tourism. (2013). *Tourism Statistics Bulletin Tourism Statistic of Tourism 2009–2012. (Issue 10)*.

Federal Ministry of Culture & Tourism. (2016). *Tourism Statistics Bulletin (2012–2015)* (Issue 11).

Fyall, A., Garrod, B., & Leask, A. (2012). *Managing Visitor Attractions: New Directions*. Taylor and Francis. https://doi.org/10.4324/9780080496368

Getahun, B. T. (2016). Historical Survey of Tourism Industry in Ethiopia and its Potential for Economic Development: The Case of Lake Tana Region. *The International Journal of Business & Management*, *2*, 422–428.

Gnamo, H. A. (2002). Islam, the Orthodox Church and Oromo Nationalism (Ethiopia). *Cahiers d'études africaines*, *137*, 99–120. https://doi.org/10.4000/etudesafricaines.137

Gudina, M. (2003). The Elite and the Quest for Peace, Democracy and Development in Ethiopian: Lessons to be learnt Merera. *Northeast African Studies*, *10*(2), 141–164.

Hussien, A. (2001). *Islam in the Ninetenth-Cuntry, Wallo, Ethiopia: Revival, Reform and Reaction*. Brill.

Insoll, T. (2017). First Footsteps in the Archaeology of Harar, Ethiopia. *Journal of Islamic Archaeology*, *4*(2), 189–215. https://doi.org/10.1558/jia.35273

Insoll, T., Khalaf, N., Maclean, R., & Zerihun, D. (2017). Archaeological Survey and Excavations, Harlaa, Dire Dawa, Ethiopia January-February 2017. A Preliminary Fieldwork Report. *Nyame Akuma*, *87*, 32–38.

Jeenah, N. (2004). Abstract: BILQIS – A QUR'ĀNIC Model for Leadership. *Journal of Semitic Studies*, *13*(I), 47–58. http://library1.nida.ac.th/termpaper6/sd/2554/19755.pdf

Khalaf, N., & Insoll, T. (2019). Monitoring Islamic Archaeological Landscapes in Ethiopia Source Satellite Imagery. *Journal of Field Archaeology*, *44*(6), 401–419. https://doi.org/10.1080/00934690.2019.1629256

Kidane-Mariam, T. (2015). Ethiopia: Opportunities and Challenges of Tourism Development in the Addis Ababa-upper Rift Valley Corridor. *Journal of Tourism & Hospitality* *4*(4). https://doi.org/10.4172/2167-0269.1000167

Kurt, A. (2013). The Search for Prester John, a Projected Crusade and the Eroding Prestige of Ethiopian Kings, c.1200–c.1540. *Journal of Medieval History*, *39*(3), 297–320. https://doi.org/10.1080/03044181.2013.789978

Labouisse, J. P., Bellachew, B., Kotecha, S., & Bertrand, B. (2008). Current Status of Coffee (Coffea arabica L.) Genetic Resources in Ethiopia: Implications for Conservation. *Genetic Resources and Crop Evolution*, *55*(7), 1079–1093. https://doi.org/10.1007/s10722-008-9361-7

Morrison, G. E. (1971). *Prester John and Europe's Discovery of Eas Asia*. Australian National University Press.

Neima, A. (2018). *Assessment Of Al-Nejashi Religious Tourism in Tigray Regional State, Ethiopia*. Master's Thesis, Addis Ababa University.

Ramos, M. J. (2003). The Myth of Prester John and Iberian visions of Ethiopia. *Proceedings of the International Seminar on Pedro Páez in 17th Century Ethiopia*, December, 9–11.

Ramos, M. J. (2005). Ambiguous Legitimacy: the Legend of the Queen Sheba in Popular Ethiopian Painting. *Annale d'Ethiopie*, *21*, 85–92.

Rubenson, S. (2009). A Christian Island? The Impact of Colonialism on the Perceptions of Islam and Christianity in Nineteenth Century Ethiopia. In Sünne Juterczenka and Gesa Mackenthun (Eds.), *The Fuzzy Logic of Encounter: New Perspectives on Cultural Contact* (pp. 117–126). Münster.

Selamawit, K. (2013). *Thirteen Month's of Sunshine: Improving Ethiopia's Image As A Tourist Destination*. Centria University of Applied Sciences.

Semu, K. T. (2016). Dynamics of the Cult of Sheik Hussein of Bale, Ethiopia: Its Course and Curse of the Extremists, a Historical Perspective. *Ethiopian Journal of the Social Sciences and Humanities*, *12*(1), 63–101.

Shanka, T., & Frost, F. A. (1999). The Perception of Ethiopia as a Tourist Destination: An Australian Perspective. *Asia Pacific Journal of Tourism Research*, *4*(1), 1–11. https://doi.org/10.1080/10941669908722025

Sisay, A. (2009). *Historical Development of Travel and Tourism in Ethiopia* Kuraz

Steen, W. M., & Constitution, E. (1936). *The Ethiopian Constitution*. Ethiopian Research Council.

Tasci, A. D. A. (2009). A Semantic Analysis of Destination Image Terminology. *Tourism Review International*, *13*(1), 65–78. https://doi.org/10.3727/154427209789130648

Tola, S. (2009). *The Conservation of Dirre Sheikh Hussein Heritage Site*. Oromia Culture and Tourism Bureau.

Trimingham, J. S. (1952). *Islam in Ethiopia*. Oxford University Press.

Tucker, C. M. (2011). *Coffee Culture: Local Experiences, Global Connections*. Routledge Taylor and Francis Group.

World Bank (2006a). *Ethiopia: Towards a Strategy for Pro-Poor Tourism Development. (Report No 38420 –ET)*. Addis Ababa:Ethiopia: World Bank

World Bank. (2006b). *Ethiopia: Towards a Strategy for Pro-Poor Tourism Development (Report No. 38420 –ET)*. Addis Ababa, Ethiopia: World Bank.

5 Challenges and Prospects to Halal Tourism Development

Focus on Ethiopia

Research Objectives

The general objective of this thesis is to appraise the potential, challenges and prospects of halal tourism development in Ethiopia. The book has the following objectives: (a) analyzing definitional and conceptual ambiguities of halal tourism and related typologies and proposing terminologies for halal and Islam (b) assessing whether tourism, by its very nature, is unIslamic from the viewpoint of the Quran and Sunnah, especially to appraise what has been written in the Quran and Hadith concerning travel and tourism; (c) assessing the knowledge and attitudes of local people and stakeholders toward halal tourism development in Ethiopia; (d) inventorying and assessing the potential of halal tourism resources in Ethiopia; (e) identifying and mapping halal tourism routes in Ethiopia and (f) identifying opportunities and barriers to halal tourism development in Ethiopia. These objectives are addressed throughout the book.

Basic Research Questions

The following basic research questions have been derived from the preceding specific objectives. The basic research questions, therefore, more or less correspond to the specific objectives of the study. (a) What are the definitional and conceptual ambiguities of halal tourism, and what should be the proper definition of halal tourism? What knowledge and attitudes do the local people and stakeholders have toward halal tourism development in Ethiopia? (c) Is tourism unIslamic by its very nature? (d) Are there adequate halal tourism resources in Ethiopia? (e) What are the potential halal tourism routes in Ethiopia? (f) What are the opportunities and barriers to halal tourism development in Ethiopia?

Research Methodology

This study was both exploratory and descriptive. An exploratory approach and qualitative techniques help elicit complex data that would not be described by using quantitative research methods. This study aimed to assess

DOI: 10.4324/9781003355236-6

the nature and feasibility of halal tourism development in the Ethiopian context and generate fresh insight into the field. The study, therefore, employed an exploratory approach and qualitative techniques to appraise the complex data that would not be possible through quantitative methods. The study seeks to identify halal visitors' attractions and propose halal routes. According to Stebbins (2019), exploratory research helps produce basic knowledge, sheds light on relevant concepts and identifies themes. As Stebbins further describes, an explorative approach is the preferred methodological approach when the problem under consideration has received little or no systematic empirical scrutiny and aims to generate new ideas and weave them together to form a theory. Battour (2019) claims that the inductive approach is appropriate for conducting an exploratory study, and therefore, the inductive approach was used. The inductive approach helps to induce knowledge from empirical data instead of testing preset theories. An exploratory approach was chosen because no previous studies have been conducted on the subject in Ethiopia. Qualitative methods are appropriate for theory building instead of theory testing.

As its very name indicates, qualitative research methods and techniques give rise to qualitative data in the form of words, images and sounds (Veal, 2018). This method helps generate rich, thick and deep information. Qualitative research includes collecting, analyzing, and understanding data based on observations, focus group discussions and face-to-face interactions with the research participants. It helps learn how people feel and what they think about the issue under discussion. The general premise of qualitative techniques is that the people personally involved in halal tourism can appropriately describe and explain their experiences or feelings in their own words (Cater & Low, 2012; McGehee, 2012; Ribeiro & Foemmel, 2012). The qualitative method helps collect nonverbal data. Nonverbal data are very important in tourism studies but are mainly overlooked. Nonverbal data is mainly gathered from facial expressions such as smiles and grimaces of visitors or the local people (Veal, 2018) and gestures such as hands and head movements as well as eye contact are means of collecting nonverbal data. Notes have been taken on such behavior as they occur. During interpretations, the recorded participants' videotape behavior helped the researchers enrich descriptions and interpretations.

Until recently, there was a tendency for researchers to prefer quantitative to qualitative methods in tourism research (Cater & Low, 2012). However, scholars such as Veal (2018); McGehee (2012) claim that since the 1980s, researchers have leaned toward a qualitative method for leisure and tourism research because qualitative methods enable researchers to sense the very experiences of visitors and services at each touchpoint. The qualitative method is not inherently good over the quantitative, but the former is appropriate for the present study. As noted by Battour (2019), the choice of methodology is not a question of the quality of one method over another but a matter of suitability to the particular study because both qualitative and quantitative methods are equally important. However, according to Veal

(2018), qualitative research has advantages over quantitative research in tourism. It is well suited to investigate emotions, symbols and gestures that matter a lot in tourism study. Qualitative methods are most appropriate when the focus of interest is the qualitative experience of leisure or tourism, personal leisure or tourism. It is also advisable to use qualitative methods when symbols, gestures in tourism contexts, and people's tourism needs and aspirations are essential in the study. The qualitative research method helps gather sophisticated details about the study under consideration and to explore the emotions and feelings associated with halal holidays. Generally, the qualitative approach is preferable to answer questions such as when, why, who and how of a particular phenomenon in their natural settings.

Participants of the Study

Participants of this study were chosen carefully because participants have a very powerful impact on qualitative research. The study participants included purposefully selected local communities living in the study area, such as religious leaders, government officials, investors, people employed in the tourism sector in the study area, tourism professionals and scholars, tour operators in Addis Ababa and both domestic and foreign tourists. In this study, terminologies such as participants, informants and interviewees will be used interchangeably.

Sample Size and Sampling Techniques

Convenience and purposive sampling techniques are the main sampling techniques in qualitative studies (Veal, 2018). Because of the scarcity of resources and time, the involvement of the entire study population is impossible in reality. Therefore, the sampling system is used to draw representatives of the entire population. Qualitative research pays attention to the quality of data but does not concern with the number of cases or participants. Hence, samples were purposefully selected (Jennings, 2005); however, there is no defined mechanism to predetermine the number of samples ahead of data collection. Qualitative data collection continues until the qualitative informational isomorph or theoretical saturation is achieved. It could be said that theoretical saturation is reached when information from participants becomes repetitive, no new ideas are generated, and no new themes emerge. At that time, data collectors could stop collecting data from additional participants because additional informants would no longer generate new ideas or make a difference. Jennings (2005) also noted that the principle of theoretical sampling determines qualitative data gathering. Therefore, the sample size of qualitative research is determined by data saturation.

The participants were selected based on a purposive and convenience sampling approach. The Snowball sampling method was also used to reach tourism professionals who had a better experience in halal tourism research. Convenience sampling is widely used during exploratory research and is perhaps the best way of collecting basic information efficiently. Therefore, these various approaches were used to draw appropriate samples. The samples were purposely selected based on convenience and purposive sampling techniques. Convenience sampling applies to making the sample from a group of people easy to access or contact. For example, the researchers collected data at an airport and star-rated hotel from halal-conscious inbound tourists about halal tourism development in Ethiopia.

Samples have been selected based on their experience, exposure, role and influence on policymaking in the tourism industry of the study area. Accordingly, 25 foreign tourists, 50 domestic visitors, 50 residents, 7 people from the culture and tourism bureau of the study area and 6 individuals from the Ethiopian Islamic Affairs Supreme Council (Mejlis), 2 people from the Ethiopian investment commission, 10 tour guides, 5 tour operators, and 17 tourism and business professionals and scholars were interviewed. Totally, 172 individuals were interviewed in different parts of Ethiopia, and 61 other individuals were engaged in eight focus group discussions (FGDs). Most of the interviews were conducted between April 2019 and October 2019 in various settings such as interviewees' homes, places of work, and at different places mainly where visitors are available such as airplanes, cafeterias, resorts, airports, star-rated hotels, and different offices and at visitor sites. Some religious leaders have been interviewed at mosques. Interviews have been conducted in airplanes and cars while traveling. Interviews lasted between 30 to 120 minutes.

Regarding demographic profile, of the total 233 interviewees and group discussants, most of the participants 201 were Muslims, 32 non-Muslims, 150 were males, and 83 were females. They were between 18 and 80 years old. Non-Muslims were interviewed in order to learn about their attitudes toward halal tourism. On top of that, important information was gathered through informal interviews and discussions as well as from mainstream media and social media. Therefore, 233 participants directly participated in this study as key informants.

Study Area

The study was conducted in Ethiopia. Ethiopia is a horn African country comprising 11 regional states, namely Tigray, Afar, Amhara, Oromia, Somali, Benshangul Gumuz, South Nation Nationalities and Peoples, Gambela, Harari and Sidama, South West Ethiopia Peoples' Region and two federal city Administrations, namely Addis Ababa and Dire Dawa. Ethiopia was selected because of the following reasons: (1) Ethiopia is endowed with Islamic Heritages. The country is rich in tangible and intangible Islamic heritages that greatly assist in developing halal tourism. Being the first country in the world next to Saudi Arabia to welcome Islam, Ethiopia consists of several antique Islamic heritages. (2) As someone born and raised in Ethiopia, the principal researcher identified research problems in Ethiopia. Moreover, as a participant observant, the researcher had good knowledge about halal

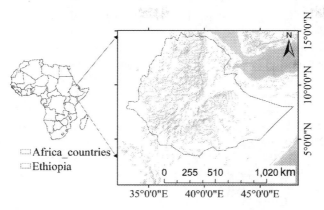

Map 5.1 Map of the study area, by the researchers.

tourism potential in Ethiopia. (3) These days, the Ethiopian government envisages utilizing tourism as a development tool. Hence, it is crucial to make halal tourism one important niche.

Data Collection Procedures

During the initial data collection phase, the researchers compiled relevant statistics, policy documents and existing research on Ethiopian and halal tourism and traced key informants. This mainly entails the consultation of the existing literature and additional archival research in libraries, archives and the internet to learn about experiences and trends of halal tourism development. This strategy helped the researchers see the study in a broader context and avoid the duplication of research that had already been conducted elsewhere. It also helped the researcher identify gaps in the existing similar works. The researchers made an in-depth comparison between secondary and primary data that were gathered in the later phase. At the end of this stage, the researchers created and tested interview protocols.

Based on the developed protocol, semi-structured and unstructured interviews were prepared and addressed to the participants (see Appendix). These interviews help explore the available enabling situations, what people think about halal tourism development, and why they hold these images, perceptions and attitudes toward it. The researcher recorded and transcribed the interviews.

The researchers got cooperation letters from Izmir Katip Celebi University. They contacted key informants at Bole International airport, the ministry of culture and tourism, the Ethiopian investment commission, Bilalul Habesha Community Museum and Exhibition Center, the Ethiopian Islamic affairs supreme council (*Mejlis*), tour operators and travel agencies, government officials and hotel companies. After contacting the selected institutions, the researcher got permission from all these institutions to conduct the research. The field data collections were in two phases. The first phase of the data collection period lasted from April 2019 to October 2019, whereas the second phase lasted from August 2020 to October 2020. The research employed qualitative and exploratory semi-structured and unstructured interviews and group discussions. The field research was conducted sequentially in two ways: the first is observation and the second is interviews consisting of in-depth focus group discussions and individual interviews. Before the face-to-face interview phase, the research objectives were explained to the study participants. The interview data were also compressed into similar themes per the research objectives to identify convenience themes in the interview course.

Another important data employed in this study is known as virtual data. Virtual data means data collected by using the internet or online platforms. These days, many researchers collect data through the internet without face-to-face contact between the researcher and participants. Especially after the coronavirus (COVID-19) had emerged, researchers have changed ways of collecting data from face-to-face to virtual/internet. Though there was no direct contact between the researchers and the participants, the researchers were able to provoke the responses of the participants. Hence, a 'virtual' discussion or a 'virtual' focus group was also used in the data collection process. The use of phone and video interviews allowed the researchers to contact informants from across the globe easily, probe for more information and clarification when needed through additional questioning and gather rich data about the subject under consideration. All interviews and group discussions were conducted in English and Amharic.

Ethical Consideration

Qualitative studies mainly employ human beings as the participants and the researchers. Therefore, in addition to working on issues such as finding data and enhancing reliability and validity, serious measures were taken to avoid any physical or psychological harm to the participants. Before the interviews or discussions were carried out, the participants had been oriented about the purposes of the study. Derogatory and culturally taboo terminologies had been avoided as much as possible. While interpreting qualitative data, consideration was taken to keep the security and confidentiality of transcripts and digital files. Veal (2018) alleges that as a precaution, research material should use pseudonyms or codes instead of the real names of participants. Accordingly, the author has employed codes instead of real names throughout this thesis.

Data Collection Techniques

The data were collected through qualitative methods such as interviews, observation, FGD and content analysis. These qualitative methods helped the researcher gather deep and varied data; secondly, they allowed the participants to describe their thoughts and feelings. This, in return, helped the researcher include the actual feeling, attitudes and perceptions of research

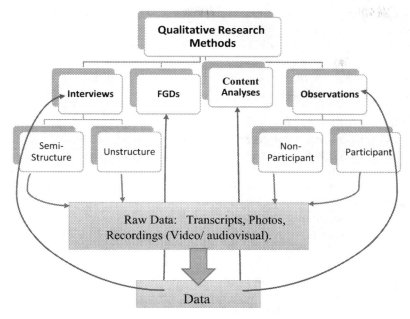

Figure 5.1 Research method design.
Source: By the Authors.

participants. Especially in-depth interviews were utilized to elicit deep, thick and rich data from participants about their expectations of halal holidays, halal products and demands (Battour, 2019). Therefore, various types of qualitative techniques (multi-methods) have been employed and triangulated in the study under discussion.

Quran and Sunnah are primary sources of the study under consideration because Islamic jurisprudence is derived from thereof. Content analysis has been widely utilized to interpret the Quran and Sunnah from the viewpoint of the current study. Data collection and analysis have taken place mainly concurrently, and writing up is often evolutionary and ongoing rather than a separate process, unlike the quantitative one that mainly takes place at the end of the project (Veal, 2018).

Interview

An interview is the most common qualitative data-gathering method (Jennings, 2005; McGehee, 2012). It helped the researchers obtain the participants' natural perceptions and attitudes to the issues. Interviewing ranges from informal 'chats' to highly structured interviews. McGehee (2012) recommends maintaining an appropriate social space between the researcher and the research participants. The interview is believed to be the most appropriate in tourism research because persons engaged in tourism are often in a position to share their discretionary time with researchers while they are on vacation. The researchers believe that the subject under discussion was properly addressed through a qualitative interview in which participants share their thoughts and experiences with the researcher directly in their own words. It has been proved that qualitative interviews are usually effective methods to gather detailed data in tourism studies. It also enables interviewees to reveal their internal picture of the subject under consideration as openly and fully as possible.

To conclude, interview techniques allowed the researcher to appraise obstacles and opportunities of halal tourism development in a deep, rich and detailed manner. As true for other methods, careful attention was paid, and the interview course was passed through appropriate procedures to minimize its limitations and maximize its strengths.

According to Jennings (2005), the interview can be classified into unstructured, semi-structured and structured interviews. However, only semi-structured and unstructured interviews were used in this study.

Semi-structured

Interview questions are loosely structured, allowing flexibility to explore various issues. The semi-structured interview is commonly used to address key themes and specific questions. A semi-structured interview is flexible and helps the researcher respond to the interviewees' answers and develop the themes and issues as they arise. Idea generator interviews are usually applied at the set out of a research project to discover and explore issues from a particular group or community.

Unstructured Interview

This method has been widely used in the study under discussion to explore the full breadth of a topic. As stated by Veal (2018), an in-depth interview is usually conducted with a relatively small number of participants where a checklist of topics is used to guide the course of the interview instead of legal questions. Hence, several checklists that address the objectives of this thesis were used.

Focus Group Discussion

Focus group discussion, also known as group interviews, is a qualitative data collection tool conducted with a group of mainly 6 to 12 discussants (Cater & Low, 2012). Most of the time, the discussion is managed by a facilitator, mainly researchers or co-researchers who oversee the discussion. Accordingly, the researcher has overseen all the focus group discussions. Free interaction between discussants was encouraged to generate deep and thick data. Group discussions have been recorded and transcribed. In all focus group discussions, the researcher had the opportunity to interact directly with participants in a social setting. This, in turn, enabled the researcher to sense the participants' actual feelings and natural responses. As someone who lived and grew up in the study area, the researcher was familiar with the culture of the discussants and was able to create a more relaxed atmosphere for further discussion. Therefore, information gathered from discussion groups is often more varied, deep and factual than if participants had been interviewed on a one-to-one basis. FGD also has an advantage over one-to-one interviews in that the former provides in-depth information from several individuals simultaneously, and intragroup members' discussion may give rise new dimension to the subject under consideration.

Eight focus group discussions were conducted from April 2019 to October 2019. Generally, 61 discussants participated in eight FGDs, and invaluable data were generated from that place. The questions and themes addressed during a discussion group are more or less similar to the interviews. The questions aim at fact-finding and idea-generating and are exploratory and experiential. The discussants were asked relevant and open questions so that the discussions could broaden, more ideas were generated, and new themes emerged. The researcher encouraged and captured emerging ideas in the discussion. At the same time, it has been tried to ensure that the discussion focuses on the key themes.

Observations

Observation is a systematic way of watching and listening to a phenomenon (Ribeiro & Foemmel, 2012). There are two types of observation: participant and non-participant.

Participant Observations

Ribeiro and Foemmel (2012) and Veal (2018) claim that participant observation is an important data collection instrument in tourism. For example, it would be difficult to learn the actual and factual attitude of the locals toward halal tourism and to identify halal tourism resources by using only questionnaires and interviews. Being a part of the local community and involved in its activities is the best way to learn the natural and genuine interest and perception of the community and local resources. Moreover, a researcher involved in the study could use tourist facilities and amenities as well as a sense attitude of the host toward tourism development. As someone who was born, lived, grew up and worked in the study area, the researcher was able to collect data through participant observations. If researchers are to study tourist destinations, they must inevitably be visitors to those destinations (Ribeiro & Foemmel, 2012). It is very difficult to understand the depth and width of the halal tourism development obstacles and opportunities unless the researcher personally faces and tests them because sometimes the participants would not be genuine for different reasons. Participant observation helped the researcher understand the very nature and prospects of halal tourism development in Ethiopia. In tourism development, participant observation could allow the planners to identify sites, map tourist routes, reallocate resources and improve facility use. Therefore, participant observation as a methodology has played a significant role in the study under consideration. The researcher has a prolonged interaction and iterations with the people being researched, and he has immersed himself into the participants' local environment in order to learn more about the identified topic from the real perspectives of the lives and culture of the host community. As a participant-observer, he not only observed but also faced the actual challenges in person and therefore, the researcher was able to overcome participants' natural mistrust of outsiders, which, in turn, enabled him to collect not only detail but also genuine data that would be difficult if not impossible to obtain in other techniques.

Non-Participant Observation

Non-participation observation is a type of qualitative data collection technique when a researcher does not get involved directly in the activities of the research study but remains a passive observer. In some areas, the researcher collected data as a passive observer. Whenever participant observation was impossible, non-participation observations were widely employed.

Content Analysis

In the present research, the Holy Quran and Sunnah were the two important documents to be analyzed from the perspectives of tourism. Therefore, content analyzes were employed to interpret verses of the Quran that touch tourism and travel directly and indirectly and some hadith texts that deal with tourism and travel. Moreover, related journal articles, books, conference papers, tourism promotion brochures and magazines, annual governmental reports, itineraries and moto were analyzed.

The Interview Guiding Questions and Checklists

While guiding questions were used for semi-structured interviews, the checklists were employed for unstructured interviews, in-depth interviews and FGDs. As mentioned earlier, before commencing the interviews, a literature review of the existing studies related to halal tourism development was carried out. This review helps to formulate appropriate interview questions and checklists. Based on the previous similar research and the present research questions, interview guiding questions and a checklist have been developed to maintain the interview's focus and ensure that all themes and issues were covered. This short list of questions and themes was also useful to begin the discussion and ensure that the discussion does not deviate from the scope of the study. The questions were designed to encourage participants to express their thoughts and feelings freely. However, it does not mean that the questions in the interview guide were necessarily asked in the same order. Questions were asked without keeping their order, and additional questions were asked based on the reply of the interviewees.

The interviews were recorded and transcribed. Most of the data for the study under discussion were collected through a series of in-depth unstructured interviews. As its name indicates, in-depth interviews tend to be longer, deeper and more detailed than structured and semi-structured interviews (Veal, 2018). Therefore, the interviews lasted from half an hour to three hours. Moreover, some participants were interviewed more than once. During all interviews, participants were encouraged to discuss, ask additional questions and freely explain their thoughts and feelings.

Data Interpretation

The collected data were presented in different forms, such as photos, objects, audio, videos and transcripts. These raw empirical materials were interpreted using qualitative descriptions and principles of grounded theory. Since this research is a qualitative study, it was guided by the grounded theory approach, whereby explorative research leads to develop new theories.

There are some known procedures to analyze qualitative data. The initial steps in qualitative data interpretation are to classify and organize the information collected. Reading transcripts and listening to or viewing audio and video materials are the preliminary tasks in qualitative analysis. The researcher read transcripts and watched the audiovisual materials as soon as the empirical material collection was completed. Accordingly, a large body of collected information was sorted and geared into common themes through inductive reasoning. Then grounded theory interpretations, content analysis and empirical material interpretation were deployed.

Qualitative data obtained from interviews, field notes, observations and analysis of documents were identified and grouped into common themes. As Veal (2018) argues, identifying themes is part of analyzing qualitative materials. Themes in qualitative research are considered as the variables in quantitative research. The themes were derived from the conceptual framework and the basic research questions. Themes have been framed before data collection, in the course of data collection and after the data collection process. After identifying themes, a cataloging approach was used to group participants' comments associated with particular themes. Data was collected by using different instruments analyzed under themes that fit better. Then, the collected information was analyzed through qualitative descriptions.

Methodological Integrity and Trustworthiness

In qualitative research, triangulation helps to ensure the research's trustworthiness, transferability, integrity and credibility. Data triangulation implies collecting information from different participants using different data collection tools. According to Creswell and Miller (2000), triangulation refers to employing different data sources and examining shreds of evidence. Bashir et al. (2008) argue that triangulation refers to employing different sources of information to increase the credibility of a study. They argue that employing multimodal qualitative methods helps to ensure the research's trustworthiness, transferability and credibility. Creswell (2003) claims that spending enough time in the field and employing multiple data collection strategies could minimize the biases of qualitative findings. Knox and Burkard (2009) argue that employing multiple methods such as observation, interviews and [focus groups] ensures the trustworthiness and quality of qualitative findings. Accordingly, multimethod qualitative research has been employed in this study to produce credible and consistent results. Qualitative methods such as interviews, focus group discussion, observation and content analyses were simultaneously employed. Therefore, to ascertain the reliability of the data, data obtained by one data collection tool were cross-checked by other tools. For instance, information obtained from interviews was cross-checked by focus group discussion, observation or document analyses, and the other way round.

Problems Faced during Data Collection

Several problems emerged during data collection. The most serious of these was the challenge of identifying institutions and key informants. Initially, it was challenging to identify the ideal participants for this study. It was challenging to convince organizations such as airports, star-rated hotels and even individual participants. It was also difficult to access some sites and attractions. The researcher had to wait a week or more to go to some destinations due to the prevalence of violent demonstrations and instability around some sites. This process was both time-consuming and enervating. The prevalence of instability, civil uprising, and strikes heavily affected the data collection process of this study. There have been serious civil disobedience and violent demonstrations since 2012 in Ethiopia. These disobediences were expressed in boycotts and road blockades. These violent activities forced the researcher to postpone some of the scheduled group discussions, observations and interviews.

Moreover, the instability also posed security threats during data collection. Another critical challenge during data collection was the newness of 'halal tourism' for many participants. Many Ethiopians, especially non-Muslims, did not want to hear the term 'halal tourism' because they considered it to propagate Islam. Hence, the researcher faced serious challenges from government officials and other stakeholders in this regard. Even though this situation helped the researcher learn the level of their knowledge and attitude about halal tourism, it was a tedious task to orient and convince them. Finally, the last stage of data collection was challenged by the COVID-19 pandemic. Even though more than 95% of data was collected during the coronavirus pandemic breakout, the pandemic impacted the data collection process. Especially in the final term of data collection, which lasted from September 2020 to October 2020, coronavirus had a negative impact.

However, the following remedial steps were taken to maintain the study's quality and credibility: scarifying the time and money it requests. The first problem was solved by scarifying time and conducting a pilot study. Therefore, concerned institutions and key informants were identified. Snowball sampling was utilized to reach some tourism scholars who know halal tourism. In such a way, key informants were identified.

The second problem was addressed by convincing those identified institutions and individuals. Hence, they were convinced by explaining the very objectives of the thesis. Series orientation was given to the participants about the concept of halal tourism and the study's objectives. In such a way, the existing misunderstandings, misconceptions and suspicions were curved. Finally, the challenge caused by COVID-19 was changed into opportunities. The researcher could access sites by using public transport and spending nights at farmers' homes when there is no transportation in some countryside. The researcher collected the remaining data through online platforms such as zoom, skype, telegram and WhatsApp.

Data Interpretation and Findings

In the previous section, the organized aspect of this thesis was discussed. This section will describe the study's findings in systematic, thematic and detailed ways. The themes that emerge from the analysis of qualitative results will be highlighted.

Halal Tourism Knowledge and Awareness

The first set of questions aimed to discern the extent of participants' knowledge about halal tourism and assess their attitude toward halal tourism development in Ethiopia. Accordingly, research participants were asked whether they had some prior knowledge, concepts and awareness about halal tourism.

When asked about what he knew about halal tourism, one participant (Muslim) argued as follows:

> We need the development of halal tourism […]. […] no doubt that I have known about halal tourism. I sometimes travel to resorts and entertainment centers to refresh my body and soul on weekends, and I saw some Muslims suffer from a lack of halal services and products there. I think people in Ethiopia do not understand what halal services and products mean. In other words, men and women were mixing, which did not give comfort to Muslims. They would also need halal services, but there was no one to offer them. My friends and I have a plan to invest in halal tourism.

This quote implies that Muslims not only understand halal tourism but also ask for it. Some non-Muslims also know halal tourism. For example, the owner of one tour operator company states as follows:

> Not only are we aware of the concept of halal tourism, but also of the huge potential for halal tourism development in Ethiopia. We have halal tourism packages and customers of halal visitors from Pakistan, India, Sudan and Turkey. I know halal tourism does not contradict other non-Muslim Ethiopians' and/or Ethiopians' values. It is rather in favor of our very culture. Though the fact about halal tourism is this one, it does not mean that some people do not hold a negative attitude towards the term halal. By considering the term halal as Islamic, some people consider halal tourism a business of Muslims for Muslims. However, this is a faulty generalization. I am not Muslim, but I am engaging in halal tourism. Halal tourism is a very lucrative business. I will specialize in halal tourism.

The preceding quote indicates that people with a better knowledge of tourism hold a positive attitude toward halal tourism and its establishment in Ethiopia.

The results of individual and group interviews indicate that although most participants, mainly Muslims, are familiar with the halal tourism concept, some Muslims and most non-Muslim participants have limited knowledge of halal tourism. When the participants were asked what they knew about halal tourism, most Christian participants reported that they had never heard about it. As far as non-Muslims are concerned, only people who have exposure to the tourism business know about halal tourism. For them, the term 'halal' only refers to the Islamic slaughtering system. Therefore, most non-Muslim participants perceive halal tourism as the Islamic way of slaughtering animals or poultry. On the contrary, a significant number of Muslims know about halal tourism and only a few Muslims associated halal tourism purely with food, mainly the slaughtering system.

Some Christian participants consider halal tourism identical to Islamic tourism, designed only for Muslims. They believe that halal tourism development would bring division between Christians and Muslims. For instance, when one participant is interviewed about his understanding of halal tourism, he responds: 'I do not agree with the establishment of halal tourism in multi-religious countries like Ethiopia. Halal tourism may fit Arabs, but it creates religious-based fractures among Ethiopians. I believe halal tourism excludes non-Muslims.' This interviewee tried to associate halal tourism not only with Islam but also with Arabs. Indeed, many Ethiopians associate Islam itself with Arabs.

Another non-Muslim participant argues:

> Ethiopia is a country of Muslims and Christians. We do not need halal tourism, which I think excludes non-Muslims. These days, Muslims are

establishing their own Islamic Banks, and now you are talking about halal tourism; it is also an Islamic business, so I'm afraid I disagree with this project.

According to this interviewee, some people are suspicious of halal business, so they resist halal tourism development in Ethiopia. Few non-Muslim government officers and other informants similarly reflect such views. This indicates that some non-Muslims consider halal tourism as an Islamic business that excludes non-Muslims. They also fear that Islamic values will dominate the country's public space. However, such explanations overlook that halal tourism has nothing to do with religion.

Compared with non-Muslims who are not in the tourism business or are not tourism experts, non-Muslims who are engaged in the tourism business or tourism experts hold a positive attitude toward halal tourism. Few of them have participated in the halal tourism business. The responses of tour operator participants indicate that they knew what the halal concept means and what halal tourism includes. In contrast, only a few participants from tour operators do not know about it.

The study participants' responses reveal that Muslims and non-Muslims have different attitudes toward halal tourism. Many Muslims seem well aware of the concept of halal tourism. Some Muslims can even identify the country's potential for halal tourism. Specially educated Muslims seem very aware of the lucrativeness of halal tourism, and some Muslims show a high interest in investing in halal tourism. Even though Muslim participants understand halal tourism's concepts, potentials, opportunities and challenges, some non-Muslims have misconceptions and misunderstandings about halal tourism.

Tourism in Islam

A debate has long prevailed concerning whether there is a contradiction between the very principle of Islam and tourism. The place and status of tourism and travel in the Islamic scriptures of the Quran and Sunnah were rigorously addressed in Chapter 2. The opinions of Muslim scholars concerning the issue of tourism and travel in Islam were presented as follows. Participants of this study (Muslim religious leaders) were asked to explain whether tourism is allowed in Islam and/or whether Islam discourages visitation. The overwhelming majority of participants felt that there is no contradiction between tourism and Islam. According to some informants, there are also situations where tourism becomes mandatory in Islam. For instance, one participant says, 'Tourism could become an *ibadah* [worship] if traveling intends to please Allah and if one can avoid the transgressions on principles of Islam throughout his way and at the destinations.' This claim implies that tourism is not only permissible in Islam, but also Islam encourages its adherents to encourage halal tourism.

One interviewee (Mosque Imam) reinforces the claim above as follows:

> [...] tourism can even be an *ibadah* if traveling is for the sake of blessing Allah and if the travelers can avoid wrongdoings throughout their journeys. If what they see, where they stay, what they consume and what they do are halal. Islam prohibits Muslims from consuming pork and drinking alcoholic beverages. Therefore, visitors should refrain from consuming such things.

This quote also indicates no inherent contradiction between tourism and Islam. However, activities and products during visitations matter a lot. For instance, Muslims are forbidden to visit a site where haram services and products are served.

Another participant also argues, '[...] travel and tourism in Islam should not be hedonistic but purposeful.' According to this participant, Muslims should not spend their time on irrelevant activities when they engage in tourism. This, however, does not mean that their visitation is necessarily religious but must be purposeful. Another participant from Ethiopian Federal *Mejlis* states the following:

> Tourism is permissible in Islam and part and parcel of Islam itself. One of the five pillars of Islam is the hajj. Hajj is nothing but halal tourism. In our office, we have a department that facilitates hajj. This implies that tourism is not only allowable in Islam but also part of Islam. Halal tourism in Islam is recommendable; in some situations (when a Muslim can do so), it could be obligatory, for instance, hajj. However, in Islam, tourism is allowed with preconditions. When I say preconditions, the visitation must be halal. People should not transgress the sharia principles. As far as no factors affect their religious practice, Muslims are allowed to travel and enjoy themselves. Our sharia is clear. People are encouraged to see what Allah creates and contemplate. You can observe what Allah creates and praise Him!

The opinion of the majority of participants was similar to the above quote.

One participant expressed his concerns as follows:

> [...] I do not think Islam does contradict tourism inherently. However, people made tourism anti-Islam. Nowadays, tourism has become synonymous with bars, alcoholism and gambling. These things are unequivocally forbidden in Islam. Unless it changes its present forms and practices, tourism could be haram to Muslims.

According to the above statements, though tourism, by definition, is not anti-Islam, activities that accompany tourism could make it anti-Muslim. A lot must be done to liberate tourism from such anti-Muslim practices. Put another way, halal tourism is one mechanism to liberate tourism from haram

Challenges and Prospects to Halal Tourism Development 161

activities and products. Some participants expressed their concerns about the halalness of halal tourism. The result of the focus group discussion also reveals that there has been almost a consensus among Muslim scholars over the permission of halal tourism in Islam. Most participants state that tourism is not only allowed in Islam but also encouraged. Some discussants argue that Islam encourages its adherents to travel for secular or religious reasons. However, all discussants recommended that Muslims should use halal products and services, and they should not ignore religious duties while traveling. It is worth noting that travelers are exempted from some religious duties and have privileges over others (see Chapter 2). The interviewees and the discussants have raised tourism status in the Ethiopian context. Almost all of the Muslim scholar participants in the study criticize how tourism is operated in Ethiopia.

One interviewee expressed his feeling in this regard as the following:

> [...] unfortunately, tourism has been synonymous with bars and prostitution in Ethiopia. There are no services and products offered for halal-conscious visitors. Hence, practicing Muslims have been systematically excluded from tourism because, on the one side, there are no halal products and services. On the other side, anti-Muslim products and activities surround tourism. Because of these factors, tourism in Ethiopia is now unwelcoming for practicing Muslims. However, it does not mean that tourism inherently contradicts Islam. The way we use it could make tourism a cursed or a blessed activity. If we use it without transgressing the tenets of Islam, tourism can be not only permissible but also a religiously rewarding act, *Ibada* or worship. However, if haram activities surround tourism or there are no halal products and services, tourism could be forbidden for Muslims [...].

According to the above statement, Muslim scholars have confirmed the positive relationship between tourism and Islam. However, they expressed that the way people implement tourism is anti-Islam. Especially in Ethiopia, those who engage in the tourism business associate tourism with anti-Islam activities such as alcoholism, prostitution and gambling.

Another participant argues:

> Tourism is one pillar of Islam. [...] indeed, tourism did not contradict Islam by its very nature, but eventually, it adopted some unIslamic practices. Allah (SWT) has ordered people to travel, visit His creatures, and perform a pilgrimage to Mecca. Prophet Muhammad (PBUH) also encourages people to visit [...]. Tourism subsumes Hajj, which is one of Islam's fifth pillars. Without Hajj, Islam cannot be full.

Hence, tourism is not only allowable but also a must-do activity in this case.

Overall, there is a consensus among participants (mainly religious leaders) that there are no inherent contradictions between the very principle of Islam and tourism; however, tourism currently deviates from its very purpose by incorporating haram products and services as if they are a core part of tourism. They, more or less, agree that Islam encourages its adherents to engage in halal tourism for religious or secular purposes. The participants recommend the development of halal tourism in Ethiopia. They want tourism stakeholders to invest in halal tourism.

Experiences and Reflections of Halal-Conscious Travelers

The knowledge and attitude of participants have been discussed in the preceding section. The section below critically examines the real-life experience of halal-conscious visitors. Halal-conscious visitors who once upon a time engaged in tourism were asked to share their experiences and challenges they faced. Almost all Muslim interviewees express their discontent with alcoholic drinks in public spaces of various touchpoints such as tourism sites, shopping malls, hotels and parks. They were unpleased when they saw people drinking alcohol in common areas of the hotel. They proposed that airline and hotel operators should designate non-drinking spaces. Even Christian participants were concerned about the safety of their children when they were around alcohol drinkers, and they feared their children might be accustomed to alcoholic beverages.

One of the participants expressed his experience as follows:

> [...] I had seen when some kids a bottle of beer and drink it. The one who put the beer in rooms disappointed me because children cannot differentiate the disadvantages and advantages of alcoholic beverages. I believe that children should not be exposed to such alcoholic beverages. Therefore, hoteliers should not put alcohol in rooms without the customers' request. If they could not abandon selling alcohol, at least they should designate specific places for alcohol users [...].

Other participants' responses also indicate that people who travel with children prefer an alcohol-free environment. These experiences indicate that travelers with children were also discontented with the presence of alcohol in their rooms or around. Therefore, it is most likely that people with children prefer halal tourism to other forms of tourism.

Halal-conscious visitors were also asked about Islamic dress codes. Most of the interviewees reported that they prefer to have hostesses and waitresses with a moderate dress code. Muslim travelers prefer waitpersons wearing modest *hijabs* (headscarves) and unexposed dresses. Most Muslim interviewees said they felt free when the female staff at hotels dressed *Hijab* and appropriate dresses. However, these suggestions could be difficult to apply in liberal Ethiopia, where the wearing of *hijab* is not even allowed in some public areas and some big institutions such as Ethiopian Airlines and star-rated hotels. In Ethiopia, *Hijab-clad* women are not allowed to work in some institutions such as Ethiopian Airlines and star hotels. Moreover, some interviewees suggested it would be better for employees to be Muslims.

Practicing Muslim participants suggest hostesses and waitpersons to wear moderate dresses instead of tight clothes.

> Hijab with moderate dresses is advised to be the dominant dress in the halal destination and no free shows (naked or semi-naked bodies) in public places [...] I would appreciate it if there were no statues or pictures of naked people in and around halal hotels.

Most practicing Muslims want the waitress to wear *hijab* and moderate dress. They recommend moderate and cultural dressings if the hotel is not halal. Another observant Muslim argues:

> [...] I have traveled to different parts of Ethiopia but was disappointed with some issues. For example, I wish the hotel employees could turn friendly to Muslims. Still, most of the time, they did not respect *Hijabist* [a woman with an Islamic headscarf] and *Nikabist* [the one who veils her face except her eyes] Muslim women. Therefore, it will be better if they [the employees] get training about handling Muslim customers.

According to the above participants, some hostesses and waitresses disrespect the Islamic dressing system. This shows that there has been a phobia against Islamic dressing by some hostesses and waitresses.

Almost all participants, irrespective of their religion, damned the availability of voyeurism and sexual permissiveness. For instance, one participant alleges, '[...] in the hotel, I would love if there is no voyeurism around my room. I do not want to experience such unIslamic and unethical activities. It is a disgrace that some hotels provide prostitutes!'

More than 98% of Ethiopians are believed to be adherents of either Christianity or Islam. Therefore, they are most likely conservative and condemn sexual permissiveness irrespective of their religion because adultery and voyeurism are sins in all religions and are taboo in Ethiopian culture.

Another participant advocates the above claim:

> [...] couples such as boyfriend and girlfriend and sometimes prostitutes interact and show affection in public. Such indecent activities are not only transgressions of religious virtues but also unethical and against the Ethiopian culture. Such things harm the ethics of children irrespective of their religion. To be honest, it may be difficult to control such activities. I know it is very hard to control. However, there must be a designated place for the customers who want to enjoy such things.

The preceding discussions reveal that Ethiopians have vastly discouraged sexual permissiveness, open kissing and voyeurism. These activities are against the very principle of halal tourism. Hence, it is most likely that most Ethiopians (both Christians and Muslims) will prefer halal tourism, especially when they travel with children.

One interviewee complains about the presence of haram food, such as pork and alcohol and the absence of prayer places. He argues:

> I would feel more comfortable if the hotels and restaurants were free from alcoholic beverages and any swine products [...], I wish I could perform my prayers timely and freely with other fellow travelers [...], and as parents, I wish we had not been concerned about cooking or finding halal food. However, it is unfortunate that in nearly all star-rated hotels in Ethiopia, there are alcohol and pork but no space to pray.

Most interviewees share the absence of prayer space as the major obstacle in most star-rated hotels in Ethiopia. They suggest that at least they had to assign one room for prayers because Muslims must pray five times a day. They claimed the hoteliers never considered the interest of practicing Muslims.

One foreign tourist speaks:

> [...] indeed, I am not a halal customer. Nor am I a practicing Muslim, but I would like to see good morality in public spaces and parks regarding the relationship between sexes, such as no public kissing. It must be clear that there are kids and elders in such places. Kids should not be exposed to such activities, and elders deserve respect.

Women visitors claim the absence of women-only facilities. A practicing Muslim woman states:

> [...] separate swimming pool, where females can wear whatever they want [...] should be provided. Women should have opportunities to enjoy in the same manner a man does because [...]. Still, practically by not offering women-only facilities, women, especially Muslim women, are systematically excluded from enjoying swimming in many hotels in Ethiopia.

Another woman claims:

> For me, halalness is having halal foods and beverages and having a separate pool. However, most hotels, including those that claim halal, have no such facilities. When I travel, I want to enjoy the swimming pool; the same is true for my sisters and friends. We all would like to swim in the pool without a headscarf, but it is unfortunate that in Ethiopia, hotels have no female-only pools or entertainment centers.

According to the preceding two participants, Muslim women could not enjoy swimming because of the unavailability of separate swimming pools. Therefore, the hotelier had to arrange female-only swimming pools, or they could have arranged it by shift, and halal tourism could help overcome such issues.

Tour operators also highlighted the provision of women-only facilities. One tour operator says, 'Having female-only services must be an aspect of the holidays that most practicing Muslims appealed to have, but, unfortunately, we are not offering such services yet.' Some tour operators admitted the importance of separate swimming pools or entertainment centers for men and women. Therefore, it is expected that the development of halal tourism in Ethiopia will solve such problems.

To sum up, most halal-conscious visitors speak that there was no conducive environment to practice their religion during their visitations. They recommend that the practices, products and services of halal destinations should be sharia friendly and must be halal. Most interviewees claimed that there have to be halal holidays in Ethiopia to help Muslim visitors enjoy their holiday without compromising their religious values. Many participants also believe that alcoholic beverages should not be served at the resort, and hotel and hostesses and waitresses should wear modest dress codes. Many domestic halal visitors have complained about the presence of women in very inappropriate wearing.

Especially people who travel with children highly prefer halal products and services. Some non-Muslim travelers with children prefer halal hotels and destinations to keep their children away from undesired activities such as alcoholism and voyeurism. They demand to enjoy a halal holiday that avoids religiously prohibited, culturally taboo services and products to save their children from being exposed to haram and taboo practices. For many Muslim travelers with their children, their main consideration during visitation was protecting them from haram and unIslamic activities.

As indicated in the preceding discussions, Muslim travelers, including non-practicing Muslims, give due attention to halal foods. When participants were asked to describe their expectations regarding facilities and food on a halal holiday, halal food, an alcohol-free environment, separate male/female pools, a gym and a prayer room or mosque were repeatedly fulfilled. In addition to discussing what facilities and food they desired within a halal holiday, interviewees were also asked to describe what they did not want to have on a halal holiday. Among others, many interviewees suggested voyeurism, alcoholic beverages and pork to be avoided by halal hotels and restaurants. Nearly all Muslim participants want to distance themselves, especially their families, from alcohol, pork and voyeurism. In contrast, they demand to have a place of prayer, halal beverages, halal food and halal entertainment.

In Islam, females and males are expected to have separate facilities and services except with the allowed individuals (brothers, father, father-in-law, sons, grandsons, son-in-law, and the like) (Battour, 2019). Therefore, the availability of separate facilities and services was among the issues raised by participants. The participants demand that a halal holiday should provide women-only facilities. Practicing Muslims consider this as the main criterion for choosing hotels over others. Women participants described how having such women-only facilities gave them the freedom to relax and enjoy their holiday. Male travelers also complained about the absence of separate facilities for males and females. They explained the importance of such women-only facilities. Practicing Muslims described the advantage of having such segregated facilities needs for males because Muslim males are also not allowed to mix with naked women. Some participants also explained that women might receive intimidation and sexual attack if there are many people at the beach.

Overwhelming participants, both Muslims and non-Muslims, have acknowledged the importance of an environment that is fit for families and children. Many agreed on the need to keep their children away from alcohol and voyeurism, which Muslims very much emphasize. Muslims are very concerned about seeing other tourists drinking and want to distance their children from such things. Non-Muslims with children also prefer to spend in hotels with no alcoholic beverages and voyeurism. Even non-Muslims who drink alcohol do not want their children to see people drinking alcohol and want to distance their children from such an environment. Most participants agreed that an alcohol-free environment is a family-friendly environment. They recommend that hotels, resorts and other entertainment service providers arrange an alcohol-free environment for Muslims and people traveling with their families. Moreover, most people discourage voyeurism, such as open kissing, especially between the same gender or couples in front of them and/or their family members. Almost all participants expressed deep concern about their children seeing other tourists kissing in public and recommended that a halal holiday provider think seriously about such issues.

Identifying and Mapping Potential Routes of Halal Tourism in Ethiopia

First, the concept of tourism routes was discussed. Then, five potential halal tourism routes and their respective nodes of attractions were presented. After inventorying the available attractions, the next step is identifying and mapping appropriate halal tourism routes.

Tourism routes are major concepts in tourism development. A tourism route is defined as a network system that connects multiple natural and cultural nodes to provide a diversified tourism product at a time and one route (Chountala et al., 2019). Route planning has become one of the most significant steps in tourism development (Görmüş et al., 2017). Tourism routes help destination managers develop non-promoted sites with high tourism resources into tourists' destinations. Commercial viability is among the determinant criteria in proposing new routes. Tourism routes tie up several nodes of attractions that would separately not have the power to attract visitors. Therefore, identifying and mapping tourism routes is important for developing fragmented attractions to attract tourists. The thematic routes refer to the row of natural, historical or cultural attractions, making them accessible to different transport forms around a chosen topic or theme (Csapo & Berki, 2014).

The aim of developing halal tourism routes in Ethiopia is to create interrelation and interconnection between diverse and separated visitor attractions

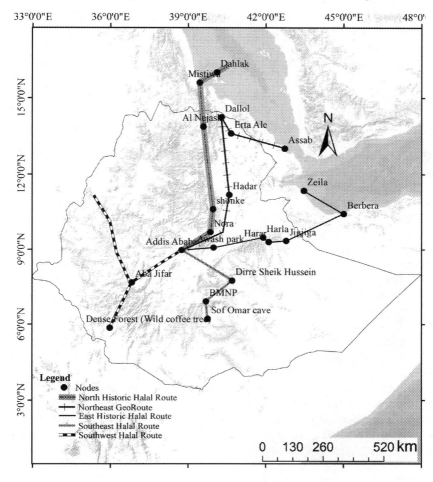

Map 5.2 Halal tourism routes of Ethiopia, prepared by the researchers.

by creating historical, economic and cultural linkages between individual attractions. This, in turn, enables visitors to enjoy rich experiences and enriches their consumption. Itineraries of a particular visitor route also offer particular advantages in promoting tourism as a spatial development strategy. Demand and expenditure can be diffused to various nodes instead of concentrating on saturated attractions. According to the opinion of tourism experts, tourism routes have long been shown to provide the impetus for developing a range of new attractions and facilities along with the ways. Therefore, the first halal visitor attractions were identified and described. Then, countrywide distribution attractions become important nodes to propose nationwide halal tourism routes. These routes will reveal not only halal itineraries but also Ethiopia's natural and cultural corridors that would fit the interest of halal-conscious visitors.

The first tourism route established in Ethiopia was the historic north route that includes the historical sites of BahirDar, Gonder, Lalibela and Axum (Sisay, 2009; Tafesse, 2016). This historic route was established in the 1960s and has recently attracted most of the country's visitors. This route, however, did not include Islamic heritage. Even iconic Islamic heritage, such as the historic site of al-Nejashi were not included in this route. Another example of a successful commercial route is the south ethnographic route, in which iconic Islamic heritages like the palace of Aba Jifar were not considered. The current proposal for halal tourism routes involves resourceful but historically disadvantaged communities in tourism route development. The role of halal routes in developing halal tourism in Ethiopia was unanimously shared among all participants of tourism experts. Forming routes in collaboration with local stakeholders makes economic sense from a marketing, networking and economic perspective.

The proposal of all routes was based on the principle of tourism development that tourism development could be sustainable only when it involves the local communities and consider the very interest of the indigenous people (Briedenhann & Wickens, 2004). Accordingly, the local communities' representatives, investors and tourism experts were consulted during the route-proposing process. According to tourism theories, tourism developments are unlikely to succeed if they do not adopt a 'community-based approach in which local communities can be decision-makers in the project's courses. Unfortunately, impracticable political promises of employment opportunities have made some people doubtful about engaging in such a project. There were also widespread feelings of inequality, fear, distrust and resentment that affected successful community participation. Some people perceive such kinds of development initiatives as exploitative and political. Conflict of interest often occurs between the indigenous community and the industry actors. During the development of new tourism, it is obvious that mistrust between various groups is inevitable since the potential benefit to one sector of the community might marginalize others.

Finally, five main halal tourism routes were identified and proposed using the 'thematic route' design and geographical actuation zone. These are the north historic halal tourism route (Al-Nejashi historic route), the Northwest halal geo-route, the Eastern historic halal tourism route (Harar historic route), the Southeast halal eco-route and Southwest halal eco-route (Aba Jifar route). The viability, feasibility and long-term sustainability of these routes were well considered.

The North Historic Halal Tourism Route (Al-Nejashi Historic Route)

The north historic halal tourism route, also called the Al-Nejashi historic route, is a border-crossing route from Addis Ababa, Ethiopia, toward the north as far as Massawa and Dahlak Islands of Eritrea. This route transcends not only international borders but also geographical diversity. It connects historic sites and Islamic heritages in Ethiopia and Eritrea. The Al-Nejash route

Challenges and Prospects to Halal Tourism Development 169

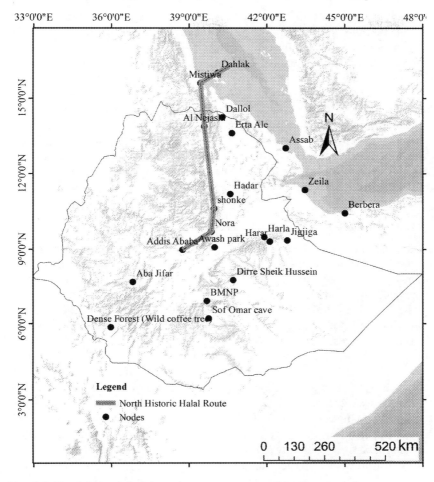

Map 5.3 North historic halal tourism routes, prepared by the researchers.

provides a unique tourism experience that links Ethiopia's Islamic heritage to Eritrea's Islamic heritage and coastal areas. The route starts from Addis Ababa and heads through the Islamic archaeological sites of North Showa and literary landscapes of Wollo to Tigray, open historical sites of Al-Nejashi, before heading north to the tourism sites of Eritrea, Massawa and the Dahlak archipelagoes. This route will transcend to Saudi Arabia by tracing the footprint of the *Sahabas* (companions of Prophet Mohammed), who conducted the first Hijra toward Habesha in 615.

The Al-Nejashi historic route covers most of the northern part of Ethiopia. The Islamic archaeological and heritage sites of the Showa, particularly Ifat Sultanate in North Showa, the heritages buildings of Shonke residential complex and Mosque in Wollo and the historic mosque and religious sites of Al-Nejashi in Tigrai Wukro are proposed to be the major nodes of this route.

Secular sites such as the battlefield of Adwa, where Ethiopians defeated Italians in 1896, and breathtaking landscapes of Northern Ethiopia will be supplementary assets of this route. Adwa is a historical place where the black defeated the white imperialist force for the first time in history. Therefore, halal-conscious visitors will enjoy visiting this historic battlefield.

The Al-Nejashi historic route consists of overlapping nodes and therefore has more capacity to capture the visitors' attention. This route has a comparative advantage over others for having overlapping Islamic heritages throughout the way and the availability of the historic north route in the same direction. These factors could increase the value of this route. The promotion of the proposed route is an integral part of route formation. Otherwise, visitors may hardly be aware of this route.

The Northwest Halal Geo-Route (The Danakil Geo-Route)

As discussed earlier, Northeast Ethiopia, mainly the Afar region, is rich in geological and archaeological visitor attractions. After studying the attractions, it is also necessary to assess how to interconnect these sites and make them accessible to visitors.

The Northwest halal route or the Danakil geo-route is a border-crossing route that runs northeastwards from Addis Ababa, Ethiopia, as far as Assab, the port of Eritrea. This route connects tourism resources of the Afar regional state, mainly geological and archaeological sites such as Hadar archaeological sites (where Lucy was discovered), the Erta Ale active volcano and the Dallol depression, and transcends international borders toward Assab port. It connects visitor attractions of the Afar region with Addis Ababa and Assab. The Danakil geo-route provides a unique tourism experience, mainly geological, geomorphological and archaeological sites. The route starts at Addis Ababa and leads through the lower Awash_Hadar, Ertale and Dallol before heading north to the tourism sites of Eritrea and Assab port.

The East Historic Halal Tourism Route

A legendary long-distance trade route in Eastern Ethiopia connected East Ethiopia with central Ethiopia. This historic long-distance trade route had realized the economic, cultural, political and religious interactions between Eastern Ethiopia and other parts of Ethiopia and the port cities of the horn of Africa. The proposed route will more or less follow the pattern of this historic route.

The proposed Eastern historical route, or the Harar historic route, will run from Addis Ababa eastward to the historic city of Harar, with a possible extension as far as Zeila and Berbera. The Eastern historic halal route comprises historic cities of Islamic sultanates and follows the trend of the historic long-distance trade. This route will connect several nodes, such as Awash national park, the archaeological sites of Harlaa, and the historic walled city of Harar, and lead to the ports of Berbera and Zeila through Jigjiga. Just like

Challenges and Prospects to Halal Tourism Development 171

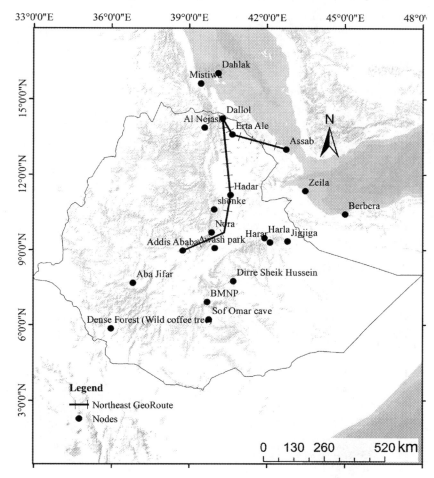

Map 5.4 North East halal route, by the researchers.

other routes, the visitation will start from Addis Ababa and continue to pass through the following destination nodes.

Bishoftu and its volcanic lakes: the visitors will enjoy observing some of the unique birdlife and experimenting with ornithologist attractions. *The Awash Park*: In addition to the park, the visitor will enjoy the cultural lifestyles of *Kereyu* pastorals. Harlaa is an abandoned Islamic city located between Harar and Dire Dawa. The visitor will have a good time at Harlaa and spend the night at Dire Dawa. Dire Dawa, the so-called 'the New Harar,' was established in 1902 following the construction Djibouti-Addis Ababa railway and has now become an important cosmopolitan city of Eastern Ethiopia. *Harar*, the sub-developed destination with some amenities and rich historical and cultural attractions in Eastern Ethiopia, will be a major node in this route. As discussed earlier in this paper, the walled city of Harar serves as the main attraction for

172 *Challenges and Prospects to Halal Tourism Development*

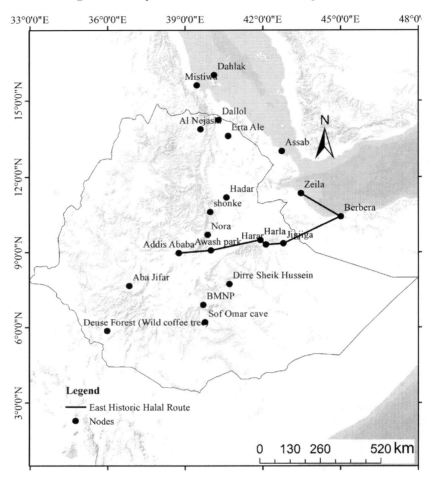

Map 5.5 The East historic halal route, by the researchers.

visitors visiting Eastern Ethiopia. Babile and Gursum (the Dakhata Valley and the Kundudo Mountain) will be important nodes of this route.

The head of Babile culture and tourism bureau states:

> [...] in addition to the walled city of Harar and many other attractions, new visitor attractions are being discovered in East Ethiopia. The famous Abyssinian Elephants sanctuary in Babile is another quality of this area. Due to these qualities, the construction of a Halal lodge in Babile or Gursum is strongly recommended.

According to the interview conducted with the Somali region culture and tourism bureau manager, in times of political calm, this route will transcend

Challenges and Prospects to Halal Tourism Development 173

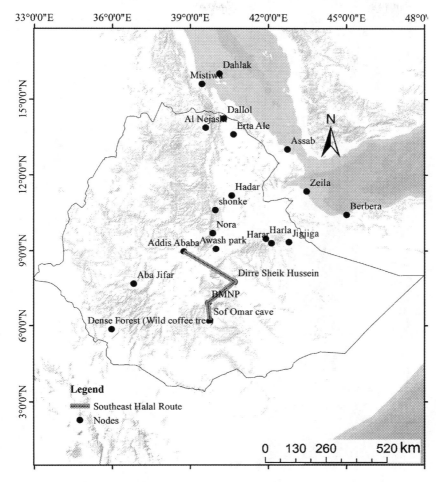

Map 5.6 Southeast halal route, by the Researcher.

toward Hargeisa, Zeila and Berbera of Somalia. In such a way, this route will be extended as far as the sea outlet so that the visitor may come to this route by ship directly from abroad and visit from the frontier to the interior.

The Southeast Halal Route (Bale Eco-Route)

The Southeast Halal Eco-Routes runs from Addis Ababa toward southeastern parts of Ethiopia, Bale zone. These routes have three major nodes: the Bale mountains national parks, Dire Sheik Hussein historical and religious sites, and Sof Omar cave system. However, visitors could enjoy visiting other attractions in the area.

174 Challenges and Prospects to Halal Tourism Development

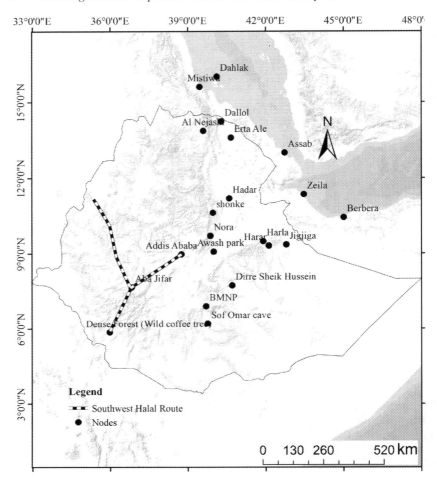

Map 5.7 The Southwest halal route: by the researcher.

The Southwest Halal Tourism Route (The Aba Jifar Eco-Route)

This route runs from Addis Ababa toward Southwestern Ethiopia. The Palace of Aba Jifar and wild coffee forests are the major attractions of this route. This route will include various natural resources and forests of Southwestern Ethiopia. Most of Ethiopia's forest resources are found in this country. When fully utilized, this route will be connected with Senkelle Swayne's Hartebeest Sanctuary, Oromo National park, Mago national park and Gambella national park. This route will also reach the Grand Ethiopian Renaissance Dam (GERD).

Generally, this section discusses the availability and viability of halal sites and routes in Ethiopia. Sites and routes are the core elements of any tourism development. Based on geographical zones and locations, halal visitor attractions were categorized into five clusters: the north cluster, the northeast cluster, the eastern cluster, the southeast cluster and the southwestern cluster. Each cluster comprises important natural, historical, cultural, archaeological and geological attractions. The location of these attractions was identified using the Global Positioning System (GPS) and Geographic Information System (GIS) and plotted on a map. Data obtained from fieldwork and google earth were employed to identify the geographical location of these attractions. After identifying visitor attractions with a greater potential to attract halal-conscious visitors, viable halal tourism routes have been identified and proposed. Generally, five major halal tourism routes were identified and proposed for further development. These routes are the north historic halal routes, the northwest halal geo-routes, the east halal historic route, the southeast halal eco-route and the southwest halal eco-route. The north historic halal route (Al-Nejashi historic route) interconnects great archaeological and historical sites of Ethiopia and even Eritrea. This route more or less follows the footprint of the pioneer Sahabas who immigrated toward Habesha during the first Hijra in 615. Hence, this route will transcend as far as the Gulf States, such as Saudi Arabia. This route may be very fit for religious and history-lover visitors.

The Northeast halal geo-route will mainly interconnect the geological attractions from Afar region. This route could be very attractive and conducive for nature-lover visitors and adventurers. The southeast halal eco-route connects three major attractions of the Bale area: Bale mountains national park, Sof Omar cave system and Dire Sheik Hussein religious and historic site. The southwest halal eco-route leads toward Aba Jifar palace of Jimma and the nature-based attractions of Southwestern Ethiopia. This route will take environmentalist, eco-friendly and nature-lover visitors to the point of their suit. GIS technology was used to plot these routes and their respective nodes on a map.

The Ethiopian government, industry players, and local people should develop and promote tourism resources and halal routes. The study identifies marginalized and the most ignored tourism resources of the country. Most of these attractions are on the brink of destruction and extinction. Hence, the government, the local community and other stakeholders should work together to maintain these heritages. Facilities and ancillaries must be set up, and halal services must be offered at these sites along the proposed halal routes. These attractions and halal routes should be branded, promoted and introduced to mainly halal customers.

Ethiopia's Comparative Advantages and Opportunities to Develop Halal Tourism

In the previous sections, the knowledge and experiences of participants about halal tourism and their perceptions and attitude toward halal tourism have been discussed. Moreover, halal tourism routes were proposed. This section will investigate Ethiopia's opportunities and comparative advantages in halal tourism development.

Comparative advantage refers to what a certain destination has over other fellow destinations (Algieri et al., 2018). This advantage would be gained because of the relative availability of endowments such as natural, historical and cultural resources. Comparative advantage allows Ethiopia to entice visitors more than its competitors and realize stronger revenues. However, Ethiopia must exploit its endowments efficiently and effectively to become competitive. The interviewed key informants state that a country specializing in its comparative advantage can compete successfully in international tourism markets, raise profits and support job creation. According to interviewed tourism experts, though Ethiopia has strong comparative advantages, it has not exploited its competitive advantage. It is likely that although Ethiopia has a potential comparative advantage, it will remain untapped unless its competitive advantages, such as infrastructure deficiencies or skill shortages, are properly addressed. Some countries could benefit from the tourism industry by exploiting competitive advantages without having comparative advantages. They overcame the lack of natural and environmental resources and ranked among the top tourist destinations. However, it is fortunate that Ethiopia is endowed with halal tourism resources and, therefore, has a strong comparative advantage over its competitors. It is endowed with high-quality Islamic heritages and natural resources that help it to specialize in halal tourism. These findings were derived from the following comments of the research participants.

When asked about Ethiopia's comparative advantages and opportunities in developing halal tourism, one participant alleges as follows:

> [...] Ethiopia is lucky. It is endowed with Islamic history and heritage but we Ethiopians have not properly exploited and utilized our resources. Geographically, Ethiopia is located at the heart of Muslim countries, and Ethiopia is rich in halal tourism resources, but we have not been utilizing it. The country has comparative advantages over its neighbors in developing halal tourism. Firstly, Ethiopia is the land of the first Hijra, the land of King Al-Nejashi, the land of Bilal and many more *Sahabas*. Therefore, it has a good image and history in the Islamic world. Secondly, Ethiopia has a round-year conducive climate, so visitors from the Islamic world want to spend their summer here in Ethiopia. Thirdly, Ethiopia is located in a strategic position in the Islamic world. Look, most of our neighbors are Muslim countries. The flight to the Gulf states takes less than 3 hours. These are all the opportunities we have at hand to develop halal tourism. Ethiopia has other privileges to halal tourism in that it has a great domestic demand for halal tourism. Half of the 115 million population are Muslims. However, there is no single halal resort and entertainment center to accommodate the interest of this large Muslim population.
>
> (Tourism Expert Participant, 2019)

According to the above quote, Ethiopia is competent regarding halal tourism resources in the bid for halal tourism development. Moreover, the interviewee indicates that there is also a huge domestic demand for halal tourism in Ethiopia. The conclusions of the focus group discussions are also similar to the above quotes.

The results of the two group discussions were synthesized as follows:

> Regarding halal tourism development, Ethiopia possesses a comparative advantage but needs more effort to be a competent halal destination. We have ancient Islamic heritage cities and great Islamic histories. We have internationally renowned heroes and heroines like Al-Nejashi and Emu-Ayman. Ethiopia is endowed with natural resources: it has incredible landscape scenes in the north, the south, the east and the west. Ethiopia is the birthplace of coffee and the only country that preserve wild coffee trees to date. The fauna and flora resources in the southern part of Ethiopia could draw the interest of halal-conscious visitors.

According to data gathered from interviewees, FGD discussants, personal observation and secondary sources, Ethiopia's comparative advantage opportunities over its competitors to develop halal tourism have been geared into the following themes.

The Availability of Unique Islamic History: Selling Stories and Legends

Participants were asked whether Ethiopia has a comparative advantage in developing halal tourism over its neighboring countries. Almost all participants believe Ethiopia has a strong comparative advantage over other countries in developing halal tourism because it has unique Islamic history, stories and legends. One participant states his opinion as follows:

> [...] Ethiopia has a unique place in Islamic history, so that it can sell its legends and histories to halal-conscious visitors. Ethiopia is a historic country blessed by the Prophet himself, so Ethiopia has room in Islamic history. For its historical contribution to Islam, Ethiopia has been known among the Muslim world. For instance, Turks and Palestinians hold a positive attitude toward Ethiopia. Prophet Muhammad called Ethiopia 'the land of peace and 'the land of truth.' Hence, it is possible to claim that Ethiopia is the only country promoted by the Prophet Muhammad as a destination. Most importantly, Prophet Mohammed blessed and promoted Ethiopia for its hospitability.

The conclusions of the focus group discussions also prove Ethiopia has a unique Islamic history of attracting Muslim visitors. Other African countries, even countries in the world, have no Islamic history like that of Ethiopia. Hence, Ethiopia has a comparative advantage in selling its Islamic history and legend to Muslim visitors. Therefore, Ethiopia could sell its unique and rich Islamic history and legend to attract and retain halal Muslim visitors.

The Land of the First Hijra

Ethiopia is known in Islamic history as the land of the first Hijra, where the first persecuted Muslims migrated toward it in 615. One participant gives his opinion in this regard as follows:

> [...] I have been to many Muslim countries in the Middle East and Turkey, and many Muslims have known Ethiopia as the land of the first Hijra. Many Muslims remember Ethiopia for giving asylum to Muslims. Hence, Ethiopia could be branded and promote its halal tourism as 'the land of the first Hijra.' Ethiopia could position itself as a halal destination. Westerners have known Ethiopia as a strong Christian state in Africa. Still, Muslim countries, mainly Arabs and Turks, have known Ethiopia as a holy land of Muslims, where the pioneer Muslims took asylum and saved Islam itself. Therefore, Ethiopia is a holy country that saves Islam when it faces fatal threats from Quraysh and is distributed to the rest of the world.

The focus group discussants also unanimously agreed that Ethiopia could be sold to halal-conscious visitors as 'the land of the first Hijra,' 'the land of truth,' 'the land of peace,' and 'the land of justice, therefore, in promoting and marketing halal tourism, it is possible to brand Ethiopia as 'the land of the first Hijra' so that several Muslim visitors from both near and distant neighbors and the Middle East could visit Ethiopia.

The Homeland of Great Muslims: King Al-Nejashi, Bilal Al-Habesha and Baraka

Many participants allege that Ethiopia is the land of prominent Muslims. They argue that King Al-Nejashi, Bilal Al-Habesha and Barakah (Emu Ayaman) were the most influential Ethiopian Muslims in Islamic history. According to participants, these great personalities excelled in their contribution to Islam and introduced Ethiopia to the rest of the world, especially the Muslim world. They allege that in several Muslim countries, the name of Ethiopia (Habesha) is strongly associated with the name of these three icons.

Marketing experts and practitioners highlight that images of famous personalities can influence a country's image. An image can be transferred from a notable individual to their country of origin. The associative network theory states that images can transfer from a great personality to a country. Great personalities can play as brand ambassadors during tourism development in their country of origin. This could ease the promotion of the tourism industry. The strength of the association in a consumer's mind between a famous person and his/her country of origin determines their choice of destination. Likewise, prominent people such as King Al-Nejashi, Bilal Habesha and Baraka could have a significant role in promoting Ethiopia as a halal destination.

King Al-Nejashi was an Ethiopian king who welcomed the first pioneer *Sahabas* when they faced persecution and brutalities from the Quraysh of Mecca in 615 (Cerulli, 1971; Erlich, 1994, 2013; Sihab ad-Din Ahmad, 2003). Nejashi, also known as As-ham bin Abjar and later as Ahmed Al-Negashi, shortened to Nejashi, accepted Islam and ultimately converted to Islam. As noted in authentic hadith, when the persecution against his followers increased, Prophet Muhammad understood that he could not have safeguarded his followers from the attacks and said, 'Flee to the Habesha. There, there is a king who never tolerates injustice. There is justice in his kingdom. Habesha is the land of truth. Therefore, go there until we achieve victory with the help of Allah' (Cerulli, 1971; Trimingham, 1952). By offering precious gifts, the Quraysh tried to convince Nejashi to hand over the Muslims and expel them back to Mecca. However, the king rejects their offer by saying, 'If you gave me a mountain of gold, I would not give up these people who have taken asylum with me.'

Moreover, Nejashi has given full protection to those Muslim migrants and said to them, 'Go and live in peace. If someone mistreats you, he will pay for it' (Erlich, 1994). Inspired by the hospitality and benevolence of King Nejashi, Prophet Muhammad (PBUH) ordered his followers to respect and protect Ethiopia and live in peace with Ethiopians. To reciprocate the Nejashi's benevolence, the Prophet the following important and ever-lasting hadith: *'utruku al-habasha ma tarakukum* (leave the Ethiopians as long as they leave you)' (Cerulli, 1971; Erlich, 1994, 2013; Trimingham, 1952). In addition to preaching peace to Ethiopia, the Prophet has called Ethiopia 'the land of peace,' 'the land of justice,' and 'the land of truth.' Hence, because of the kindness of King Al-Nejashi, first, Prophet Muhammad blessed Ethiopia. Second, the Prophet promotes Ethiopia as the world's land of peace, justice and truth. The most important point here is that the speeches of the Prophet are Sunnah, which is a core lesson in Islamic education to transmit through generations as a guiding principle. Hence, his speeches about Ethiopia transcended not only countries but also transcended generations. The speeches of the Prophet are timely and geographically unbounded. The statement of the Prophet Muhammad about Ethiopia is an ever-lasting promotion for Ethiopia. As a memorial to king Al-Nejashi of Ethiopia, nowadays, several countries designate their highways and institutions after his name. Several countries have named their highways and institutions after King Al-Nejashi. This, in turn, has a paramount role in introducing Ethiopia to halal investors. Ethiopian Airlines also named one of its airplanes after his name.

Due to the very nature of halal tourism, most of the potential customers of halal tourism are Muslims. Hence, introducing Ethiopia as the country of Bilal al-Habesha to the Muslim world could come to fruition because every single Muslim has known about Bilal. An Ethiopian Bilal Rabah, the first Muezzin of Islam, was another icon. Even the name Bilal is attached to the term 'Habesha' (Bilal Al-Habesha); Habesha was another name for Ethiopia. Nowadays, there are hundreds of institutions and organizations named after Bilal Habesha. The researcher has listened to Neshida and religious songs in the name of Bilal Al-Habesha in Turkish. Such activities play an invaluable role in introducing Ethiopia as a halal destination.

In addition to Nejashi and Bilal, great female personalities such as Baraka (Emu-Ayman) played a great role in introducing Ethiopia to the Muslim world. The histories of these great personalities could contribute a lot to building a positive image of Ethiopia as a halal destination. Baraka Tha'alaba was among the pioneer companions of the Prophet Muhammad (PBUH) (Erlich, 2013). She was among the closest women to the Prophet and the first person to clasp him when he was born. She cared for the Prophet until he married Khadija (Erlich, 1994). She is known to have been the woman who never stopped caring for the Prophet. She is also said to have been the second woman to accept Islam. Hence, Ethiopia is known among the Muslim world with men of great personalities, such as King Al-Nejashi Bilal, and women of great personalities, such as Baraka. Therefore, destination marketers could use such great personalities to build the image of Ethiopia as a halal destination.

The Availability of Ancient Islamic Cities and Landscapes

As inventoried and discussed earlier, Ethiopia has Islamic heritage, ancient Islamic cities, Islamic archaeological sites and landscapes. When participants were asked about the opportunities and comparative advantages of Ethiopia in the bid for halal tourism development, the availability of Islamic cities and historic landscapes were mentioned as great assets. Since Islam has introduced in Ethiopia before any country, Islamic heritage cities were founded in different parts of Ethiopia, aged as early as the 7th century. Independent Islamic kingdoms and sultanates in different parts of the country left their legacies and prints behind. Hence, nowadays, Ethiopia is rich in Islamic archaeological sites and cities distributed in different parts of Ethiopia. Harar is a typical example in this regard (see the detail in Chapter 4). Hence, the availability of these ancient Islamic cities and archaeological sites could help draw the attention of halal-conscious visitors to Ethiopia.

The Geostrategic Location of Ethiopia to the Muslim World

To express the importance of geostrategic location, Tobler said, 'everything is related to everything else, but near things are more related than distant things' (Tobler, 1970, p. 236 cited in Waters, 2017, p. 1). Distance decay theory also suggests that demand for any good or service declines exponentially as distance increases (Ho & McKercher, 2014). McKercher and Mak (2019) confirm in their finding that 56% of all international travel occurred among countries that shared a land border and that 93% of all departures were to destinations within 2,000 km of the source market country. In the study conducted in Hong Kong, Ho and McKercher (2014) approve that, ceteris paribus, visitors opt for short-haul destinations over long-haul destinations. The preceding theories and research findings endorse that geographical location, mainly the distance between countries of origin and destination, affects the demand for tourism.

Since immemorial times, there has been a flow of people from Muslim countries, mainly the Middle East, to Ethiopia (Erlich, 1994). This influx of people has continued after the birth of tourism in the form of tourists, mainly business tourists. Due to its geopolitical and geostrategic location, Ethiopia has been attracting the attention of the Muslim world's travelers and investors.

Ethiopia is geographically located at the center of Muslim countries. Therefore, Ethiopia holds a geostrategic and decisive geopolitical position in the Muslim world. For Middle East visitors, Ethiopia is a short-haul destination, mainly less than three-hour by flight. One participant (tourism expert) expresses the geostrategic situation of Ethiopia as follows:

> Since most halal tourism customers are Muslims, Ethiopia has a God-gifted opportunity to develop halal tourism. In addition to its huge potential domestic customers, Ethiopia is found in an appropriate location and position to capture foreign halal-conscious visitors. Located only a few miles from Ethiopia, Gulf States visitors are expected to be the major halal market for Ethiopia's halal tourism industry.

A tour operator participant in Addis Ababa states:

> Today there is a high demand for halal tourism. There are interests of halal-conscious visitors and investors from the Middle East, such as Turkey, Gulf-Countries and Pakistan. There are actual and potential visitors from neighboring countries, such as Sudan and Djibouti. However, we have no halal-friendly facilities and services to meet their needs. In the future, we plan to establish independent halal tour packages to capture this lucrative but untapped and marginalized business.

According to the Ethiopian investment commission, Muslim countries such as Turkey, the UAE and Saudi Arabia have appeared to be top foreign investors in Ethiopia (Ethiopian Investment Commission, 2019). These forces could be counted as customers of halal tourism. Generally, its geostrategic position has enabled Ethiopia to capture the Middle East's business tourists. Inbound and outbound tourism is available in the Middle East and the UAE. According to participants from the Ethiopian federal Mejlis, more than 15 thousand Ethiopian pilgrims travel to Saudi Arabia to make Haji and *Umra*. For instance, in 2019, more than 10,000 outbound pilgrims traveled to Saudi Arabia through the federal Mejlis; this figure includes only hajj pilgrims. It is believed that, on average, each pilgrim has spent 160,000 Ethiopian birrs. However, there are no halal tour operators to run this business in Ethiopia.

To conclude, Ethiopia and the Middle East have intermingled in terms of culture, history, religion and geography. The establishment of halal tourism could further strengthen the interrelation between the two regions. It could bring about economic yield and political, social and diplomatic gains.

The Availability of Conducive Weather Conditions and Fertile Land

Scholars of tourism have examined the manifold relationships between tourism and climate. The relationship between climate and tourism has a significant influence on visitors' decision-making, the travel experience and the marketing of destinations. Climate is among the prime factors to be considered by visitors in visiting a certain destination. Ethiopia has been endowed with conducive climate and weather conditions throughout the years. As a matter of chance, the origin of the halal tourism market, the Middle East countries have harsh and unconducive climate and weather conditions. Ethiopia could sell its conducive weather conditions to the Arab world, mainly the senders of halal-conscious visitors. Hence, Ethiopia has a comparative advantage in terms of climate and weather.

One visitor from the Gulf countries states:

> [...] during summer, the temperature is very warm and suffocated in the Middle East, so many people from the Gulf countries want to spend their vacations in the countries like Ethiopia. If there were halal lodges, resorts and hotels, Ethiopia could attract many halal tourists from the Gulf counties [...].

The opinion of the interviewed Gulf Countries' visitors was similar to the preceding quote.

Ethiopia is also endowed with fertile and arable land that most Middle East countries do not have. According to the Ethiopian investment commission, several investors from the Middle East invest in agriculture, industry and infrastructure. For instance, Turkey, Saudi Arabia, and UAE are among the top foreign investors in Ethiopia (Ethiopian Investment Commission, 2018). According to the Commission, Turkey was the third-largest investor next to China and India in 2018 and 2019. There were about 229 Saudi investors in 2019. Saudi investors have invested over 18.3 billion USD in capital on over 200 investment projects in Ethiopia (Ethiopian Investment Commission, 2018). United Arab Emirates (UAE) also invested more than 3 billion USD in Ethiopia only in 2018. These are potential customers of halal businesses and halal tourism.

The Availability of Huge Domestic Demand

The role of domestic visitors has been neglected in many parts of the world while developing tourism. Previous studies show that many developing countries have generated a significant local tourist population of a sizeable middle class. Many domestic visitors from developing countries have also shown interest in participating and investing in their country's tourist attractions. During the tourism development process, domestic demand should be properly addressed than international demand because it helps create tourism awareness and culture that can sustain tourism in the long term (Butler, 2008).

One interviewee expresses his opinion about Ethiopian Muslims and their strong interest in halal tourism as follows:

> In the past couple of decades, Ethiopian Muslims' awareness of the principle of their religion [Islam] has been steadily mounting. Today, many Ethiopian Muslims want to refrain from what has been prohibited by their religion, the so-called haram activities. Simultaneously, their interest in engaging in entertainment/tourism has been increasing. Most people ask for halal products and services to reconcile these two emerging interests of Ethiopian Muslims. Previously, many people considered tourism unIslamic, but now many Muslims, including religious leaders, want to engage in a halal form of tourism. Some people show interest in investing in halal tourism. Therefore, I believe developing halal tourism in Ethiopia is timely and advisable.

According to Ghimire (2001), domestic tourism helps link local economies and diversify the economy. Domestic tourism helps secure citizens' right to holidays, know their own countries and strengthen national conscience and solidarity (Ghimire, 2001, p. 21). Additionally, domestic tourists are believed to use locally produced products that diminish leakages. Domestic visitors are more likely to purchase local products and services and use small businesses. This, in turn, increases linkage and reduces leakage rates. As Sindiga (1996) notes, domestic tourism helps destinations minimize seasonality and leakage and maximize linkages. It also reduces dependency on a few international markets and is less negatively affected by some shocks.

One participant (tour guide) of this study argues:

> About half of the 115 million Ethiopian population are Muslims. Recently, the interest of Muslims in visiting has been steadily increasing. Especially urban dwellers and educated Muslims want to engage in tourism without compromising their religion, and only halal tourism can address the demand of this segment of the population. Therefore, it is possible to conclude that halal tourism has many domestic customers, and the demand for halal tourism is very high among Ethiopian Muslims.

Participants were asked whether they wanted to engage in tourism if halal services and products were offered at destinations. Most of those interviewed plan to engage in tourism if halal products and services are provided. Few interviewees were engaged in tourism but were dissatisfied because of the unavailability of halal products and services.

One participant speaks as follows:

> There are many Islamic attractions, including historic cities, archaeological sites and ancient Islamic learning centers, and I wanted to visit these attractions with my spouse and children. However, halal services were not available around these sites. Nor are halal hotels available to spend nights. If halal tourism starts to function in Ethiopia, many friends and I will engage in tourism. Ethiopian Muslims are passive in tourism because tourism is attached to some activities, such as alcoholism and voyeurism. Such activists are against the very principle of Islam. Hence, there must be facilities and services in the tourism business that help Muslims to engage in tourism.

The above quote indicates that many Ethiopian Muslims desire to participate in halal tourism and know about halal attractions. The following comment given by another participant reinforces the claim above.

> Sometimes I take my children to resorts and historical sites, but what I encountered there was not good, especially for children. These areas have been surrounded by haram activities such as alcoholic beverages and voyeurism. Therefore, such things have deterred me from visitation. There has been voyeurism, such as public kissing, which negatively affects the behaviors of children. Hence, I recommend the stakeholders arrange halal areas for halal-conscious visitors.

A tour operator claims, 'I do not doubt that there are no problems of a market for halal tourism. Many Ethiopians demand halal services and products. The problem is that there are no halal accommodations and services.'

As the preceding quotes show, there is a high demand for halal tourism in Ethiopia. Many Ethiopian Muslims are interested in and able to engage in halal tourism. Still, they have been constrained by the availability of haram activities around the sites and the absence of halal services and products. Those who visited also complained about the absence of halal services and products in the destinations.

The focus group discussions show that millennial Muslims especially want to engage in tourism. The millennials are educated and awaked both academically and religiously. This section of the population understands that the very nature of tourism is no longer against Islamic principles, and they want to visit the countries' manmade and natural attractions. Simultaneously, this population wants to practice their religion even during traveling. They want to enjoy holidays with their spouses and children outside their villages. However, for the time being, most of them cannot engage in tourism anymore because they are halal consumers, and halal services and products are not provided at accommodations and destinations. Hence, this portion of the population is a sustainable market for halal tourism.

To conclude, over the past couple of decades, there has been a dramatic increase in Muslims' interest in participating in tourism. This has proved the feasibility and sustainability of halal tourism in Ethiopia. Both primary and secondary data have shown that Ethiopia has a comparative advantage in terms of domestic customers of halal tourism. Ethiopia not only has a large Muslim population, but the interest of Muslims in engaging in tourism is also exponentially mounting. Many Ethiopians seriously complain about offensive tourism business operations in Ethiopia and have asked to establish halal tourism. Millennials especially seem very enthusiastic about engaging in halal tourism.

The Birthplace of Coffee Arabica

Researchers unanimously approved that Ethiopia is the genesis of coffee Arabica and coffee culture (Tucker, 2011). Being the origin of coffee was one factor in adopting the phrase 'the Land of Origins' as a national motto of Ethiopian tourism. Coffee domestication in Ethiopia was begun in the 9th century (Tucker, 2011). The Oromo people of Ethiopia are said to have discovered and used coffee for the first time (Pritchard, 1985). It is also believed that coffee comes from a small town in Southwest Ethiopia called Kaffa. In Ethiopia, coffee is known as 'Bun' or 'Bunna.' These terms are also used in some Arab countries like Yemen. Coffee is the country's most important export cash crop (Labouisse et al., 2008). Over 4 million householders in Ethiopia are involved in the cultivation of coffee plants. However, with those employed in ancillary activities to coffee production, even more, households depend on coffee for part of their livelihoods.

Coffee Culture as Niche Halal Tourism Product

Linking coffee and coffee culture with halal tourism is a lucrative business but has been marginalized. In Ethiopia, the origin of coffee and coffee culture, many activities and experiences can connect coffee with halal tourism. After serious focus group discussions with stakeholders (mainly tour operators), some feasible ways of linkage of halal tourism and coffee tourism have been proposed. History and legend of coffee, experiences of wild coffee at the field, the coffee culture, traditional coffee drinking and various coffee festivals are viable niche products of coffee tourism.

As the birthplace of coffee (Tucker, 2011), Ethiopia has special privileges in coffee history and legend. Ethiopians have been utilizing wild coffee for centuries, and the Ethiopian coffee preparation process has become part and parcel of Ethiopians' culture. Today, Ethiopia is the only country in the world that has wild coffee. One participant argues as follows:

> [...] the coffee-growing areas of Ethiopia could offer visitors the opportunity to experience coffee at its origins and to gain insights into the

growing, harvesting and production processes. Not only hearing the story of coffee, halal visitors who visit Ethiopia will enjoy the actual experiences of wild coffee and the ways of coffee cultivation from tree to cup, and they will visit the relationship between coffee and the local people. The fresh air from the wild coffee and other creatures could also add value for the visitors.

Therefore, it is logical to conclude that Ethiopia, the coffee tree's and coffee culture's birthplace, could offer various coffee-related activities for halal visitors. In addition, visitors meet the local people and learn about the production process of coffee, and their visit generates additional income for the local community. In such a way, a halal coffee tour could provide an excellent example of how tourism may positively contribute to local, sustainable development.

According to the study participants, coffee is more than just a source of income or beverage; it is a spice of social cohesion in Ethiopia. From tree to cup, coffee preparation in Ethiopia is accompanied by various celebrations, performances and traditions transmitted from generation to generation. Therefore, coffee has become a part of being Ethiopian. Coffee is not just a drink but also a symbol of daily social activities. Drinking it with other people is of social significance. Ethiopia has had unique coffee processing, preparation and drinking cultures for centuries. Coffee in Ethiopia has economic, social and cultural implications. It is the most customary beverage during social events such as family gatherings, spiritual celebrations and times of mourning. A lot of experiences and traditional gastronomic activities accompany accompanied Ethiopian coffee culture.

One participant speaks:

> Roasting and drinking the original coffee in its birthplace could be a great experience for halal-conscious visitors. Among others, the traditional Ethiopian food of roasted grain known as Kolo is consumed while drinking traditional coffee. The special aroma of *ittan* (incense) and the green grass, locally known as *Ketiema*, make the coffee culture colorful. All these cultures go along with the principle of halal tourism; therefore, such cultural activities of coffee preparations could create special experiences for halal visitors.

In recent years, there has been growing interest in visiting Ethiopia as the birthplace of coffee Arabica. However, promoting Ethiopia as the birthplace of coffee is one of the most neglected areas by destination marketers.

Another participant states the following:

> In the absence of alcoholic beverages, tasting and drinking original and organic coffee could be good for halal-conscious visitors. Visitors can access and enjoy consuming the original coffee in modern star-hotels, small restaurants, or street vendors.

The experiences of coffee-growing destinations approved that coffee festivals are important tourist attractions. For instance, during the coffee weeks held in 2007, Dak Lak Province of Vietnam attracted many halal-conscious visitors. This coffee-week celebration included a model coffee farm, a coffee road with cafes, coffee games and meetings about the coffee industry, exhibitions and films on coffee production and cultural performances from the coffee-producing region.

There are also some initiations in Ethiopia too. One participant from the Ethiopian Investment Commission states:

> Ethiopia has begun showing its coffee culture and ceremonies at different trade fairs. For instance, during the annual coffee festival held in Saudi Arabia on 18 April 2018, Ethiopia demonstrated its untapped potential in the area. In the festival organized by Renald Arabia Exhibition and Conference Center in Jeddah on public display for ten days, Ethiopians could display coffee's historical and cultural linkage with Ethiopia and Ethiopians. During the festival, which lasted for ten days, Ethiopians' coffee ceremony, traditional costumes, dances and pictorial exhibits of various tourist destinations were demonstrated. Moreover, gastronomic tourism activities, such as Ethiopian traditional and staple food Injera made from teff flour and *wot* (sauce), were provided. This festival was able to attract more than 5000 Saudi halal visitors. These people promised to come to Ethiopia, taste traditional Ethiopian aromatic coffee, and popularize Ethiopian coffee among the Saudis.
> (Ethiopian Investment Commission, 2019)

Ethiopia has a comparative advantage over many countries because of coffee, culture, and wild coffee. It has been known that shopping is a popular tourist activity, and coffee-related tools have the potential for the production of souvenirs for tourists. Hence, it is feasible in Ethiopia that coffee festivals can draw the attention of numerous halal-conscious visitors and satisfy them.

Barriers to Halal Tourism Development in Ethiopia

As discussed in the preceding sections, several favorable conditions exist to develop halal tourism in Ethiopia, but it is not without its challenges. In this section, barriers to halal tourism development in Ethiopia will be discussed rigorously.

The Perceived Image of Ethiopia as a 'Christian Island'

With its long and deep Christian legacy, Ethiopia is traditionally known as the 'Christian Island in a sea of Muslims,' where more than half of its population is Muslim (Desplat & Østebø, 2013). Notwithstanding, Ethiopia is a holy country for both Islam and Christianity. Half of its population are Muslims, and the county has been promoted as 'a Christian Island.' Scholars delineate that the destination image is shaped based on historical, political, economic and social information about that destination, which in turn affects the travel decision of individuals.

One participant argues:

> Since priest-kings ruled Ethiopia from the 4th century until the last quarter of the 20th century, Ethiopia was promoted as 'a Christian Island' to the outside world. Even these days, only Christian heritages and churches have been displayed in different international exhibitions and trade fairs to promote Ethiopia as a visitor destination. Moreover, mainstream media promote mainly Christian heritages and festivals. Muslims are not represented in the promotional materials of Ethiopia. Because of such factors, Ethiopia's image is associated only with Christianity.

In addition to the preceding testimony, the UK parliament member who spoke about the Ethiopian conflict in December 2020 stated that Europeans support and visit Ethiopia because Ethiopia is a Christian country in Africa. Ethiopia is, therefore, a strong partner of Christian Europe in Africa. This man did not visit Ethiopia, but his mental image of Ethiopia was built based on the limited promotion and biased history of Ethiopia. While the researcher was in Abuja in 2018, he asked one Polish tourist concerning his perception and impression of Ethiopia as a destination. The Polish tourist said that Ethiopia was an important Christian country in Africa, and he would visit Ethiopia for Ethiopia was a 'Christian Island.' Even some Muslims have known Ethiopia as a Christian Island. One participant from Tunisia said that he knew Ethiopia as a Christian state. He thought that less than 10% of the Ethiopian population were Muslims. Even some Ethiopians still insist on the slogan 'a Christian Island,' which affects not only the halal tourism development but also such perception is an existential threat to Ethiopian Muslims. Most European and Western travelers visualize Ethiopia as a Christian Island. Several tour operator companies do not include Islamic heritage in their promotional materials. Nor do they take visitors to Islamic heritage and sites.

Another reported problem was the lack of promotion of Islamic heritages and Muslim-friendly destinations. For example, one tour guide claims:

> We take most tourists to the Rock-hewn Church of Lalibela and Tigray, to Gonder and Bahir Dar. Given that other sites such as Jugol and Shonke, Aba Jifar and Dire Sheik Hussein were not promoted, most visitors have no idea about these Islamic heritages. Even Muslim visitors do not know about the availability of such Islamic heritages and Muslim-friendly sites in Ethiopia. They thought that Ethiopia was a Christian country with insignificant numbers of Muslims.

However, the image of Ethiopia as a 'Christian Island' is unrealistic and naïve. Potential visitors held this unrealistic, naïve image of 'a Christian Island' without ever having been to Ethiopia. Therefore, when they visit Ethiopia, they find Ethiopia a destination different from their expectation because, in Ethiopia, Muslims, Christians and non-believers coexist. Therefore, after actual visitation, people learn that Ethiopia is multi-religion, multicultural, and multilingual. For instance, one visitor participant from Germany states:

> I thought that Ethiopia was a Christian country. However, when I visited Ethiopia, the reality on the ground was different from what I perceived. Here on the ground, I learn that there are Muslims equal to Christians. There are Islamic cultures in eastern Ethiopia, such as Harar and Dire Dawa. Now I understand that I had a corrupted image of Ethiopia, so I will reevaluate my perception of Ethiopia.

Other participants shared the concept of the preceding quote. This tells that the real situation in Ethiopia is very different from the projected image. It has been approved that international visitors' image of Ethiopia often was based on induced information agents rather than personal experiences. Most of this study's participants confirm a difference between pre-visitation and after-visitation images of Ethiopia. The after-visitation of Ethiopia's image is encouraging halal tourism development.

The Availability of Islamophobia at the National and Global Level

In the past few decades, Islamophobia has become one of the greatest challenges in the tourism industry. As has been discussed, 9/11 terrorist profiling caused the proliferation of Islamophobia throughout the world. Today, Islamophobia and xenophobia have become a challenge for the travel and tourism industry. The research participants were systematically asked to learn whether Islamophobia exists in Ethiopia. The participants' responses reveal that whatever form it takes, there is Islamophobia in Ethiopia at the individual, organizational and even state levels. For instance, most security staff at Ethiopian Airlines seriously inspect Muslim travelers more than they seriously inspect non-Muslims. There are various situations in that Muslims might be the target at airports and star hotels. Islamic names, beards and wearing hijab are causing discrimination. These things are the major signals of Islamic identity.

For instance, one Muslim visitor states:

> I came to Ethiopia to spend my leisure time visiting Islamic historical sites such as Al-Nejashi, but the security forces and some police hold a negative attitude towards Muslims. Starting from Bole airport, there was a special investigation against Muslims. I looked at how police inspect travelers, and most security forces were extremely strict while investigating Muslims. Sometimes, I have seen illegal investigations against Muslims both in and outside Bole airport. The surveillance against Muslim travelers especially bearded Muslim men and *Hijabist* women, was very serious.

Even Muslims from the Western world, such as the United States and the UK, were not exempted from being victims of anti-Islamic political rhetoric. Evidence shows that the security apparatus and police forces are crucial in persecuting Muslim travelers in Ethiopia.

One participant alleges:

> I was traveling with my non-Muslim workmates in Addis Ababa. The security force inspected me within a few meters but did not inspect my friends because they did not wear a headscarf like me. I have also seen extra scrutiny in Bole international airport focusing on Muslim travelers. During my stay here, I learned that security staffers hold a negative attitude toward people in whom Islamic identity is manifested.

According to the preceding quote, Muslims have faced serious hardships because of their religious identity. Another Muslim visitor expressed her experience in Ethiopia as follows:

> Women wearing headscarves and men with long beards have undergone additional security screening. Some participants claim that in Ethiopia, Muslims are targeted for their religious identity. I have been to Europe but did not face such discriminative surveillance and inspection against Muslims.

The above quote indicates that discriminative surveillance and inspection against Muslims is a common practice and considerably impacts Muslim travelers. Addressing these discriminative acts for halal tourism development in Ethiopia is very important.

One interviewee claims:

> Especially after 9/11, Islamophobia causes racial profiling against Muslims and Ethiopia is not an exceptional country. I witnessed that airport screening has placed special attention on Muslim women who wrap their headscarves up and/ or cover more of their bodies. I have known some Muslim women who lay aside their religious clothes or traditional Islamic dress to avoid religious-based discrimination.

According to the above statement, Muslim visitors were cringed due to the act of some security apparatus and staffers against Muslim women. The following quote also reinforces the above claim.

> In Ethiopian airports, I had seen *hijabists* screened frequently. It is logical to conclude that these women were targeted because of their Islamic identity, mainly their headscarves. That fact is that these days many people associate terrorism with Muslims. That is why Muslims are targeted at many airports.

One participant claims:

> [...] in the aftermath of 9/11, Muslims have been profiled simply because of their religious identity. Even some Ethiopian are frightened when they see *Hijabists*. This shows the extent of Islamophobia in Ethiopia. I viewed the situation of Ethiopia for Muslims and Arabs traveling through Ethiopian airports and touring around cities of Ethiopia. To be honest, some security staff members seem like Islamophobes. They try to humiliate Muslims as if Muslims were terrorists. The concerned body of the Ethiopian government should take serious action in this regard. The police and security forces must be oriented to treat Muslims as equal to non-Muslims [...].

Personnel of Ethiopian airports were asked to respond to the above claims. Personnel of Ethiopian airport based at Bole airport claimed that Ethiopian Airlines had a positive outlook toward Muslim travelers and would not discriminate against any religious denomination. He spoke that the emerging Islamophobia was a challenge for every destination, and he did not think Muslims were targeted at Bole international airport or other parts of the country. He affirmed that the Ethiopian airline had been working to address such a problem by taking proactive measures. He added that Ethiopian airline is indifferent to the religious affiliation of the passenger.

Ethiopian Muslims have also claimed that the Ethiopian security sector has collected information about Muslims through extensive surveillance and monitoring of mosques and Muslim communities. Moreover, some sectors, such as the state's media, Ethiopian airlines, army and police, are not open to *hijabist* Muslims joining as personnel.

Domestic visitors also claimed that they were profiled not only by the police but also discriminated by some civilians. For instance, one female Muslim interviewee alleges:

> I usually travel to visit some historical sites. However, some people profiled me because of my Islamic identity, hijab. Some youths insult me by saying, 'Terrorist! Terrorist!' Some tour guides have no positive attitude towards women who wrap up hijab like me. To be frank, Islamophobia is increasing in Ethiopia. Whenever there were conflicts between Muslims and the government or Non-Muslim, we faced racist verbal, even sometimes physical, attacks from police and security. They used racial slurs such as የአረብዳቄላ (the Arab bastard) and terrorist to humiliate and embarrass us.

According to the key informants, systematic and extensive surveillance against Muslims is uncommon in Ethiopia. For instance, some organizations discriminate against Muslims while employing workers. Muslims are discriminated against for their name, Islamic wearing and beard. In some Christian-dominant Ethiopian cities, Muslim women have been insulted as 'terrorists' and the 'the Arab bastard.' This harassment includes visitors and inbound tourists. Recently, some areas have been a campaign and boycott against halal business sectors. This anti-halal business movement is based on the belief that the Christian majority presents itself as persecuted and excluded from marketplace resources by the emerging halal business that Muslims mainly own. By accusing Muslims of introducing Sharia law into Ethiopia, some non-Muslims seek political support from the government.

On the contrary, some non-Muslim businesspersons are ready to enter the Halal tourism business. For instance, one tour operator company's owner has already started providing halal tours and guiding services for halal-conscious visitors. Other non-Muslim businesspersons and investors are ready to invest in halal hotels and halal restaurants. For instance, one participant alleges:

> [...] I do not mind! I am not a religious person; I am a liberal man. Not only do I have no objection, but I also plan to invest in halal businesses. It is business, and religion has nothing to do with this. If someone guarantees me a certain demand for halal tourism, I will surely invest in it. I am a business first. However, one thing I want you to know is that it should not adversely affect other segments.

The above quotes reveal that there exists widespread Islamophobia in Ethiopia. The anti-Islam propaganda that rejuvenated following the terrorist act of 9/11 caused the proliferation of Islamophobia in Ethiopia. Verbal and/or physical attacks against Muslims, mainly Muslim women are not uncommon in the public space of Ethiopia; this has been manifested in Ethiopia, especially from 2012 to 2020. The findings of this study reveal the proliferation of islamophobia at state, organizational and individual levels. Some parts of the country also have tendencies to boycott halal products. Therefore, the prevalence of Islamophobia in Ethiopia could adversely affect all kinds of halal business in general and halal tourism development in particular. Hence, the Ethiopian government should note that in addition to causing detectable negative socio-cultural, diplomatic and political impacts, Islamophobia has undesirable consequences on the Ethiopian economy, and the government should address the issue timely. Due to widespread negative sentiments against Islam and Muslims, terminologies such as Muslim, Halal, Sharia and Islam have become frightening for some businesspersons and government officials. Even some Muslim stakeholders in Ethiopia have resisted the development of halal tourism.

The Availability of Tourismophobes

The preceding section discussed how Islamophobia has evolved globally and transcended to Ethiopia. The next section will look at the evolution of tourismophobia and its likely effect on halal tourism development.

The journalist of the *El Pais* newspaper in Madrid coined the term 'tourismophobia' (Egresi, 2018). Consequently, media and researchers have adopted the terminology. In addition to Islamophobia, tourismophobia could be an obstacle to developing halal tourism in Ethiopia. According to this study, two factors cause the birth of phobia against tourism. The first reason is the mass flow of inbound visitors to Europe, which causes overcrowding, congestion and inflation. Because of this, some people tend to be tourismophobes, which sometimes have xenophobia characteristics. Second, in some culturally and religiously conservative countries, people turn out to be tourismophobes because they assume that the very nature of tourism is against their religion and culture. They thought that activities in tourism deviated from the principle of their religion.

Currently, in popular tourist destination cities such as Paris and Barcelona, over-tourism deteriorates the quality of the local community life and is blamed for causing inflation. This undesired host-guest relationship caused by over-tourism eventually led to tourismophobia in well-developed destinations. In contrast, the strong connection of tourism with haram activities such as alcoholism, gambling and voyeurism brings about tourismophobia in many Muslim countries. In developing countries, tourism has been accused of poisoning the religion and culture of the indigenous people. In Ethiopia, some spiritual and traditional community leaders tend to be tourismophobes.

Some pious Muslims openly objected to the proposal of developing halal tourism. For instance, one Imam claims, 'tourism is not Islamic whatever form it takes, [...] not at all. [...] it is against the very principle of Muslims. I never thought that tourism could be halal in Islam. I never advise any Muslim to participate in Tourism.'

This Imam seriously objects to the development of tourism in Ethiopia. According to him, Muslims are not allowed to participate in any tourism, whether it is halal or not. Similarly, another Da'e (preacher) alleges the following:

> [...] I do not support tourism, whether halal or not, because it paves the way for *Shirk* (idolatry or polytheism). If you start halal tourism, it is most likely that some Muslims will start to visit tombs and Mausoleums and venerate them, which is a *shirk* and strictly forbidden in Islam. It is the greatest sin in Islam. Islam teaches us to avoid any action that leads humankind toward sin. Therefore, I do not want halal tourism to develop.

According to this participant, tourism per se may not be a problem, but it paves the way for evil activities. Another participant also expresses his concern as follows:

> I think tourism is the culture of Westerners. It is a device to impose their culture and haram activities upon the Muslim world. Tourism introduced and/or induced most evil deeds such as alcoholism, prostitution and voyeurism to Muslim countries. Therefore, I dislike tourism, and I never support the development of any type of tourism in Ethiopia.

Ethiopian Muslims largely hold a positive attitude toward tourism, but it does not mean there are not a few pious people who develop a phobia against tourism.

Another participant stated:

> Islam allows Muslims to visit only three places: Mecca, Medina and Jerusalem. There is also an accurate hadith in this regard. As registered by authentic hadith Bukhari, Prophet Mohammed (PBUM) said Muslims should not travel to visit holy sites except to the three Mosques: Masjid Al-Haram (Mecca), Masjid al Nebawi (Medina) and Masjid al-Aqsa (Jerusalem). According to Islamic teaching, the Kaaba, Masjid an-Nebawi and Al-Aqsua Mosques are the holiest places. Other than these three holy places, Muslims are not allowed to visit any place, and I do not agree anymore with the development of halal tourism in Ethiopia. Two or three years ago, the federal *Mejli*s had arranged a trip towards Al-Nejashi for pilgrims that were anti-Muslim action.

However, the above participant misplaced the hadith. He considered halal tourism a pilgrimage. According to other Muslim scholars, these places were mentioned to refer to travels conducted only for worship (see Chapter 2). Whatever the reason is, this interviewee develops a phobia against tourism.

Generally, the preceding quotes indicate the availability of tourism phobia among a few Muslim religious leaders. Previous studies, however, have failed to consider the impact of tourismophobia on tourism development. As noted in the preceding quotes, it is unfortunate that a few Ethiopian Muslims seem to have low awareness about the very nature of tourism. Non-Muslims opposed the development of halal tourism because they feared that halal business would dominate their business and halal tourism would cause the spread of Islamic culture in Ethiopia. In contrast, few Muslims are tourismophobes because they think that tourism is against Islam. Even though these challenges should be considered a barrier to establishing halal tourism and orientation about halal tourism must be continuously given, the number of these people is insignificant to halt the development of halal tourism in Ethiopia.

Lack of Muslim-Friendly Infrastructures

In Ethiopia, the researcher identified twofold challenges as far as tourism infrastructure is concerned. First, as is true for developing economies, there is a lack of general tourism infrastructure. Second, the existing limited infrastructures are not Muslim-friendly; they have been tailored to suit the taste of Western visitors. Hence, in addition to the overall shortage of tourism infrastructures, the existing limited infrastructures are not welcoming to halal-conscious visitors. Based on the participants' claims, these infrastructural pitfalls of halal tourism development have been discussed in the following subsections.

Lack of Muslim-Friendly Airports

The findings of this study reveal that challenges facing halal-conscious visitors at airports while traveling include Islamophobic staff; lack of inclusive and accessible airports; lack of Muslim-friendly restaurants, hotel rooms, shops, and public spaces and unavailability of information about halal foods and Muslim-friendly attractions on brochure and websites.

Airports are among the prime touchpoints of entry to a destination and the last point of departure. Therefore, facilities and services offered at airports matter a lot because services at airports are the first encounter to visitors and leave the last impression on the visitors. The main facilities Muslim travelers demand at airports are the availability of prayer facilities such as prayer rooms, proper ablution facilities and halal meal options or halal restaurants. As to the researcher's observation, most Ethiopian airports do not provide Muslim-friendly airport services and facilities for Muslim travelers. Even though there is a single prayer room at Bole international airport, there are no proper ablution facilities. During an interview with one international visitor at Bole airport, he claims as follows:

> Bole international airport seems very great, but there are no proper toilets and ablution facilities for Muslim travelers. I saw many Muslim travelers wandering here and there to search for ablution at the airport. I was also searching for ablution facilities but could not find them. Moreover, I could not find halal restaurants in and/or around the airport. I did not expect such a big airport have no ablution facilities. This shows how they undermine their Muslim customers.

The opinion of other participants also reinforces the above claim. A domestic Muslim traveler interviewed at Bole International airport alleges the following:

> [...] it is a paradox that there is a huge influx of Muslim visitors, but there are no halal services and products in the Ethiopian airports. Not only Bole international airport but also all airports in Ethiopia do not provide facilities for prayers, including *wudu* (ablution) facilities. The toilets are not Muslim-friendly. They had to arrange some toilets and ablution facilities for the Muslim customers, but they did not consider Muslims while setting up such facilities at the airports. Numerous Muslim investors and visitors frequently use the Ethiopian airport and many Muslims transit through Bole international airport. By considering such facts, they have to reconsider their facilities and services. There are no Mosques near the Airport where Friday prayers would be conducted.

The preceding participant argues that the Ethiopian airports did not consider Muslim travelers' religious needs and wants. This directly influences the effort of halal tourism development in Ethiopia. Another international Muslim traveler claims:

> [...] generally, Muslim passengers have no halal food outlets and prayer facilities in all terminals of Ethiopian airports. The toilets at the airports are also fixed in a way that does not fit Muslims' traditions. [...]. Put another way, Ethiopian airports are not Muslim-Friendly.

However, the airport authorities claimed that if there were a demand for halal food, the airport would consider the establishment of halal-only restaurants. They would welcome collaboration with the halal investors on the halal market segment. Personnel of Ethiopian airports mentioned that Ethiopian Airlines and airports had been providing Muslim-friendly services to the passengers. They were also looking at providing Muslim-friendly toilets and wudu facilities. For instance, a prayer space was designated at Bole international airport.

Nowadays, Muslim visitors are more vocal in expressing their preferences and requirements regarding halal food and prayer facilities at airports or accommodations. Additionally, the ever-increasing of Muslim travelers has been compelling the travel industry to sit and discuss the needs of Muslim travelers. This would involve dining establishments displaying the identical halal logo across Ethiopia.

Lack of Muslim-Friendly Accommodations

Muslim visitors interviewed for this study said that halal accommodation was their primary concern while traveling. Contrary to this fact, Ethiopia has no star-rated halal hotels or accommodations. One traveler has expressed his disappointment with the lack of halal services as follows:

> In Ethiopia, hotels do not fit Muslim customers. They have no place to pray, halal food, or a halal beverage to drink [...]. The toilets are also not Muslim-friendly. There are beers and unnecessary pictures in the room of some hotels. There are no places of entertainment for Muslims.

The preceding claim indicates that most star-rated hotels do not provide Muslim-friendly products and services. The following comment of one research participant also reinforces this claim.

> As far as accommodation is concerned, halal food is a very important consideration for many Muslim tourists. Some destinations worldwide seem to understand this and have started identifying this potential. They are adapting their products and services to meet the needs of Muslim visitors. Japan can be mentioned as an example in this regard. To draw the attention of Muslim travelers, the Japanese Government has encouraged the availability of Muslim-friendly products and services, such as halal food. Ethiopia

does not exert any effort to attract Muslim tourists even though half of its 115 million population are Muslims. There is not even a single-star-rating hotel that provides full halal services. Ethiopia seems unaware of the economic and socio-cultural contribution of the halal business.

According to the foregoing argument, in Ethiopia, stakeholders did not try to adapt halal services to the existing hotels' services to meet the needs of Muslim travelers or establish separate halal hotels.

Participant from Ethiopian (federal) *Mejlis* claims as follows:

> There is no halal hotel in Addis Ababa. We have been facing a serious challenge in welcoming our guests from different countries because there are no standard halal accommodations in the country. Sometimes, our guests spend nights at private homes. Even we are suffering from a lack of halal hotels to run conferences and meetings. We usually use 'Uma Hotel,' but this hotel is insufficient and not a standard one. There is a huge demand for halal accommodations from both domestic and inbound visitors, but the concerned bodies are not doing their job in this regard. We have branches in each region, but most areas have no halal accommodations. For instance, there are no Muslim-friendly accommodations in metropolitan cities such as Bahrdar, Gonder, Hawassa and Mekele.

Major concerns raised by interviewed participants on the unavailability of prayer facilities in accommodation seem to be a common problem for most participants. Moreover, the availability of voyeurism and alcoholism at accommodations, especially at star-rating hotels, were serious concerns to Muslim travelers.

A Muslim visitor participant alleges:

> I spent some nights at a star-rating hotel in Addis Ababa. However, to be honest, the environment within and around the hotel was not comfortable. There has been alcoholism, loud music and voyeurism. Due to the availability of such activities, I did not feel comfortable. These things are against the very principle of my religion.

Another participant has reinforced the above complaints as follows:

> I always dream of traveling with my spouse and children on weekends and holidays. However, most of the destinations have no halal accommodations or cafeteria services. My friends also planned to visit, but the absence of halal accommodation has constrained us from traveling. The Ethiopian hospitality and hotel industries generally are repulsive against Muslims.

All in all, the responses of the interviewed participants and the group discussants reveal that although the demand for halal tourism seems very high, there is a serious shortage of halal accommodations in Ethiopia. The researcher, personally, has also faced such challenges. He has participated in Ethiopian Universities' annual research conferences. Though there were Muslim participants, including the researcher, the hoteliers or the conference organizers did not provide halal food and beverages. Even they have never understood whether halal-conscious visitors need halal foods and beverages. For Ethiopia to develop halal tourism, serious attention must be paid to awareness creation. It is especially important to draw investors' attention to invest their capital in this area. Turkish, the UAE and Saudi investors could be potential investors in halal accommodations.

Lack of Halal Recreational Centers and Leisure Facilities

As noted by many interviewed participants of the study under consideration, the number of Ethiopian Muslims who want to engage in recreational and leisure activities has been increasing exponentially. Especially urban dwellers, millennials, and educated Muslims want to travel in-group with their families and alone. Simultaneously these portions of Muslim populations do not want to compromise their religion. They demand halal recreational centers and leisure facilities. Unfortunately, there is no single halal recreation center in Ethiopia. One interviewed participant speaks:

> I want to refresh my body and soul on the weekends or holidays, but there are no recreation centers in and around Addis Ababa. My children always ask me to take them somewhere for refreshments. Still, I cannot travel with my children because what is available in recreational areas is not good for Muslims and children. I know some resorts on the outskirt of Addis Ababa, but non-halal services and products surround them. Though I have a desire, time and capacity to enjoy myself at some recreational centers, the absence of halal services and products constrained me from enjoying myself in such areas.

Other interviewed participants have shared the preceding concern. This implies that there has been a high demand for halal resorts and entertainment in Ethiopia, but there is a huge gap on the supply side. Another interviewed participant argues:

> In the past couple of years, the demand for Muslims (mainly educated and urban dwellers) to engage in entertainment/tourism has been increasing. Simultaneously, Ethiopian Muslims' awareness of the principle of their religion [Islam] has been steadily rising. These days, most Ethiopian Muslims want to refrain from haram activities but want to participate in tourism. Previously, many people considered tourism unIslamic, but now many Muslims, including religious leaders, want to engage in a halal form of tourism. Therefore, I advise that attractions and entertainment centers should begin to provide prayer rooms and halal food.

The preceding opinions and quotes indicate that though there is a high demand for halal entertainment and halal recreation, there is no supply to entertain such demands. Most of the interviewed participants and discussants of the focus groups seemed very enthusiastic about engaging in halal entertainment and resorts. However, the existing limited entertainment centers lack halal services and have been surrounded by anti-Sharia activities such as voyeurism, open kissing and loudly played music. There are also religiously prohibited products, such as pork and alcoholic beverages. Therefore, the lack of halal entertainment centers could be an immediate obstacle to halal tourism development.

Absence of Muslim-Friendly Tour Operators and Tour Guides

There is no doubt that tour operators and tour guides play a crucial role in the shaping destination image, retaining visitors and increasing revisit demand. This study's findings reveal that no tour operators provide Muslim-friendly holidays in Ethiopia. Only a few conventional travel agents and tour operators try to offer tour packages to Muslim travelers. There are also no tour guides who understand and accommodate the values and culture of Muslim travelers. Ethiopian tour guides do not know Arabic/Islamic terminologies. Tour guides are supposed to be ambassadors of destinations who serve as cultural and social mediators between the host and the guest. Their services potentially influence the visitors' perception of the image of the visited destination and the decision to revisit.

One interviewed study participant speaks the following:

> Ethiopia is a country of celebrated Muslims such as Bilal al Habesha and King Nejashi. Ethiopia is also known to be the land of the first Hijra. Having such information, I thought Ethiopia was rich in Islamic heritage and history. Therefore, I decided to spend my holiday in Ethiopia. However, when I visited it, I could not find halal tour operators who took me to Islamic heritage areas. The existing tour operators do not know Muslim-friendly destinations and attractions. There are no tour guides to interpret Islamic heritages, legends and histories.

According to the preceding interviewee, there are no tour operators and tour guides that promote and market Ethiopia's Islamic heritage. This, in turn, negatively affects the movement of halal tourism development.

Another participant alleges:

> In Ethiopia, there are no halal tour operators, travel agencies or tour guides. Even though there have been numerous Islamic heritage sites that would attract halal-conscious visitors, no itineraries indicate the location of Muslim-friendly attractions and destinations. Iconic Islamic heritage sites and attractions have not been included in the itineraries of tour operators. Islamic heritage sites have neither been promoted for potential

visitors nor visited by the actual ones. There have been tens of thousands of outbound pilgrims toward Saudi Arabia. However, there are no halal tour operators and travel agencies to facilitate the tour for those pilgrims. The federal *Mejlis* arranges pilgrimages for the pilgrims.

Absence of Halal Promotion and Halal Websites

Tourism could be promoted through different materials such as travel brochures, websites and online booking platforms (Benjamin et al., 2020). The promotion provides general information about a destination that ultimately shapes a visitor's perception of a destination and affects their travel decision-making. Through a content analysis of the county-level brochures and advertisement materials, the researcher has confirmed that the tourism promotional materials of Ethiopia lack diversity and continue to persuade homogenous Western audiences. This lack of inclusiveness in promotional materials could cause challenges to halal tourism in Ethiopia. Halal tourism resources have been generally marginalized in Ethiopian tourism promotion and marketing. Ethiopia's current tourism promotion methodology is one-size-fits-all-visitors – excluding a large portion of the country's tourism resource and ignoring significant market segments. Tourism promotional materials have adversely affected halal tourism activities in Ethiopia by not including pictures and information about Muslim-friendly tourism destinations or touristic activities in the country. In addition to being ignored in national promotional materials, halal tourism activities in Ethiopia have not been promoted through the internet or website. For instance, one participant claims that:

> I have been searching about Ethiopian heritage and itineraries of Islamic heritage sites and Muslim-friendly destinations in Ethiopia. Ethiopia has precious Islamic heritage sites but fails to promote them to targeted customers. It must design an appropriate website, promote them […], and introduce them […].

The focus group discussion participants also confirmed that there were no state or private media to promote Islamic heritage or target halal visitors.

Halal tourism resources and Muslim-friendly attractions should be included in promoting and marketing touristic destinations, activities and spaces. Historically, halal customers have not been considered a target market by the Ethiopian government and the private sector. This study confirms that though there is some improvement, this tradition has continued. As noted by Benjamin et al. (2020), promotion is not just about introducing and selling products and attractions; it also conveys representations of social groups and societies and/or it can also marginalize social and cultural groups. Hence, Ethiopian Muslims should be represented in national tourism promotional materials by including their rich heritage.

Lack of Halal Healthcare Facilities and Services

The lack of halal healthcare facilities and services will constrain halal tourism development in Ethiopia. Although Muslim women want prenatal and postnatal care in a health facility, they often encounter challenges obtaining Muslim-friendly services in many health centers. These difficulties emanated from the contradiction between their religious obligation and how services have been delivered to Muslim Women. Especially the maternal healthcare services (both government and private) are designed to meet the needs of mainstream non-Muslim women.

One participant alleges:

> I believe a pregnant mother must go to go to the hospital. However, many healthcare centers are not Muslim-friendly. Most doctors who examine women are males, which is against our culture and religion. Ethiopian Muslims demand halal healthcare, especially for maternal check-ups and delivery.

Several personal narrative accounts from participants indicated that the available healthcare centers are not Muslim-friendly. Nor do doctors understand sharia and Islamic culture.

> Some Muslim women go to the hospital neither for maternal checkups nor to give birth because there is no Muslim-friendly environment in hospitals. It is not allowed for a Muslim woman to expose her naked body, especially her private parts, to men in both culture and religion. Hence I highly recommend the establishment of a halal health care center.
> (Discussant Woman, FGD)

Several participants noted that halal healthcare is one critical challenge in establishing halal tourism. Halal visitors would want to receive sharia-friendly treatment and halal medications. However, there are no such facilities and services in Ethiopia.

One participant also argues:

> Getting halal medication, food, and a place to pray in Ethiopian healthcare centers is difficult. Most women did not attend maternity care nor deliver at the hospital because of the unavailability of Muslim-friendly healthcare centers. This is not good, especially for those who are observant Muslims. In the hospital, patients and staff need private space to pray, and it would be better if they had quiet places for prayers.
> (Discussant, FGD)

Several interviewed participants stated that a serious shortage of Muslim-friendly healthcare centers adversely affects halal tourism development in

Ethiopia. Visitors may face illness and seek a Muslim-friendly healthcare center like everyone else. The existing healthcare centers have not accommodated the values and beliefs of Muslim patients. The challenges Muslims have faced in healthcare centers include but are not limited to the absence of prayer places, halal food and halal medication or pharmaceuticals, and lack of knowledge about Muslim culture among healthcare providers.

Lack of Awareness about the Practice and Concept of Halal Tourism

The lack of appropriate knowledge about the practices and concept of halal tourism is the genesis of most of the challenges mentioned above. Since halal tourism is a nascent industry, stakeholders misunderstand the concepts and practices of halal tourism. Many stakeholders do not dare to invest in halal tourism, and some develop a negative attitude toward halal tourism. The foregoing quotes show that the government official, industry stakeholders and the wider community have not understood halal tourism in Ethiopia. They consider it an Islamic business designed only for Muslims. However, the fact is that halal tourism is a sharia-compliant secular business open to Muslims and non-Muslim visitors. Many people confine the term 'halal' to the slaughtering system. Therefore, a lack of awareness may affect investment in halal tourism, which highly affects halal tourism development.

Moreover, until recently, Interest-Free Banks (IFB) were prohibited from operating in Ethiopia. This prohibition also adversely affected halal developments and investments. In halal tourism, financial issues at the accommodations, restaurants, travel organizers and airlines should comply with halal regulations. However, the Ethiopian government has recently allowed interest-free banks to run in Ethiopia. Accordingly, at this time, at least two interest-free banks, namely ZamZam Banks Sc. and Hijra Bank Sc. have been opened.

SWOT Analysis of Halal Tourism Development in Ethiopia

SWOT is an abbreviation of strengths, weaknesses, opportunities and threats. SWOT analysis is a widely used method of evaluation in tourism development. The internal strengths and weaknesses, as well as external opportunities and threats to halal tourism development in Ethiopia, will be discussed.

Internal Strengths

Internal strength refers to the internal positive forces to develop halal tourism in Ethiopia. The first strength of Ethiopia to be a halal tourism destination is its geostrategic location with the Muslim world. Its proximity to the Muslim world, which is commonly expected to be the major senders of halal-conscious visitors, is an imperative asset in developing halal tourism. Its near and distant Muslim neighbors surround Ethiopia, presumed to be senders of halal visitors. Second, the strength of Ethiopia is related to its rich manmade and natural resources. Ethiopia can provide unique tangible and intangible Islamic heritages found nowhere in the world to halal-conscious visitors. The other strong point of Ethiopia to host halal tourism is its variety of Islamic archaeological sites and heritages, rich Islamic history and legends. Moreover, the burgeoning huge potential domestic customers ease the task of halal tourism development. The findings of this study show that there is high initiation among Muslim Ethiopians to participate in halal tourism as both investors and visitors.

Internal Weaknesses

There are also internal challenges that adversely affect halal tourism development in Ethiopia. The first internal challenge is the lack of institutions taking the initiative in Ethiopia's halal tourism development. The Ethiopian tourism commission still seems to undermine the role of halal tourism in the Ethiopian economy. Personnel of this office consider halal tourism as an Islamic business, and they have a negative attitude toward halal tourism. Moreover, the sector suffers from a lack of trained human power. The lack of tourism experts in general and halal tourism experts, in particular, could be obstacles to this effort. Tour operators and travel agencies are unaware of halal tourism

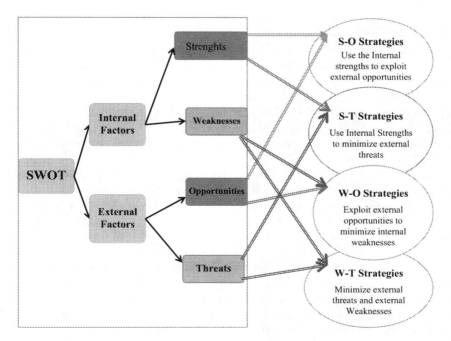

Figure 5.2 SWOT strategies.

Source: By the researchers.

and do not dare to promote Ethiopia as a halal destination. Another internal challenge would come up from bigoted Muslims and Christians. The lack of sharia-compliant infrastructures also has a negative effect. The existing infrastructures do not consider the needs of halal-conscious visitors. This poses a serious problem in developing halal tourism.

External Opportunities

Several external positive forces and favorable factors to developing halal tourism in Ethiopia exist. First, Muslim communities' interest in halal tourism has been increasing from time to time. As studies conducted by Battour et al. indicate, Muslim Millennials want to engage in halal tourism. Hence, Ethiopia could be one potential destination for this halal tourism market segment. Moreover, the number of Muslims has been steadily increasing. This assures the sustainability and profitability of halal tourism for decades to come. A study conducted on the behavior of Muslim visitors confirms that Muslim tourists spend high, stay longer and travel with family. Such behavior of halal visitors assures the profitability of the halal tourism business. The availability of huge investors from the Islamic world in Ethiopia is another enabling factor. According to the Ethiopia Investment Commission, countries such as Turkey, UAE and Qatar have huge investments in Ethiopia.

External Threats

There are also negative forces that adversely affect halal tourism development in Ethiopia. The first of these unfavorable factors is the proliferation of Islamophobia. Following the terrorist act of 9/11, there has been a series of character assassination campaigns against Muslims and their institutions. These campaigns add fuel to the preexisting Islamophobia. This 'Western-made' Islamophobia has pervaded different parts of the world, and Ethiopia is not an exceptional country. Hence, Islamophobia could adversely affect halal tourism devolvement in Ethiopia and elsewhere. Second, the proliferation of terrorism will also tackle halal tourism development. Westerners deliberately associate terrorism with Islam and Muslims, and by using their strong media, they induced this concept to the wider world. Given Muslims are the majority of consumers of halal tourism, the proliferation of terrorism in general and its association with Muslims and Islam in particular adversity affects the halal tourism development project. The entrance of experienced and strong countries such as Turkey and Malaysia into halal tourism may stiffen the competition. With ancient Islamic heritage and advanced infrastructure, superstructure, better human resources and experiences, Turkey has a comparative and competitive advantage over Ethiopia in developing halal tourism. Ethiopia, therefore, could face stiff competition from such countries. Another external negative factor is the prevalence of violent insurgency, instability and civil war in the Islamic world. The anti-government protests, uprisings and armed rebellions in the so-called Arab Spring that

Table 5.1 SWOT Analysis Summary

Internal		External	
Strengths	Weakness	Opportunities	Threats
• Ethiopia is globally recognized for being the land of the first Hijra	• Lack of halal Muslim-friendly infrastructure and qualified human resources	• Changes in Muslim tourist preferences from Europe to Africa after 9/11	• The proliferation of terrorism. Westerners deliberately associate terrorism with Islam and Muslims
• Ethiopia has a strong reputation as a homeland of great Muslims such as Bilal al-Habesha, King Al-Nejashi and Um Ayman (Baraka)	• Ethiopia is perceived as a Christian country by outsiders	• The prevalence of a huge number of Muslims in general and educated Muslim youths who are interested in travel in particular	• The proliferation of Islamophobia, especially from 9/11 onwards
• There is huge domestic demand. Ethiopian Muslims are enthusiastic about engaging in halal tourism	• Lack of human resources, resistance from different stakeholders	• Unavailability of strong competitors in the Horn of Africa	• Expansion of halal tourism in countries such as Turkey, Egypt and the UAE region may cause stiff competition
• Ethiopia has rich Islamic Heritages, stories and legends	• The political situation in Ethiopia is uncertain. The image of an unsafe country held by potential visitors	• The increment in Muslim communities' interest in engaging in halal tourism	• The prevalence of violent insurgency, instability and civil war in the Muslim world

started in the 2010s and spread across much of the Arab world could highly affect the halal tourism sector. As of 2012, there has also been internal instability, civil disobedience and uprising throughout Ethiopia. Hence, such instabilities and uprisings could negatively affect halal tourism development in Ethiopia.

References

Algieri, B., Aquino, A., & Succurro, M. (2018). International Competitive Advantages in Tourism: An Eclectic View. *Tourism Management Perspectives*, *25*(November 2017), 41–52. https://doi.org/10.1016/j.tmp.2017.11.003

Bashir, M., Afzal, T., & Azeem, M. (2008). Reliability and Validity of Qualitative and Operational Research Paradigm. *Pakistan Journal of Statistics and Operation Research*, *1*, 35–45.

Battour, M. (2019). *Halal Tourism: Achieving Muslim Tourists' Satisfaction and Loyalty*. Author. https://books.google.com.tr/books?id=Jx-lyAEACAAJ

Butler, R. (2008). Butler Tourism Development Revisited. In S. Babu, S. Mishra, & B. B. Parida (Eds.), *Tourism Development Revisited: Concepts, Issues and ParadigmsIssues and Paradigms* (pp. 55–64). SAGE Publications Ltd.

Benjamin, S., Bottone, E., & Lee, M. (2020). Beyond Accessibility: Exploring the Representation of People with Disabilities in Tourism Promotional Materials. *Journal of Sustainable Tourism*, *29*(2–3), 295–313. https://doi.org/10.1080/09669582.2020.1755295

Briedenhann, J., & Wickens, E. (2004). Tourism Routes as a Tool for the Economic Development of Rural Areas-Vibrant Hope or an Impossible Dream? *Tourism Management*, *25*(1), 71–79. https://doi.org/10.1016/S0261-5177(03)00063-3

Cater, C., & Low, T. any. (2012). Focus Groups. In L. Dwyer, A. Gill, & N. Seetaram (Eds.), *Handbook of Research Methods in Tourism Quantitative and Qualitative Approaches* (pp. 352–365). Edward Elgar Publishing Limited.

Cerulli, E. (1971). *The Most Salient Parts, Mainly Focused on Ethiopia: Islam Yesterday and Today*. Roma Istituto Per'Oriente.

Chountala, V., Chountalas, P., Magoutas, A., & Mavragani, E. (2019). The Cultural Route of Hercules: Mapping the Tourist's Perspective. *International Journal of Tourism Policy*, *9*(2), 131–154. https://doi.org/10.1504/IJTP.2019.102638

Creswell, J. W., & Miller, D. L. (2000). Determining Validity in Qualitative Inquiry. *Theory into Practice*, *39*(3), 124–131.

Csapo, J., & Berki, M. (2014). *Existing and Future Tourism Potential and the Geographical Basis of Thematic Routes in south Transdanubia, Hungary To cite this version: HAL Id: halshs-00516130*.

Desplat, P., & Østebø, T. (2013). *Muslims in Ethiopia: The Christian Legacy, Identity Politics, and Islamic Reformism* (P. Desplat & T. Østebø, Eds.; Vol. 4, Issue 1). Palgrave Macmillan.

Egresi, I. (2018. September 20-23). *"Tourists Go Home!" – Tourism Overcrowding and "Tourismophobia"in European Cities (Can Tourists and Residents still Co-Habitate in the City?)*. Paper presented at the International Conference on [CO]HABITATION TACTICS Imagining future spaces in architecture, city and landscape, Kashar Albania.

Erlich, H. (1994). *Ethiopia and the Middle East*. Lynne Rienner Published Ltd.

Erlich, H. (2013). *Islam, Christianity, Judaism, and Ethiopia: The Messages of Religions*. Haggai Erlich.
Ethiopian Investment Commission. (2018). *Ethiopia: #Turkish Investments Roaring in Ethiopia*.
Ethiopian Investment Commission. (2019). *Saudi Arabia Reaffirms to Enhance Ethio-Saudi Business Partnership*.
Ghimire, K. B. (2001). The Growth of National and Regional Tourism in Developing Countries: An Overview. In K. B. Ghimire (Ed.), *The Native Tourist: Mass Tourism Within Developing Countries* (pp. 1–29). UNRISD/Earthscan.
Görmüş, S., Atmiş, E., Günşen, H. B., Özkazanç, N. K., & Artar, M. (2017). The Importance of Mapping Natural and Cultural Routes in Rural Tourism: Bartın Case. *Research Journal of Agricultural Sciences*, *10*(1), 32–38. www.nobel.gen.tr
Ho, G., & McKercher, B. (2014). A Comparison of Long-Haul and Short-Haul Business Tourists of Hong Kong. *Asia Pacific Journal of Tourism Research*, *19*(3), 342–355. https://doi.org/10.1080/10941665.2012.746235
Jennings, G. (2005). Interviewing a Focus on Qualitative Techniques. In P. Burns & W. R. Ritchie (Eds.), *Tourism Research Methods Integrating Theory with Practice* (pp. 99–155). CABI.
Knox, S., & Burkard, A. W. (2009). Qualitative Research Interviews. *Psychotherapy Research*, *19*(4–5), 566–575. https://doi.org/10.1080/10503300802702105
Labouisse, J. P., Bellachew, B., Kotecha, S., & Bertrand, B. (2008). Current Status of Coffee (Coffea arabica L.) Genetic Resources in Ethiopia: Implications for Conservation. *Genetic Resources and Crop Evolution*, *55*(7), 1079–1093. https://doi.org/10.1007/s10722-008-9361-7
McGehee, N. G. (2012). Interview Techniques. In L. Dwyer, A. Gill, & N. Seetaram (Eds.), *Handbook of Research Methods in Tourism: Quantitative and Qualitative Approaches* (pp. 352–364). Edward Elgar Publishing Limited. https://doi.org/10.4337/9781781001295
McKercher, B., & Mak, B. (2019). The Impact of Distance on International Tourism Demand. *Tourism Management Perspectives*, *31*(March), 340–347. https://doi.org/10.1016/j.tmp.2019.07.004
Ribeiro, N. F., & Foemmel, E. W. (2012). Participant Observation. In L. Dwyer, A. Gill, & N. Seetaram (Eds.), *Handbook of Research Methods in Tourism: Quantitative and Qualitative Approaches* (Issue 3, pp. 392–403). Edward Elgar Publishing, Inc.
Pritchard, J.C. (1855). *The Natural History of Man: Comprising Inquiries into the Modifying Influence of Physical and Moral Agencies on the Different Tribes of the Human Family*. London: H. Bail- lière.
Sihab Ad-Din Ahmad, A. al-Q (2003). *Futuh Al-Habasha: The Conquest of Abyssinia (English Translation)*. Tsehai Publishers.
Sindiga, I. (1996). Domestic Tourism in Kenya. *Annals of Tourism Research*, *23*(1), 19–31. https://doi.org/10.4324/9781849770057
Sisay, A. (2009). *Historical Development of Travel and Tourism in Ethiopia* (Kuraz (ed.)).
Stebbins, R. (2019). What Is Exploration? In *Exploratory Research in the Social Sciences* (Thousand O, Issue January). SAGE Publications, Inc. https://doi.org/10.4135/9781412984249
Tafesse, A. (2016). The Historic Route in Ethiopian Tourism Development. *African Journal of Hospitality, Tourism and Leisure*, *5*(2), 0–13.
Trimingham, J. S. (1952). *Islam in Ethiopia*. Oxford University Press.

Tucker, C. M. (2011). *Coffee Culture: Local Experiences, Global Connections*. Routledge Taylor and Francis Group.

Veal, A. J. (2018). *Research Methods for Leisure and Tourism* (5th ed.). Pearson Education Limited.

Waters, N. (2017). Toblers FirstLaw of Geography. In D. Richardson, N. Castree, M. F. Goodchild, A. Kobayashi, W. Liu, & R. A. Marston (Eds.), *The International Encyclopedia of Geography* (pp. 1–13). John Wiley & Sons, Ltd.

Conclusion, Recommendations and Implications

This section will summarize the results of the interviews, FGDs and personal observations presented in the preceding sections. The research objectives posed at the beginning of the study process are revisited, and the findings are discussed. The theoretical and practical implications of the research findings are presented. Furthermore, recommendations have been forwarded.

This study aimed to assess the feasibility and viability of halal tourism development in Ethiopia. The thesis has tried to address the following six objectives: (a) analyzing definitional and conceptual ambiguities of halal tourism and related typologies and proposing cogent terminologies for halal tourism and Islamic tourism; (b) assessing whether tourism, by its very nature, is unIslamic from the perspective of the Quran and Sunnah; (c) assessing the knowledge and attitudes of local people and stakeholders toward halal tourism development in Ethiopia; (d) inventorying and assessing the potential of halal tourism resources in Ethiopia; (e) identifying and mapping halal tourism routes in Ethiopia and (f) identifying opportunities and barriers to halal tourism development in Ethiopia.

In order to address the aforementioned research objectives, a qualitative research method was employed. Primary data were collected through personal observations, focus group discussions and individual interviews. Semi-structured and unstructured interview-guiding questionnaires were designed for FGDs and face-to-face interviews. The qualitative data were collected through interviews with 172 participants and eight focus group discussions with 61 discussants in Ethiopia. A particular strength of this study is that it includes the perspectives of several stakeholders, such as tourism experts, visitors, the local community, government officials, and industry players, such as tour operators and guides, religious leaders and traditional leaders research participants. It must be clear that the study has been primarily concerned with Islamic heritage and Muslim visitors. However, this does not mean that this study excludes non-Muslims and other heritages and attractions of Ethiopia.

Terminologies such as Islamic tourism, sharia tourism and Muslim-friendly tourism have been employed interchangeably with halal tourism to denote tourism that complies with the principles of Islam and meets the religious and secular needs of Muslims. However, this study indicates the

DOI: 10.4324/9781003355236-7

210 Conclusion, Recommendations and Implications

differences between halal tourism and these terminologies. The study tries to redefine halal tourism and Islamic tourism. For instance, the following definitions were proposed for halal and Islamic tourism.

> Halal tourism comprises the activities of any person (Muslim or non-Muslim) who obeys Sharia law and principles and consumes halal products and services, traveling to and staying in places outside his/her usual environment for not more than one consecutive year for secular and/or religious purposes.
>
> Islamic tourism comprises the activities of practicing Muslims who strictly abide by Sharia law and principles and consume only halal products and services, traveling to and staying in places outside their usual environment for not more than one consecutive year for sacred or religious purposes.

The contents of the Quran and hadith that deal with tourism and travel were also consulted to assess the place of tourism in Islam. The study discerns numerous verses of the Quran that encourage Muslims to travel and visit various sites. In several verses of the Holy Quran, Allah encourages people to travel, visit, and contemplate His creation. There are verses of the Holy Quran that recommend humankind visit historical sites and learn a lesson from the deeds of their ancestors. Prophet Muhammad (PBUH) also advises Muslims to visit various places. However, the following two hadiths of the Prophet Muhammad (PBUH) have been used out of context to indicate as if tourism is discouraged in Islam. As registered by authentic Hadith al-Bukhari, Prophet Muhammad (PBUM) ordered that people should not travel to visit places except the three Mosques: Masjid Al-Haram (Mecca), Masjid al Nebawi (Medina) and Masjid al-Aqsua (Jerusalem). The other one is the statement of the Prophet that traveling could be seen as torture because it prevents people from sleeping and eating. These two hadiths have been interpreted out of context as if they contradict tourism. However, the first one intends to indicate that one should not travel for pilgrimage, worship, or venerate other than the three holy mosques. Regarding the second one, it indicates how much traveling is tiresome, but it does not mean that tourism is haram. Moreover, thanks to technology, these days, traveling is no longer an activity of torture.

As one of its objectives, this thesis assesses participants' general attitudes, knowledge and practices toward halal tourism. Accordingly, the perceptions and attitudes of participants toward halal tourism development in Ethiopia were assessed. The study also tries to assess the prior halal tourism knowledge of participants. The results of the FGDs and interviews indicate that there are significant differences in attitudes between Muslims and Christians. The findings show that Muslims have a relatively good knowledge of halal tourism and hold a positive attitude toward halal tourism development. The study proves that many Muslim participants have complained about the lack of halal travel services and products. This investigation confirms that the demand for Ethiopian Muslims to participate in halal travel and tourism has recently been skyrocketing. Simultaneously, religiosity has been increasing among Ethiopian Muslims. Especially educated Muslims and urban dwellers want to engage in tourism without compromising their religious identity and values and without transgressing the very principle of Islam. Some practicing urban dwellers and educated Muslims have been enjoying tourism. However, they have encountered twofold challenges: First, the existing tourism activities have been surrounded by anti-Islam activities such as alcoholism and voyeurism. Second, halal products and services have not been provided in major visitor touchpoints such as airports, hotels, resorts and attractions. These factors have caused dissatisfaction among those who have already visited and constrained those who have a desire and a capacity to participate in tourism. Hence, Muslim participants cordially support the proposal of a halal tourism development project in Ethiopia. Non-Muslim Ethiopians have limited knowledge about tourism, and they seem suspicious of the development of halal tourism in Ethiopia.

Some non-Muslims consider halal tourism development as a project of Muslimism and Islamization. This kind of attitude and misconception seems to emerge from the triple factors. First, the ongoing Islamophobia negatively shaped their attitude as far as Islam and Muslims are concerned. The media bombardment against Muslims and Islam at the national and global level has loosened the trust between Muslims and non-Muslims. Second, the lack of knowledge about halal tourism among non-Muslims made them resist halal tourism development, especially the Arabic term 'halal' caused suspicions among Christian Ethiopians. Some non-Muslims deliberately boycott halal businesses in Ethiopia. The last one seems to emerge due to the current tension and competition between Muslims and Christians. Recently, there has been unhealthy competition in all sectors, including trade and investment between Muslims and Christians. Hence, some Christians have considered halal tourism as a business of Muslims for Muslims. However, there have also been favorable responses from non-Muslims as well. Some non-Muslims show interest in investing and participating in halal tourism. The Pentecostals especially appreciate the development of halal tourism in Ethiopia. Therefore, it has been approved that though there are objections, there are also demands from non-Muslim Ethiopians to engage in halal tourism as both investors and visitors.

The study proves that Muslims do not have a uniform way of practicing Islam. According to the findings of this study, there are three major behaviors of Muslim travelers: non-practicing, mildly practicing and conservative Muslims. This finding matches with the findings of Mastercard-CrescentRating (2018). Therefore, halal tourism developers are advised to consider such variations even within Muslim communities while developing and marketing halal tourism. They should differentiate between those who strictly observe Islamic rule, those who mildly practice and those who do not practice at all. Halal tourism should be promoted during hajj and umrah, where important segments of halal tourism are gathered.

The study assesses the resources (attractions) of halal tourism attractions in Ethiopia. In this section, major attractions that could attract halal visitors have been identified, described and mapped. Based on their direction and dimension, these attractions have been categorized into five clusters, each consisting of multiple individual attractions. The clusters are the north cluster, the northwest cluster, the east cluster, the southeast cluster and the southwest cluster. The north cluster consists of very age-old Islamic heritages, Islamic archaeological sites such as Nora, and historic religious sites such as Shonke and al-Nejashi. Some religious sites, such as al-Nejashi, have already been visited by domestic halal visitors and inbound halal tourists. The northwest cluster consists of mainly geological, geomorphological and archaeological attractions such as Erta Ale, Dallol and Hadar. There is also a tendency that halal visitors would prefer these attractions. The east cluster comprises well-known Islamic archaeological sites such as Harlaa and renowned historic cities such as the walled city of Harar and Dire Dawa. The southeast cluster includes three major attractions, namely Bale mountain national parks, Sof Omar cave system and Dire Sheik Hussein Shrine. The southwest cluster contains the palace of Aba Jifar, wild coffee trees and dense forests. This cluster comprises the fauna and flora resources of southwest Ethiopia. This study, therefore, confirms the availability of untouched, untapped and undeveloped halal tourism resources in different parts of Ethiopia. These heritage sites should be preserved, promoted to visitors and transmitted to the next generations.

After identifying halal tourism resources, the study proposes and plots five halal tourism routes. The first proposed halal route is the North historic halal route. This route runs from Addis Ababa northwards by joining important Islamic heritage sites and shrines. It is an international route that lies as far as Massawa and Zeila, with possible extensions as far as Gulf states, mainly Saudi Arabia. Nora Islamic archaeological sites, Shonke historical and religious sites, as well as the al-Nejashi shrine, are the major nodes of this route. This route is proposed based on the footprints of the *Sahabas* who migrated to Ethiopia in 615. Therefore, this route is proposed to memorialize the first Hijra.

The second proposed route runs from Addis Ababa toward northwest Ethiopia as far as the Assab port of Eritrea. This route is a geo-route that will connect geological and archaeological attractions. Attractions such as Hadar archaeological sites, the active volcano of Erta Ale and Dallol are major nodes of this route. The third one is the historic east halal route that runs from Addis Ababa eastwards as far as Berbera and Zeila. This route also transcends the international border that connects the Islamic heritage sites of Ethiopia with neighboring Somalia. This route coincides with the ancient long-distance trade route of Ethiopia. The fourth route is the southeast halal route. This route runs from Addis Ababa southeastward to the Bale area. This route provides a combination of natural and cultural attractions. Bale mountain national park, Sof Omar Cave System and Dire Sheik Hussein Shrine have been identified as the major nodes in this route. The last route is

Southwest Eco-route. It runs from the capital city to southwest Ethiopia. The palace of Aba Jifar, dense forest and wild coffee trees have been identified as the major attractions on this route. This route provides a variety of natural attractions to nature-loving visitors. These routes should be further developed, promoted and introduced to target customers.

This study has identified major comparative advantages and opportunities Ethiopia possesses in developing halal tourism. Ethiopia has a glorified Islamic history that sets her above others as far as halal tourism is concerned. Ethiopia is a holy country that warmly welcomed the pioneer Muslim immigrants in 615. The then Ethiopian king called Nejashi gave protection to these Muslim immigrants. Therefore, Ethiopia is the first country where Muslim immigrants took asylum for the first time in human history. Accordingly, as a visitor destination, Ethiopia could be branded as the land of the first Hijra. This benevolence in favor of Islam helps Ethiopia to be renowned among the Islamic world. The Prophet Muhammad himself has given testimonies about Ethiopia. Some catchphrases of the Prophet, such as the land of truth, the land of justice, and the land of peace, have a paramount role in promoting Ethiopia as a halal destination. Besides these, prominent Ethiopians are known to have been starring in Islamic history.

Personalities such as Al-Nejashi, Bilal al-Habesha and Emu Ayman were internationally renowned Ethiopian Muslims. The everlasting deeds and positive images of these popular Ethiopian Muslims could help Ethiopia to be introduced as a halal destination. Furthermore, these histories and legends could be sold to halal-conscious visitors as a halal tourism product. Therefore, it is highly recommended that in order for Ethiopia to develop halal tourism, it should be branded as the Land of First Hijra. Other catchphrases, such as the land of peace, the land of truth, the homeland of Bilal al-Habesha, the homeland of Al-Nejashi, and the homeland of Emu Ayman could be utilized. Its geostrategic location is also a God-gifted opportunity for Ethiopia to develop halal tourism. Given that most halal tourists are Muslims, its strategic location in the Muslim world enables Ethiopia to capture inbound halal tourists.

Moreover, Ethiopia is also surrounded by its neighboring Muslim countries, namely Sudan, Djibouti, Somalia and Eritrea. These countries could send a significant number of halal tourists to Ethiopia. Another important comparative advantage of Ethiopia is the availability of a conducive climate and fertile soil compared to the Muslim world. Most Muslim countries have arid climates and infertile land. Therefore, for one thing, tourists from Arab countries could choose Ethiopia to spend their summer vacations. The other thing, Arab countries could invest in Ethiopia. Several investors from Turkey, the UAE and Saudi Arabia have already invested in Ethiopia. These investors and their employees are customers of halal tourism.

Furthermore, the findings of this study show that these countries tend to invest in halal tourism in Ethiopia. The availability of huge domestic customers also shows the viability of halal tourism development in Ethiopia. The findings of this study reveal that many educated and urban dweller Muslims have the interest and the capacity to participate in halal tourism. One of this study's most significant findings is that many Ethiopians want to participate in tourism without compromising their religion. This is the most important coincidence of the flourishing halal tourism in Ethiopia. Ethiopian Muslims seem tired of the monotonous one-size-fits-all type of Western tourism. Participants seriously claimed that mainstream tourism, ingrained in and tailored to Western culture and style, no longer accommodates their culture, religion and values. Hence, halal tourism could be the best alternative for Muslims and other halal-conscious visitors. Therefore, the prevalence of such strong demand for halal tourism is another opportunity for halal tourism developers. The extant of pro halal tourism resources, such as coffee, help Ethiopia diversify its halal tourism products. Being a cradle of coffee Arabica, Ethiopia could entice more Arab visitors, who are, by default, halal visitors. For Ethiopia to develop halal tourism and to be competitive, it should properly exploit its comparative advantages and opportunities.

Finally, this study identified barriers and hurdles to halal tourism development in Ethiopia. Even though Ethiopia has comparative advantages and opportunities, some pitfalls also challenge halal tourism development. The perceived naive image of Ethiopia as a Christianity Island has been identified as a hindrance to halal tourism development. This naïve image of Ethiopia affects the promotion of Ethiopia. The availability of Islamophobia at the national and global levels and the prevalence of tourismophobes will also challenge the halal tourism development project. This study's findings indicate a proliferation of hatred against Islam and Islamic culture. Muslims with Islamic manifestation have faced discrimination and mistreatment at different touchpoints such as airports, hotels and attractions. Muslim travelers have been targeted for their Islamic manifestations, especially by their headscarves and *hijabs*. They faced attacks from police, security apparatus and other personnel at hotels, attraction sites even public spaces. Another study finding shows that there is tourismophobia among Ethiopia's religious and traditional people. Some devoted Muslims have developed a phobia against tourism because they think tourism is inherently anti-Islam. They argue that tourism causes time wastage as well as exposes Muslims to anti-Islam activities. The lack of Muslim-friendly infrastructures is also claimed to be a major obstacle in halal tourism development. This study's findings reveal a lack of Muslim-friendly airports, accommodations, entertainment centers and websites. The absence of halal tour operators and halal promotion are also identified challenges.

Furthermore, the lack of awareness about halal tourism concepts and practices and the availability of ambiguities on halal tourism concepts and practices could be obstacles to halal tourism development in Ethiopia. According to the findings of this study, the existing tourism operators and hoteliers of Ethiopia are advised to provide services to cater to Muslim religious' needs by allocating places exclusively for halal-conscious visitors to pursue those activities that are required in Islam. In the long term, the construction of independent halal hotels and restaurants, halal lodges, halal entertainment centers and halal healthcare centers are highly viable and, therefore, highly recommended. Ethiopian airports are also advised to avoid any maltreatment and discrimination against Muslim travelers. Muslim-friendly toilets and ablution facilities are suggested to be installed, and it is advised that prayer rooms be assigned at airports, resorts and star-rated hotels.

A lack of knowledge about halal tourism's concepts and practices was identified as a major obstacle. There are ambiguities and confusion regarding the concepts and practices of halal tourism, even among scholars and practitioners. The negative attitudes of some non-Muslims toward halal tourism development will also adversely affect the halal tourism development project. Therefore, academics should use the term 'halal tourism' in order to avoid confusion about halal tourism with Islamic tourism. Marketers should also promote halal tourism as a secular business. Awareness creation programs should be arranged for non-Muslim tourists and locals to avoid some activities that offend Muslim societies.

The previous studies on halal tourism focus only on the economic role of halal tourism development. The economic value of tourism development tends to be a cliché concept in tourism studies, whereas halal tourism's sociocultural and diplomatic impacts have received less attention. For a country like Ethiopia, which has near and distant Muslim neighbors as well as half of its population is Muslim, the sociopolitical and diplomatic role of halal tourism is equally important as that of the economic gains. Hence, while developing halal tourism, its sociopolitical and diplomatic rule for Ethiopia should be considered.

Furthermore, this study identifies the following unique features and principles of halal tourism. First, halal tourism is environmentally friendly and socially responsible. The study approves that participants in halal tourism are environmentally friendly and socially responsible. The findings suggest directions for sustainable, people-center, and eco-friendly halal tourism development in Ethiopia. Therefore, halal tourism preserves natural and cultural heritages and respects the guests' and hosts' norms and values. Second, halal tourism heeds the values and principles of all religions. The results of this study confirm halal tourism does not contradict the very principles of other religions as well. This research proves that halal tourism never contradicts the very principle of Christianity. According to the findings of this paper, though halal tourism is Sharia-friendly, it never contradicts the very dogma of Christianity. For instance, like Islam, Christianity prohibits voyeurism, alcoholism and consumption of swine products and by-products. Therefore, even though halal tourism seems in favor of Islam, practically, it fits with the very principle of other religions as well. Third, halal tourism is open to all. Even though the raison d'être of halal tourism is to cater to the spiritual need of Muslims and some anti-Sharia activities such as alcoholism, pork and voyeurism are not allowed, it is open to all interested visitors. Put another way, services and products of halal tourism are expected to comply with Sharia, but visitors could be anyone who wishes to consume halal products and services. Therefore, halal tourism should not be promoted as Islamic tourism. Rather it should be promoted as an environmentally friendly and socially responsible secular tourism niche. A further study is recommended focusing more on the secular aspect of halal tourism and the economic, social, political and diplomatic role of halal tourism development. For the success of halal tourism, it is very advisable that the spiritual dimension of halal tourism should diminish, and it must excel as responsible tourism in terms of ecological, social and health dimensions. This perspective makes halal tourism sustainable and acceptable to all parties (Muslim and non-Muslims).

The findings of this study imply that Ethiopia should work to position itself as a halal tourism destination for historical, political/diplomatic, socio-cultural, economic and geostrategic reasons.

I   Historical: As discussed rigorously throughout this book, being the land of the first Hijra, the land of King Nejashi and the land of Mauzzin Bilal Rabah, Ethiopia could easily position itself as the halal destination. It also possesses precious Islamic heritages, which Muslim visitors find nowhere in the world. Due to the presence of Islamic civilization in Ethiopia since the 7th century, the Islamic legacy is visible in the architectural heritage and historical sites, and there are living Islamic heritages. A colorful Islamic lifestyle is inseparably intermingled with Ethiopian cultures. Therefore, Ethiopia's natural resources and cultural appeal are undeniable and enviable to halal tourism development.

II Political/Diplomatic: In the contemporary globalized world, economic and diplomatic policy objectives cannot be addressed separately. Creating a conducive external environment for all-inclusive growth in the country must be an integral component of Ethiopia's foreign policy. For many years, the availability of unjustified and erroneous perceptions of the Arab world has cost Ethiopia politically, diplomatically and economically. The status of historical hostility should be replaced by a strategic partnership and good neighbor rhetoric. Arab countries are and will remain a permanent component on the agenda of Ethiopia's policymakers. The agenda of strategic partnership and the win-win relationship could be institutionalized and materialized through halal tourism. Ethiopia could utilize halal tourism for both diplomatic purposes and economic interests. It could use halal tourism to build positive relations and peaceful cooperation with its near and distant neighbors. Halal tourism is very promising for the economic development of Ethiopia; simultaneously, government officials should view it as a vehicle for changing perceptions of its near and distant Muslim neighbors and open channels that could yield diplomatic benefits, especially in the context of Ethio-Arab relations. Ethiopia should create a conducive environment for its Muslim neighbors, and halal tourism could bridge the gap between Ethiopia and its Muslim

III Economic: The economic role of halal tourism in the Ethiopian economy has been discussed throughout this book. By establishing halal tourism, Ethiopia could absorb the dollars and dinars of Arab and Muslim countries. Hence, halal tourism could inject hard currency into the national economy and create local job opportunities. Halal tourism could also support the mainstream Ethiopian tourism industry through product diversification and curving seasonality. Moreover, the growing halal segment would contribute positively to reviving the national economy while also boosting rural tourism in the country.

IV Socio-cultural: Halal tourism also has social values in Ethiopia. These days, social tourism has become a guiding principle in tourism. Social tourism refers to the right of all individuals to participate in tourism. Every citizen has the right to enjoy his/her natural and cultural resources, and the state should avoid any obstacles to this. Article 7 of the 1999 United Nations World Tourism Organization Global Code of Ethics for Tourism, for example, includes the human rights issue in tourism development. UNWTO affirms the right to tourism and emphasizes that obstacles should not be placed against direct and personal access to the planet's resources. Tourism resources shall be equally open to all citizens. This implies that the right of Ethiopian Muslims to visit their natural and cultural resources should be assured through halal tourism development. Therefore, for Ethiopia, developing halal tourism means maintaining the rights of half of its population.

V Geostrategic Position: As has been discussed, Ethiopia holds an imperative geostrategic and geopolitical position in the Muslim World. Therefore, Ethiopia could be a strong competitor in halal tourism development. Therefore, by developing halal tourism, Ethiopia could kill many birds with one stone.

This research has the following implications. The principal theoretical implication of this study is that it proposes inclusive definitions of halal tourism and Islamic tourism. This book could provide brief hints and detailed justifications for halal tourism development in Ethiopia. Though several recent studies (Battour et al., 2012; Battour et al., 2014; Battour & Ismail, 2015; Boğan & Sarıışık, 2019; Din, 1989; El-Gohary, 2016; Jafari & Scott, 2014; Jafari & Scott, 2014) explored the potential of halal tourism, these investigations have mainly been limited to South East Asia and the Middle East. Thus, this paper could shift the focus to Africa to explore how halal tourism could be developed and implemented in multireligious, multiethnic and multicultural countries like Ethiopia. Second, this dissertation sheds light on the potential of halal tourism resources in Ethiopia. This may help investors invest in these resources. Simultaneously, concerned bodies such as the Ethiopian government and nongovernmental organizations could pay attention to these resources and participate in preserving these halal tourism resources. Most Islamic heritage sites of Ethiopia are highly endangered and need preservation. The study assesses the feasibility and viability of halal tourism and identifies potential halal routes that help stakeholders to invest in halal tourism. The study also highlights the potential barriers to halal tourism development, which helps to take proactive measures instead of reactions. The findings from this study could contribute to the current literature on halal tourism. Finally, this study could give some glimpse and will serve as a theoretical base for further research in the area.

References

Battour, M., Ismail, M. N., & Battor, M. (2010). Toward a halal tourism market. *Tourism Analysis*, *15*(4), 461–470. https://doi.org/10.3727/108354210X12864727453304

Battour, M., Ismail, M. N., & Battor, M. (2011). The impact of destination attributes on Muslim tourist's choice. *International Journal of Tourism Research*, *13*(6), 527–540. https://doi.org/10.1002/jtr.824

Battour, M., Ismail, M. N., Battor, M., & Awais, M. (2017). Islamic tourism: an empirical examination of travel motivation and satisfaction in Malaysia. *Current Issues in Tourism*, *20*(1), 50–67. https://doi.org/10.1080/13683500.2014.965665

Battour, M., Battor, M. M., & Ismail, M. (2012). The mediating role of tourist satisfaction: A study of Muslim tourists in Malaysia. *Journal of Travel and Tourism Marketing*, *29*(3), 279–297. https://doi.org/10.1080/10548408.2012.666174

Boğan, E., & Sarıışık, M. (2019). Halal tourism: conceptual and practical challenges. *Journal of Islamic Marketing*, *10*(1), 87–96. https://doi.org/10.1108/JIMA-06-2017-0066

El-Gohary, H. (2016). Halal tourism, is it really Halal? *Tourism Management Perspectives*, *19*, 124–130. https://doi.org/10.1016/j.tmp.2015.12.013

Jafari, J., & Scott, N. (2014). Muslim world and its tourisms. *Annals of Tourism Research*, *44*(1), 1–19. https://doi.org/10.1016/j.annals.2013.08.011

Appendix

Dear Participants:

I am conducting a research entitled 'Potentials, Challenges and Prospects of Halal Tourism Development in Ethiopia.' Thus, the following questions have been prepared to investigate major factors that positively or negatively affect halal tourism development in Ethiopia. Rest assured that your answer will be kept confidential. Therefore, please spend a few minutes answering these questions as accurately as possible. Your help is crucial for the success of this research.

I deeply appreciate your kind cooperation

Thank You!

Participants Background Information

Age_____

Male_____ Female_____

Educational status_____

Position _____

I. **Guide Questions Addressed to Participants of the Host community**
   1. Did you hear about halal tourism so far?
   2. Have you been engaged in tourism?
   3. What kind of service have you used?
   4. Were you satisfied with the provided products and services?
   5. Do you believe the available infrastructures (hotels, airports, and cafeterias) meet the need of practicing Muslims?
   6. How do you evaluate the general attitude of the local community toward halal tourism, in your opinion?
   7. Do you believe halal tourism development is feasible and possible in Ethiopia?
   8. What, in your opinion, are the potential resources for halal tourism development in Ethiopia?

9. Do you think Ethiopia has tourism resources/tourist attractions that can draw halal tourists? Yes, No
10. If your answer to question number 1 is yes, what are Ethiopia's halal tourism resources/tourist attractions?
11. What is the significance or value of these sites?
12. What is the quality of these sites' existing basic and halal infrastructure?
13. Would you propose halal tourism routes?
14. In your opinion, how do you evaluate the general attitude of non-Muslims toward halal tourism?
15. Have halal tourists ever been in and around your locality?
16. Do you know of any attempts to introduce and promote halal tourism resources in Ethiopia so far?
17. Do you believe that communities have a good awareness of halal tourism?
18. Do you know of any halal tourism initiatives in your locality? If yes, please specify the types and purposes of tourists.
19. Have you shared any benefits from tourism so far?
20. Are there any individuals who benefited from tourism more than others? How?
21. Do you know someone who hates, attacks, or loots Muslim tourists? If yes, who were they? And what were their purposes?
22. As per your knowledge, does halal tourism cause any benefit or cost to the local communities?
23. What do you think is the best halal tourism potential to be exploited in Ethiopia, especially in your locality?
24. In your opinion, what should be done to solve problems hindering halal tourists' flow and halal tourism activities in Ethiopia?

II. **Interview questions Addressed to the Culture and Tourism Bureau Managers/Officials/Tour Operators/Guides**
1. Do you think Ethiopia has tourism resources/tourist attractions that can draw halal tourists? Yes, No
2. If your answer to question number 1 is yes, what are Ethiopia's halal tourism resources/tourist attractions?
3. Were any attempts made to introduce and promote halal tourism resources so far? A Yes B, No
4. If your answer to question number 3 is yes, what mechanisms or media have you employed?
5. As per your knowledge, are there any benefits or costs for the local communities from halal tourism development?
6. Have halal tourists ever been to your locality so far? Yes, No
7. If your answer to question number 6 is yes, please specify the types and purpose of halal tourist tourists.
8. In your opinion, what were/are the main factors that affect halal tourists' flow toward Ethiopia?

9. Does political instability hinder the development of the halal tourism industry in Ethiopia? Yes, No
10. If your answer to question number 9 is yes, how?
11. Is there any halal tourist who has encountered any security problems in Ethiopia?
12. What factors do you think affect halal tourism development in Ethiopia?
13. What measures have been taken to alleviate the existing problems to develop the halal tourism industry and increase the flow of halal tourists? And what should be done?
14. What are the latest plans for your office concerning halal tourism? What do you propose for the future of the development of the halal tourism industry and to attract halal tourists at large?
15. Lastly, I would like to hear your thoughts on whether the development of halal tourism affects Ethiopian Christians.

III. Interview Questions Addressed to Visitors
1. How do you evaluate Ethiopia as a halal destination?
2. Do you face challenges because of your religious identity in Ethiopia?
3. Do you believe there is Islamophobia in Ethiopia?
4. Did you know about the Islamic heritage of Ethiopia?
5. Have you ever heard about First Muslims Migration to Ethiopia?
6. Do you believe Ethiopia is the land of the first Hijra?
7. Have you ever heard about Bilal al-Habesha, Al-Nejashi, and Emu Ayman?
8. Do airport hoteliers and others supply halal products and services?
9. Do you believe Ethiopia is an important destination for halal tourists?
10. Do you believe Muslims will spend their holiday in Ethiopia if there are halal products and services?

IV. Interview Questions Addressed to Religious Leaders
1. Is there any contradiction between Islam and Tourism?
2. I there any Quranic verse that objects to tourism and travel?
3. Is there any hadith that objects to travel and tourism?
4. Have you participated in tourism so far?
5. Do you believe tourism is haram for Muslims?
6. How do you manage outbound pilgrims to Haji and Umra?
7. Do you believe Haji is part of tourism?
8. Do you believe halal tourism is important for Ethiopian and Ethiopian Muslims?
9. Do you advise Muslim investors to invest in halal tourism?
10. Do you think halal tourism development affects the behavior of Ethiopian Muslims positively or negatively?
11. Can you tell me about any tourist attractions that would attract halal-conscious visitors in your area?

222 Appendix

12. Do you see halal-conscious tourists visiting these or any other places of interest in your area?
13. What do the sites you mentioned mean to you?
14. From your point of view, what would be the expected impacts if your halal products and services were offered in your area?
15. Would you have engaged in halal tourism if it had been developed in Ethiopia?
16. Would you accept halal tourism development in your area?
17. To what extent has existing tourism affected your culture and religion, either positively or negatively?
18. Will you participate if halal tourism develops in Ethiopia?
19. Have you ever seen guests to visit Islamic Heritage sites or natural areas?
20. What, in your opinion, is the stakeholders' role in a local area's Halal tourism development?

Guiding Questions (Amharic Version)

ውድ ይህንን መጠይቅ የምትሞሉ የጥናቱ ተሳታፊዎች፦

እኔ መሐመድ ጀማል አህመድ "*የሀላል ቱሪዝም ልማት በኢትዮጵያ፦ እምቅ ሐብቶች ፣ ተግዳሮቶች እና ተስፋዎች*" በሚል ርዕስ ጉዳይ ላይ ጥናት አዩሪያለው፡፡ የሚከተሉት ጥያቄዎች ጥንታዊ ጽሑፎን ለመሰረት ጠቃሚ ናቸው፡፡ ስለዚህ እንዳንዱ ጥያቄ ለሚከዩደው ጥናት ጠቃሚ መሆኑን ተገንዝበው የተወሰነ ሰዓት በመስጠት በቅንነት እንድመሉልኝ በአክበሮት እጠይቃለሁ፡፡ በተጨማሪም የሚሰጡት መረጃ በሚስጥር እንደሚያዝ መጠቆም አፈልጋለሁ፡፡

መልካም ትብብርዎን ከልብ እጠይቃለሁ አመሰግናለሁ

መጠይቁን የሚሞሉ ሰዎች መሰረታዊ መረጃዎች

የስራ ሀላፊነት_____

ጾታ፦ ወንድ_____ ሴት_____

የትምህርት ደረጃ_____

I. **በጥናቱ ለተሳተፉ የተለያዩ ባለድርሻ አካላት የቀረቡ መሪ ጥያቄዎች**

1. ከአሁን በፊት ስለ ሐላል ቱሪዝም የሚያቁት ነገር አለ?
2. በሐላል ቱሪዝም ተሳትፈው ያውቃሉ?
3. ከተሳተፉ ምን ዓይነት አገልግሎት አግኝተዋል?
4. በቀርቡት ምርቶች እና አገልግሎቶች ረክተዋል?
5. አሁን ያለት መዉረት ልማቶች (በሆቴል ፣ በአየር ማረፊያዎች እና በካፍቴሪያዎች) ሀይማኖታቸው በሚፈቅድው መልኩ የሙስሊሞችን ፍላጎት ያሟላ ብለው ያምናሉ?
6. የአከባቢው ማህበረሰብ በሐላል ቱሪዝም ዙሪያ ያለውን አጠቃላይ አመለካከትን በአርስዎ አስተያየት እንዴት ይገመሙታል?
7. የሐላል ቱሪዝም ልማት በኢትዮጵያ ውስጥ ተግባራዊ ሊሆን ይችላል ብለው ያምናሉ?
8. በአርስዎ አስተያየት ለሐላል ቱሪዝም ልማት የሚጠቅም እምቅ ሀብቶች ምን ምን ናቸው?
9. ኢትዮጵያ ሀላል ጉብኝቶችን መሳብ የሚችሉ የቱሪዝም ሀብቶች/የቱሪስት መስህቦች አሉት ብለው ያስባሉ?

Appendix 223

10. ለተራ ቁጥር 9 የሚሰጡት መልስ አዎ ከሆነ እነዚህ የኢትዮጵያ ሐላል ቱሪዝም ሀብቶች / የቱሪስት መስህቦች ምን ምን ናቸው?
11. የእነዚህን የቱሪስት መስህቦች አስተዋጽኦ ሚና ቢያብራሩልኝ?
12. በእነዚህ መስህቦች ዙርያ ሐላል ጎብኚዎችን ሊያገለግሉ የሚችሉ መሰረተ ልማቶች አሉ? ካሉ ምን ያህል ጥራት አላቸው?
13. የሐላል ቱሪዝም መንገዶች በየት በየት ቢዘረጉ አዋጭ ይሆናል ብለው ያስባሉ? ለምን?
14. ሙስሊም ያልሆኑ ወገኖች ሐላል ቱሪዝም ላይ ያላቸውን አውቀትና አጠቃላይ አመለካከት በእርስዎ አስተያየት እንዴት ይገመግሙታል?
15. ሐላል ቱሪስቶች በአካባቢያ ጎብኝተው ያውቃሉ?
16. እስካሁን ድረስ የኢትዮጵያን ሐላል የቱሪዝም ሀብቶች ለማስተዋወቅ እና ለመሸጥ የተደረገ ሙከራ ያውቃሉ?
17. ማህበረሰቡ ማለትም የአካባቢው ነዋሪዎች ስለ ሐላል ቱሪዝም አውቀትና ጥሩ ግንዛቤ አላቸው ብለው ያምናሉ?
18. በአካባቢያ ሐላል ቱሪዝምን ለመተግበር የተጀመረ ነገር ያውቃሉ? መልሰዎ አዎ ከሆነ እባክዎን የተጀመሩ ነገሮችን ቢያብራሩልኝ?
19. እስካሁን ድረስ ከቱሪዝም ያገኙት ጥቅም አለ?
20. ከሌሎች በተሻለ በቱሪዝም ተጠቃሚ የሆኑ ግለሰቦች አሉ? እንዴት?
21. ሙስሊም ጎብኚዎችን የሚጠሉ ፣ የሚያጠቁ ወይም በሙስሊም ጎብኚዎችን ለይተው ዘርፉ የሚያደርጉ ግለሰቦች አሉ? መልሰዎ አዎ ከሆነ እነዚህ አካላት እነማን ናቸው? ይሄን ሊያደርጉ ያበቃቸው ነገር ምንድን ነው ብለው ያስባሉ? ዓላማውትስ ምድን ነው ብለው ይምታሉ?
22. በእርስዎ አመለካከት ሐላል ቱሪዝም ለአካባቢው ማህበረሰብ ምንም ዓይነት ጥቅም ወይም ጉዳት ያስከትላል?
23. በኢትዮጵያ በተለይም በአካባቢያ ለሐላል ቱሪዝም ልማት በተለየ መልኩ የሚውሉ ምን አይነት እምቅ ሀብቶች እና አስቻይ ሁኔታዎች አሉ?
24. በእርስዎ አስተያየት ለሐላል ጎብኚዎች ፍሰት እና ለሐላል ቱሪዝም እንቅስቃሴ እንፉት የሆኑ ችግሮችን ለመፍታት ምን መደረግ አለበት?

II. **ለቱሪዝም ቢሮ ኃላፊዎች፣ ለአስጎብኝ ድርጅቶች፣ ለቱር ኦፐሬቶች የሚውሉ መሪ ጥቄዎች**

1. ኢትዮጵያ ሐላል ጎብኝዎችን መሳብ የሚችሉ የቱሪዝም ሀብቶች / የቱሪስት መስህቦች አሏት ብለው ያስባሉ?
2. ለጥያቄ ቁጥር 1 የሚሰጡት መልስ አዎ ከሆነ የኢትዮጵያ ሐላል ቱሪዝም ሀብቶች / የቱሪስት መስህቦች/ ምን ምን ናቸው?
3. እስካሁን ድረስ የሐላል ቱሪዝም ሀብትን ለማስተዋወቅ እና ለጎብኚዎች ለመሸጥ የተደረገ ጥረቶች አሉ?
4. ለተራ ቁጥር 3 ለጥያቄ መልሰዎ አዎ ከሆነ ምን ዓይነት ስልቶች ወይም ሚዲያዎች ተጠቅማችሁ ለማስተዋወቅ ሞክራችሁ?
5. በእርሶዎ አረዳድ ሐላል ቱሪዝም ልማት ለአከባቢው ህብረተሰብ ይጠቅማል ወይስ ይጎዳል?
6. እስካሁን ድረስ ሐላል ቱሪስቶች በአካባቢው ተገኝተው/ጎብኝተው ያውቃሉ?
7. ለጥያቄ ቁጥር 6 የሚሰጡት መልስ አዎ ከሆነ እባከዎን የሐላል ጎብኝዎችን አይነቶች እና ዓላማ ይጥቀሱ።
8. በእርስዎ አስተያየት ሐላል ጎብኚዎች ወደ ኢትዮጵያ ቢመጡ በኢትዮጵያ ህዝብ ላይ ሊያመጡ የሚችሉት ዋና ዋና ነገሮች ምን ምን ናቸው?
9. የፖለቲካ አለመረጋጋት በኢትዮጵያ የሐላል ቱሪዝም ኢንዱስትሪ እንዳይሳፋ እንቅፋት ይሆናል ብለው ያስባሉ?
10. ለጥያቄ ቁጥር 9 መልስዎ አዎ ከሆነ እንዴት? ያብራሩልኝ።

11. በኢትዮጵያ ማንኛውም አይነት የፀጥታ ችግር ያጋጠመው ሐላል ጉብኝ ያውቃሉ?
12. ካጋጠሞ በሐላል የቱሪዝም ልማት ላይ ምን ተጽዕኖ ያሳድራሉ ብለው ያስባሉ?
13. የሐላል ቱሪዝም ኢንዱስትሪን ለማዳበር እና የሐላል ጉብኝዎች ፍሰት እንዲቸምር አሁን ያሉትን ችግሮች ለማቃለል ምን ዓይነት እርምጃዎች ተወስደዋል? ለወደፊትስ ምን መደረግ አለበት ብለው ያስባሉ?
14. ሐላል ቱሪዝምን በተመለከተ የቢሮዎ ወቅታዊ እቅዶች ምንድን ናቸው? / ለወደፊቱ ለሐላል ቱሪዝምን ለማሥፋት እና ሐላል ጉብኝቶችን በበዛት ለመሳብ መሠሪያ ቤቶ ምን እቅድ አለው?
15. በመጨረሻም የሐላል ቱሪዝም ልማት በኢትዮጵያውያን ክርስቲያኖች ወይም ሙስሊም ያልሆኑ ወገኖች ላይ ተጽዕዕ ያሳድራል ብለው ያምናሉ?

III. ለጉብኝዎች የቃል መጠይቅ ጥያቄዎች

1. ኢትዮጵያን እንዴ ሐላል መዳረሻ እንዴት ይገመግሟታል?
2. በሃይማኖት ማንነትዎ ምክንያት በኢትዮጵያ ውስጥ ችግሮች ገጥሙዋት ያውቃል?
3. ሙስሊም ጠልነት በኢትዮጵያ አለ ብለው ያምናሉ?
4. ስለ ኢትዮጵያ ኢሰላማዊ ቅርሶች ምን ያክል ያውቃሉ?
5. በ615 ስለተደረገው የመጀመሪያው የሙስሊሞች ወደ ኢትዮጵያ መሰደድ ሰምተው ያውቃሉ?
6. ኢትዮጵያ 'የመጀመሪያዋ የሂጅራ ምድር' ናት ብለው ያምናሉ?
7. ስለ ቢላል አል ሀበሺ ፣ አል ነጃሺ እና ኢ.ሙ አይመን ሰምተው ያውቃሉ?
8. የአውሮፓላን ማሪፊያ፣ ሆቴሎች፣ ቱሪስት መዳረሻዎች ወዘተ የሐላል ምርቶን እና አገልግሎቶችን ይሰጣሉ?
9. ኢትዮጵያ በሐላል ጉብኝ ተፈላጊ መዳረሻ ናት/ ወደፊት ትሆናለች ብለው ያምናሉ?
10. ሐላል ጉብኝዎች የአረፍት ጊዜያቸውን በኢትዮጵያ እንዳሳልፉ የሚያስችሉ ሐላል ምርቶች እና አገልግሎቶች አሉ ብለው ያምናሉ?

IV. ለሃይማኖት መሪዎች የተዘጋጀ መሪ ጥያቄዎች

1. በእስልምና እና በቱሪዝም መካከል ተቃርኖ ይኖር ይሆን?
2. ቱሪዝም እና ጉዞን የሚቃወሙ የቁርኣን አንቀጾች አሉ?
3. ጉዞና ቱሪዝም የሚቃወሙሐዲሶች አሉ?
4. እስካሁን በቱሪዝም ተሳትፈው ያውቃሉ?
5. ቱሪዝም ለሙስሊሞች ሐራም ነው ብለው ያምናሉን?
6. ወደ ሐጂ እና ዑምራ የሚጓዙ ሀጆችን ጉብኝዎች ናቸው ማለት ይቻላል?
7. ሀጂ የቱሪዝም አካል ነው ብለው ያምናሉን?
8. ሐላል ቱሪዝም ለኢትዮጵያ እና ለኢትዮጵያን ሙስሊሞች አስፈላጊ ነው ብለው ያምናሉ?
9. ሙስሊም ባለሀብቶች በሐላል ቱሪዝም ላይ ኢንቨስት እንዲያደርጉ ይመክራሉ?
10. የሐላል ቱሪዝም ልማት በአንታ ወይም በአሉታ መልኩ የኢትዮጵያ ሙስሊሞችን ወይም ሙስሊም ወገን ያልሆኑ ወገኖችን ባህል ይነካል ብለው ያስባሉ?
11. በአካባቢያ ሐላል ተጠቃሚ ጉብኝዎችን ሊሰብ ስለሚችል ስለ ማንኛውም የቱሪስት መስህብ ስፍራዎች ሊነግሩኝ ይችላሉ?
12. ሐላል ተጠቃሚ ጉብኝዎች እነዚህን ወይም ሌሎች በአካባቢያ ያሉ ቦታዎችን ሲጎበኙ አይተዋልን?
13. እርስዎ የጠቀሷቸው መዳረሻዎች የጉብኝዎች መስህቦች ለእርስዎ ምን ትርጉም አላቸው?
14. በእርስዎ አመለካከት ሐላል ምርቶች እና አገልግሎቶች በአካባቢያ ቢቀርቡ ምን ምን አንታዊ እና አሉታዊ ተጽዕኖዎች ያመጣሉ?
15. በኢትዮጵያ የሐላል ጉብኝት ቢቻትም ኖሮ በሐላል ቱሪዝም ይስተፉ ነበር?
16. በአካባቢያ የሐላል ቱሪዝም መስፋፋትን ይደግፋሉ ወይንስ ይቃወማሉ፧ ለምን?
17. አሁን ያለው ቱሪዝም በባህላ ወይም በሃይማኖትዎ ላይ ምን ሃይል ተጽዕኖ አሳድራል?

18. እንደ ሐይማኖት አባትነዎ ሐላል ቱሪዝም በኢትዮጵያ ውስጥ ቢዳብር ሰዎች እንድነቡኑ ያበረታታሉ?
19. እንግዶች ወይም ከሌላ ቦታ የመጡ ጎብኝዎች ኢስላሚክ ቅርሶችን ወይም የተፈጥሮ ቦታዎችን እንዲጎበኙ ጋብዘው ያውቃሉ?
20. በአካባቢያ ያለውን የሐላል የቱሪዝም ሐብት እንድለማ የሐይማኖት አባቶች እና የሌሎች የባለድርሻ አካላት ሚና ምን መሆን አለበት ብለው ያስባሉ?

Index

Note: Page numbers in **bold** refer to tables; and page numbers in *italics* refer to figures.

access, communication, environment and services (ACES) model 30
Adie, B. A. 92
Ahmed, M. J. 124–125
Aji, M. H. 19
Akbaba, A. 124–125
Ali, A. A. 110
Al Jallad, N. 17–18
Allah (SWT) orders 61, 65, 67, 161
Al-Munajjid, M. S. 5, 45, 60, 64
Al-Nejashi historic route 168–170
Al-Qaradawi, Y. 17
alternative tourism 35–36, 79–80
Álvarez-García, J. 97
Ambali, A. R. 42
Amir Nur Mujahid 112, 132
Amru bin Umayah al-Damari 115
Angeline, C. 120
Annals of Tourism Research 99
Asgari, M. 17
Azikiwe, N. 118

Bakar, A. N. 42
Barich, H. 116
Bashir, M. 156
Battour, M. 5–7, 13, 17–19, 22, 25, 29, 32–33, 44–45, 55, 58–59, 62, 64, 86, 90–93, 99, 146
Benjamin, S. 117, 200
Bergeaud-Blackler, F. 38
Beydoun, K. 95
Bhuiyan, H. 33
Biancone, S. 33–34, 97
Bilal bin Rabah 111
Bilim, Y. 94, 97
Blackwell, R. 55–56, 92
Boğan, E. 13, 21–22, 28
Borzooei, M. 17
Britton, S. 79

Burkard, A. W. 156
Butler, R. 75, 82, 100

Çaki, C. 95–96
Camilleri, M. A. 16
Carboni, M. 20
Çetinkaya, M. Y. 55
challenges and prospects: basic research questions 145; content analysis 154; data collection phase 149–150; data collection techniques 150–151; data interpretation and findings 155, 157–206; ethical consideration 150; exploratory approach 145–146; focus group discussion 152–153; guiding questions and checklists 154–155; interviews 151–152; methodological integrity and trustworthiness 155–156; non-participant observation 154; participant observations 153–154; participants of the study 147; problems during data collection 156–157; quantitative research methods 145–147; research method design *151*; research objectives 145; sample size and sampling techniques 147–148; study area 148–149, *149*
Chaperon, S. 79
Chaudry, M. M. 39–41
Cieśluk, K. 131
Coccia, M. 75
Committee for Economic and Commercial Cooperation of the Organization of the Islamic Cooperation (COMCEC) 34, 98
Cook, T. 96
CrescentRating website 37
Creswell, J. W. 156

Danakil geo-route 170
Dann, G. M. S. 1
Darda, A. 33
Daricha, D.N. 124
dark tourism 36
data interpretation and findings: ancient Islamic cities and landscapes 180–182; birthplace of Coffee Arabica 185–187; 'Christian Island in a sea of Muslims,' 187–189; conducive weather conditions and fertile land 182; domestic visitors 182–185; eastern historical route 170–173; experiences and reflections of halal-conscious travelers 162–166; homeland of great Muslims 178–180; identifying and mapping potential routes of Ethiopia 166–168; Islamophobia at national and global level 189–192; knowledge and awareness 157–159; lack of Muslim-friendly infrastructures 194–202; land of the first Hijra 178; north historic halal tourism route 168–170; northwest halal route 170; opportunities and comparative advantages 175–177; southeast Halal Eco-routes 174; southwest halal tourism route 174–175; SWOT analysis 202–206, **205**; tourism in Islam 159–162; tourismophobes 192–194; unique Islamic history, stories and legends 177–178
Dawud, M. 140
Desplat, P. 117, 124
destinations and origins of halal visitors **29–30**
Din, K. H. 5–6, 20, 28, 38, 59, 62, 96, 99
Duman, T. 13, 18, 20, 22, 38, 42, 53, 60, 84, 92
Durán-Sánchez, A. 55

eastern cluster attractions, Ethiopia: abandoned islamic city of Harlaa 135; ancient walled city of Harar 131–133, *132*; basketry and handicraft products 133–134, *134*; Daketa rocks in Babile 135; heritage buildings 134–135; live culture and traditional cottage of pastoralists 136; prison house of Lij Iyasu 135–136
ecotourism 4, 35–36, 79
Eid, R. 6, 17–18
El-Bassiouny, N. 18–19, 93

El-Gohary, H. 5–6, 17–18, 23–25, 27–29, 44, 58–59, 62, 64, 90, 97, 99
Elseidi, R. I. 61
Erlich, H. 112, 115–116, 119
Erraoui, E. 90
Ethiopia: advantages and opportunities 213; arrivals by country of origin **123**; christianity in 110–111; Christian pilgrimage sites 124; eastern cluster attractions 131–136; economic and diplomatic policy 216–217; economic role of halal tourism 217; First Hijra 114; geostrategic and geopolitical position 217; heritage and historical sites 216; image of Ethiopia in islamic eyes 113–116; image of Ethiopia in the eyes of outsiders 116–120; inbound visitors arrivals and tourism receipt **122**; inventory and descriptions of halal visitor attractions 125–126; Islamic intangible living heritages 140–141; Islam in 111–112; King Solomon 108–110; Muslim pilgrimage centers 124; Muslim sultanates 112–113; north cluster 126–130; northwest cluster 130–131; Ottoman Turk 113; overview of 107–108; Queen of Sheba 108–110; religions in 110; socio-cultural tourism 217; southeast cluster 136–140; state of halal tourism development 125; tourist development 120–122
Evans, A. 17–18, 31–33, 38–39

faith-based service needs *69–70*, 84–86
Fakir, F. 90
Foemmel, E. W. 153
Frank, G. 78
Frost, F. A. 117

Gee, C. Y. 77
Gemma, M. 75
Ghimire, K. B. 183
glocalization strategy 80–82
Gnanapala, A. 4
Gobo, G. 81
Goeldner, C. R. 14
good to have faith-based service: local Muslims experiences 86; Ramadan services 86; social justice 86
Griffin, K. A. 64
Gülada, M. O. 95–96
Gundala, R. R. 81

Index

Hajj and Umrah 37, 55, 61, 67–70, 211
Hakim, R. 61
halal accommodation *vs.* conventional accommodation **43–44**
halal-conscious muslim visitors 45–46
halal-conscious visitors: characteristics of 91–92; motivation of 92–93
Halal Quality Standard (HQS) 35
halal tourism: alternative tourism 35–36; attributes of 91; birth of 28–29; characteristics of **24**; components of **87–89**; concepts and practices 215; defining 17–20; e-marketing 36–37; faith-based service needs 84; focus on Ethiopia 4–10; glocalization strategy 80–82; good to have faith-based service 85–86; guidelines for 46–47; knowledge and awareness 157–159; need to have faith-based service 84–85; nice to have faith-based service 86–87, 90; non-Muslims 31–33; principles of 90–91; products and services 37–45; and Sharia law 27–28; standardization and certification 33–35; ten destinations and origins of halal visitors **29–30**; tourism activities 13; trends and prospects of 29–30; vis-à-vis Islamic tourism 21–27; visiting relatives and friends (VRF) 22–23
halal tourism development: conceptual framework of the research 100–101, *101*; feasibility and viability of 209; glocalization strategy 80–82; identified barriers and hurdles 214; identified research gaps in the existing literature 99–100; infrastructure and superstructure 97–98; lack of awareness 94; Muslimism and Islamization 211; opportunities and comparative advantages 175–177; perceived paradox of Islam and tourism 96–97; prevalence of Islamophobia and Xenophobia 94–96; standardization and certification 98; SWOT analysis 202–206, **205**
HalalTrip aims 37
Halim, M. A. A. 34, 98
Han, H. 97–98
Hanziker, W. 14
haram 7, 17–18, 34, 38, 40–42, 45–46, 86, 160–162, 164–165, 183–184, 193, 198, 210
Harrison, D. 78–80
Henderson, J. C. 13, 20, 60, 62

Ho, G. 180
Holloway, J. C. 4, 82
Holy Quran 7, 10, 23, 27–28, 39–41, 43–44, 53, 58–68, 84–86, 90–91, 108, 115, 145, 151, 154, 159, 209–210
host-guest conflict 4, 83
Humphreys, C. 4, 82
Hussein, S. 137

Ibn Abbas 66
Ibn Battuta 116
Ibn Hawqal 116
Ibrahim, I. A. 110, 113, 132
Ibrahim, S. 137
image of Ethiopia: in the eyes of outsiders 116–120; in islamic eyes 113–116
Insoll, T. 126
intangible attributes 7
Islam and tourism 58–63
Islamic tourism 10; characteristics of **24**; defining 20–21; in Muslim destinations 21; travel of non-Muslims 25; UNWTO 20
Ismail, M. N. 19, 22, 59, 99

Jabatan Agama dan Kemajuan Islam Malaysia (JAKIM) 34, 39
Jafari, J. 20
Jamal, A. 18–19, 91, 93
Jennings, G. 147, 152
Johanson, D. 131
Jugol Wall of Harar *132*

Kadhim, M. 57
Kawata, Y. 33
Kenyatta, J. 118
Khalaf, N. 126
Khan, F. 4
Khoiriati, S. D. S. 32, 98
Khondker, H. 81
Kotler, P. 116
Krapf, K. 14

Larrain, J. 78
Lawton, L. 2, 9, 16, 82
Leslie, D. 35

Mak, B. 180
makruh 18, 38, 40
Malaysian Standard (MS) of halal foods 34
Marzuki, S. 41
mashbuh 38, 40
Maslow's hierarchy of needs *94*

Mastercard-CrescentRating 6, 29–30, 35, 37, 62, 84–87, 92, 211
McGehee, N. G. 146, 151
McKercher, B. 180
Mecca and Medina of Saudi Arabia 6, 67–70, **69**
Medlik, S. 14
Michael, I. 136
Miller, D. L. 156
Mohamed, N. 20
Mohideen, H. 23, 95
Mohideen, S. 23, 95
Moral-Moral, M. 13, 19, 28, 36, 99
Moudine, S. 120
Muhrim 46
Musa, C. 35
Musa, G. 60
Muslim-friendly infrastructures: absence of halal promotion and halal websites 200; absence of Muslim-friendly tour operators and tour guides 199–200; awareness about practice and concept of halal tourism 202; lack of halal healthcare facilities and services 201–202; lack of halal recreational centers and leisure facilities 198–199; lack of Muslim-friendly accommodations 196–198; lack of Muslim-friendly airports 195–196
Muslim-friendly tourism 17, 22, 26, *26*, 199–200
Muslim travelers behaviors 211

need to have faith-based services: halal food and beverages 84; no islamophobia 85; prayer facilities 84–85; water-friendly washrooms 85
Neima, A. 124
Nicholas, F. 81
Nkrumah, K. 118
north cluster, Ethiopia: Al-Nejashi religious and historic sites 128–129; ancient mosque and village of Shonke 127–128; Ashura Ceremony in Al-Nejashi 129–130; islamic archaeological sites of North Showa 126–127; Shrine and Mausoleums 129; story of the *Sahabas* 129
northwest cluster, Ethiopia: Dallol Volcano 130–131; Erta Ale 131; The Hadar Archaeological Site 131
Nurdiansyah, A. 97

Østebø, T. 117, 124
Öter, Z. 55

Othman, K. 45
Othman, N. A. 91
Oyelakin, I. O. 35, 42

Pădurean, A. M. 58
pilgrimage and tourism 57–58
Prophet Abraham 68
Prophet Muhammad 27, 44, 59–60, 66–67, 111–112, 114–115, 137, 179, 194
Prophet Suleiman 108

Qayum, B. 18, 25

Rahadian, B. 45
Raj, R. 64
Rashid, T. 59
Razalli, M. R. 43, 90
religious food restrictions **53–54**
religious tourism 53–56; abandoned islamic city of Harlaa 135; Al-Nejashi religious and historic sites 128–129; ancient mosque and village of Shonke 127–128; ancient walled city of Harar 131–133, *132*; Ashura Ceremony in Al-Nejashi 129–130; Bale Mountains National Park (BMNP) 136–137; basketry and handicraft products 133–134, *134*; Daketa rocks in Babile 135; Dallol Volcano 130–131; Dire Sheikh Hussein shrine 137–138; Erta Ale 131; in Ethiopia 122–141; food restrictions **53–54**; The Hadar Archaeological Site 131; heritage buildings 134–135; inventory and descriptions of halal visitor attractions 125–126; islamic archaeological sites of North Showa 126–127; live culture and traditional cottage of pastoralists 136; The palace of Aba Jifar II 140; prison house of Lij Iyasu 135–136; Shrine and Mausoleums 129; size and projected growth **56**; Sof Omar cave system *138*, 138–139; state of halal tourism development 125; story of the *Sahabas* 129
Riaz, M. N. 39–41
Ribeiro, N. F. 153
Rinschede, G. 55
Ritchie, J. R. B. 14
Roberts, L. 77
Rubenson, S. 118

Sahaba Bilal Ibn Rabah 118
Salleh, M. M. 34, 98

Samori, Z. 6, 66, 90
Sandaruwani, J. A. R. C. 4
Santos, M. 55
Sarıışık, M. 13, 21–22, 28
Scott, N. 20
seasonality 3, 83, 121, 183, 217
Secinaro, S. 33–34, 97
Selassie, H. 109–110, 136
Shackley, M. 55
Shakona, M. 90
Shanka, T. 117
Shapley, R. 80
sharia-compliant products and services: accommodation and restaurants 42–44; airports 44; entertainment services 42; food and beverages 38–42; healthcare centers 44–45; *makruh* 38, 40; *mushbuh* 38, 40
Sharia law 13, 18, 20–21, 27–28, 34, 39, 41–42, 66, 126, 192, 210
Sharpley, R. 77, 79
Sheikh Jawhar Haydar Ali 127
Sheikh Nur Hussein Melka 137
Sindiga, I. 183
Sisay, A. 120
Sofronov, B. 76
Solá, E. F. 77
southeast cluster, Ethiopia: Bale Mountains National Park (BMNP) 136–137; Dire Sheikh Hussein shrine 137–138; The palace of Aba Jifar II 140; Sof Omar cave system *138*, 138–139
Stebbins, R. 146
Suleman, R. 18, 25
Sultana, S. 32
Sunnah 27–28, 39, 58–59, 63–64, 66–67, 145, 151, 154, 159, 179, 209
Suradin, M. 31
SWOT analysis **205**; external opportunities 204; external threats 204, 206; internal strengths 202–203; internal weaknesses 203–204; strategies *203*
Syed, S. 17–18, 31–33, 38–39

Tală, M. L. 58
tangible attributes 7

Tasci, A. D. A. 116
Tebligh 24, 65
Telfer, J. 80
Theobald, W. F. 14, 16
tourism: business travelers 16; classification of visitors *15*; defining 14–17; domestic visitors 17; environmental perspective 3; in Ethiopia 7; as global industry 2; Holy Quran 64–66; labor-intensive industry 3; natural and anthropogenic shocks 1; negative impacts of 4; private travelers 16; seasonality 3; Sunnah 66–67; UNWTO 15
tourism development: consolidation phase 83; dependency theory 78–79; development stage 83; economic development 75; in Ethiopia 120–122; exploration stage 82; involvement stage 82–83; modernization theory 78; Northwest Territories (NWT) 76–77; principles of 77; stagnation stage 83; sustainable development 79–80
Tribe, J. 14, 16
Trimingham, J. S. 112

Ubaydalla bin Jahsh 115
Umayah Ibn Kalaf 111
UNWTO 2, 9, 14–16, 20, 55, 57, 76, 217
Utomo, S. B. 57

Vargas-Sánchez, A. 13, 19, 28, 36, 99
Veal, A. J. 15, 146, 150, 152–153, 155
visiting relatives and friends (VRF) 22–23

Weaver, D. 2, 9, 16, 82
Weldesenbet, G. E. 124

Yusuf, A. H. 35, 42

Zabiha 40
Zamani-Farahani, H. 60
Zawawi, M. 45
Zul-Hajjah 68

Printed in the United States
by Baker & Taylor Publisher Services